J. MARTIN

HARD WAY
JAY

ARPress
ILLUMINATING IDEAS.
EMPOWERING VOICES

ARPress
45 Dan Road Suite 36
Canton MA 02021

Hotline: 1(800) 220-7660
Fax: 1(855) 752-6001

Ordering Information:
Quantity Sales. Special discounts are available on quantity purchases by corporations, associations, and others. For details, contact the publisher at the address above.

Printed in the United States of America.

ISBN-13   Softcover   979-8-89389-896-5
                    eBook   979-8-89389-897-2

Library of Congress Control Number: 2024923871

CONTENT

Preface.. 1

Chapter 1: Farmer... 5
Chapter 2: Carol.. 9
Chapter 3: Sarah.. 30
Chapter 4: Hard Times.. 41
Chapter 5: Teenage.. 57
Chapter 6: More Better... 80
Chapter 7: Adult Responsibility.. 98
Chapter 8: Aircraft.. 117
Chapter 9: Roller Coaster.. 130
Chapter 10: Oil... 150
Chapter 11: Director... 168
Chapter 12: Nuclear Weapons.. 184
Chapter 13: Product Engineer.. 196
Chapter 14: Nondestructive Testing... 210
Chapter 15: Retirement.. 227

Acknowledgments 244
About the Author 245

HAY BALER

The sketch above of a hay baler is of the same baler design as the baler on page 10 with a man standing on the platform out over the tailpiece of the baler. His job is to feed hay into the hopper.

Preface

A True Story

The following true story is about a fellow who had his roots in farming when farming was a hard life; a hard way to go. The first time a name appears in the book, it is bolded for the convenience of the reader when refreshing his or her memory. The names have been changed to protect the guilty as well as the innocent.

There is an old, silly joke that has some merit. As the joke goes, a travelling salesman was going about his route in the countryside. He saw a farmer plowing his field. He had a mule tied to a tree, and he was pulling the plow with a rope over his shoulder. The salesman stopped and asked the farmer for a drink of water. The farmer walked over to the dug well, dropped the bucket into the well, and pulled it out hand-over-hand instead of through the pulley on the well's overhead structure. The salesman introduced himself, and the farmer said his name was Hardway Jones. About that time, a boy came out across the plowed field walking on his hands. The farmer said, "That's Hardway Junior." The salesman said, "I'll bet you got that boy in a hard way." The farmer said, "Oh, it wasn't so hard. I got him standing up in a hammock." The hard way is how Jay, the main character of this book, saw his life.

Now Wiley, Jay's grandfather, was a farmer in south central Missouri. He was born in January 1828 in Virginia. When the Civil War began, Wiley enlisted in Abe Lincoln's army. Whether Wiley saw or was told gruesome stories about the Civil War is not known; however, some were borne out as fact (e.g., cannons using rocks for shot when cannon balls were not available or chains that acted like rotary lawn mowers when used in cannons).

Wiley told his son, Joe, that some soldiers had fought all day with nothing to eat. They found a dog hide where someone had skinned the dog and ate the dog. They were so hungry they threw the hide in a pot and made soup out of it. Also, he was told that slaves on plantations had nowhere to go after the Civil War and asked the slave owner if they could stay on. Also, the slaves without last names assumed the plantation owners name.

Wiley and Lizzy

Joe and Marlene with one of their first children

Now, when Wiley came home to his farm, he learned that his neighbor, Will, had appropriated his farm and his family: a wife, a son and a daughter. Wiley did not like that much, so he and his wife divorced. Wiley moved to Illinois where he met a German lady by the name of Lizzy Falk. They were married and moved to Nebraska to farm. They had three children there. They lost two children, both girls, one at four years of age and one two days after birth. Later they moved to southeast Kansas to a farm with a log cabin and had four more children including their seventh child in 1890. He was named Joe. Joe was a frisky young lad living on that farm between Baxter Springs, Kansas, and Joplin, Missouri. He tried riding a big dog he had as a boy. The dog convinced Joe one day that he was no horse; he bit Joe. Joe's dad, Wiley, wanted to do away with the dog, but Joe talked him out of it explaining that the dog was not at fault. Joe hunted raccoons with his friends. One night Joe's dog ran out on a limb of a big tree leaning over a creek, slipped and fell into the creek. All of the dogs of Joe's friends jumped in and tore Joe's dog to shreds. No doubt Joe's dog was a raccoon to the other dogs.

One day when Joe and a friend were walking home from school, he and his friend, who was a girl, had a bet about who could pee the highest on a wall. Joe lost. Many years later, Joe and his third wife visited the friend and her husband from time to time. They usually played cards (pitch).

Joe attended a Wild West show. He was convinced that the shots at the glass balls were with bird shot; they never missed.

Wiley died when Joe was thirteen. Joe's mom could not support them both, so Joe went to live with his brother, who was several years older than Joe, in NE Oklahoma. His brother treated Joe like a slave. When Joe was twenty-one, he acquired a farm in NE Oklahoma and married a local lady by the name of Marlene. They lost their first two in infancy. They had seven children, the youngest daughter died at two years old in the family car. Does history repeat itself somewhat? Joe's parents had seven children and lost two very young.

Joe was twenty-one in the photograph at right; Marlene was nineteen. He and Marlene had a farm and did well. Joe was able to hire several farm hands to help with the farming. They had cattle, grain crops and hay. Haying took most of their summers. As soon as the grain crops were in, they began bailing hay. Much of the area was owned by Indians. The Indians were restricted from selling their land, according to Joe, but could lease it to local farmers. Joe was able to rent several native grass lands for hay. The grass was blue stem on ground that had not yet been plowed. The meadows around the mines were drilled for lead and zinc ore; they were full

Marlene 19, Joe 21

of abandoned drill holes, no casings. Some caved in, but most were just holes in the ground. Horses were at danger of breaking a leg in the holes, which were flush with the ground and hard to see. The grass on the meadows made excellent hay for cattle during winters. Also, the hay was a good cash source for Joe during the winter. Many times he hauled hay into the Arkansas Boston Mountains, sold it, and bought white oak lumber for the return trip. The lumber was used by Joe or sold for income to carry his family through the winter. In the 1930s, Joe bought a 1936 one-and-a-half-ton International truck that was designed for a tractor to pull trailers over the road. Joe lengthened the wheel base and used it for a farm truck.

Joe, Marlene, Their Family and Hired Hands

This above photo was made in the late 1920's of Joe (driver), his first wife (Marlene) holding her youngest child, their oldest living female child, their next to youngest female child, Joe and Marlene's only son on the back of the truck, and the father with several of his sons as hired hands. The truck burned sitting next to Joe's house in 1935.

Chapter 1

Farmer

Now Joe was determined to make a living at farming. He was able to accumulate a sizable farm near Quapaw, Oklahoma. It included hay meadows of native bluestem grass, pasture land, and tillable land. Included was the land leased from Indians. He hired a lad thirteen years old from the local area.

Ted

His name was Ted. Ted worked steadily for Joe and proved to be a capable and dependable farm hand. As a matter of fact, he would work all of his working life for Joe.

Joe was a hard worker. He drove his work horses and his help as hard as himself. One day in the winter, Joe and Ted were a long way from home. They were crossing a frozen creek when one of the horses slipped and fell as the ice broke up. The other horse moved ahead causing the wagon to hold the fallen horse's head under water. Joe jumped in the water, which was over waist deep, held the horse's head up while Ted unhitched the horse so he could get up. Joe walked the rest of the way home with his clothes frozen stiff.

A big Buick was Joe's transportation. Oklahoma was dry, but a neighboring state was not. The lead and zinc mines around the area were playing out. There were several abandoned open and unprotected mine shafts approximately ten feet by ten feet entrance hole along with abandoned mine shacks in the area. A man approached Joe and told him he had a job for him. He took Joe to an abandoned mine shack. The room was dark and he could not see anyone in the room. Someone asked Joe if he would like to use his big car to do some hauling for them; he would not have to do any work, just drive from the Joplin

Joe

area to where he was told in Oklahoma. Joe's German heritage kicked in. He was a bit smarter than the average man of his area. Joe could imagine his body being tossed into one of the abandoned, open mine shafts. The shafts were about four hundred feet down to where the ore was. However, most were filled to around one hundred feet from the top with water. Several people disappeared around the mines and were thought to be in one of the many open shafts; they were covered over and made safe years later. With these thoughts in mind, Joe decided to pass up the offer. He felt relieved to escape with his life because he was sure the shady characters were bootleggers.

Shown below are some photographs of what the mine tailings appeared as..

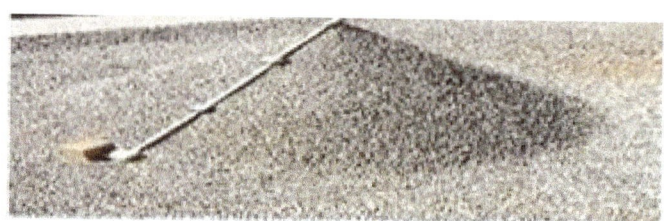

Model of Chat Pile (Mill Tailings)

Operational Mill and Chat Pile

Large Chat Pile

Life of a miner was hard; many miners came down with lung problems (miner's consumption) caused by dust when the ore was blasted loose. There was no cure for the disease. Picher, Oklahoma was the toughest of the mining towns in the area, according to the old timers. There are many tales about that town. It is now a ghost town with much of it blocked off as not safe. The pillars left by

the miners to support the overhead were stripped away; cave-in of the mines was a safety issue. Several cave-ins have now occurred.

Joe's hay meadows around the mines had many of the drill holes abandoned and unprotected. Joe baled the hay with horses and mules. Care had to be taken to keep the horses from stepping in drill holes and breaking their legs; mules were naturally cautious and shied away from the drill holes. Joe's youngest son, Jay, enjoyed dropping rocks down the holes to hear them clink down the sides and plunk into the water.

Sometimes he could see the water at the bottom when his eyes adjusted to the darkness of the holes. At a young age, Jay went to the hay fields with his dad and brother even though he was no help to baling of the hay until he was nine years old. Then he raked scraps with a black mule. The mule was an ex-Army mule with a number branded on her jaw. She was intelligent and managed to eat the lunch of some of the hay crew who left their lunch in paper sacks in the supply wagon.

Joe and Marlene were living well with modern conveniences in the 1920's in the countryside. For example, they had a coal oil (kerosene) cook stove. The tank was mounted up on the wall behind the stove for gravity feed. One day, Marlene was filling the tank for the stove. A burner was lit. The container slipped from her hand, and spilled coal oil on her as well as the stove. On fire, she ran into the yard screaming. Ted came from the barn and wrapped her in his coat smothering the flames. Marlene was burned over a large part of her body; she died that night. She was only thirty-five years old. Her youngest daughter of two years had died mysteriously shortly after Marlene died. Her next youngest child was a girl approximately three and a half years old. Her name was Vera. Of the seven children of Marlene and Joe, one boy and three girls survived.

Now Joe did not know what to do with the two older girls, Olla and Lou. He took them to the field with him. He baled hay all summer with several men helping run the baler. This was not a good situation; the girls were exposed to the rough talk, the orneriness and the meanness of the farm hands of that time. This should not have been.

Olla   Ray

The woman who took care of the younger children was said to have been a local woman. The youngsters were a boy named J R and girls named Vera and Paula, a girl who was two years old. One of Joe's daughters, said that the woman wanted to adopt the two-year-old girl, but Joe refused.

She said she was told that the woman poisoned the child. It is known that the child died in the family car

Lou and her Family

on the way to get medical help. The daughter said that Joe once told her the woman died in prison.

Joe did take another wife some four years after Marlene's death. The new wife was the sister of a couple of his hired hands. Her name was Carol.

Even though the two older girls had a rough teenage life; both married well and raised good families. They were well loved by all who knew them. They both lived in the same neighborhood as Joe for several years. Eventually, the older daughter moved to California with her husband and family.

Carol

The picture above of Olla was taken in 1978 in Hutchinson at Jay's house at that time. The picture of Ray, Olla's husband, was taken in the 1940s. Olla and Ray had three daughters and one son. The girls were very pretty in their youth. They all spent their lives in California except the son who had moved to Missouri. The picture of Lou and her family was taken in the 1950s. Her family did well in their lives.

Chapter 2

Carol

Now, Joe and Carol had much activity and tragedy. Carol was a member of the Christian Church in a nearby town. She insisted on Joe becoming a Christian if he wanted to marry her. He did and became an active member in a local country Baptist Church. He was the Sunday school superintendent. He even took the church members around the neighborhood singing Christmas carols. One farmer did not appreciate the carolers and stepped out with a rifle firing in the air.

Carol's Four Children, 7 through 10

Besides taking care of two of Marlene's children, Carol had four in a row of her own in four years starting in 1932. The oldest was Wes and the youngest was Jay. The two girls were Ellen and Bonny. In the photograph above, Ellen is on the left and Bonnie is on the right as the viewer sees them. Joe and Carol bought property near Miami, Oklahoma some six miles from where Joe and Marlene's home was. It had a nice two-story house with a barn and milking shed.

Wes 6, Jay 3

A spring beside the road adjacent to the property provided drinking and household water. The county had concreted around it and put a lid over it to keep out the road dust. Neighbors used the spring.

The economic depression of 1929 to 1942 hit essentially everyone hard. Joe took a job with the WPA with his team of mules hooked to a slip (a device for moving dirt). Joe said he was fired after a short time because he worked too hard. While others were taking it easy, Joe was working. This was a make-work project. Joe said that WPA meant "we poke along." Joe was doing alright, though. His place

First National Bank

was paid for and he had two trucks as well as other farm equipment including a hay baler and horse and mule teams.

One day, a bank president in a local town told Joe that there were some distressed cattle for sale by the bank. He encouraged Joe to buy them, fatten them and sell them in Kansas City some one hundred eighty miles away. Joe did, and took the cattle to Kansas City stock yards, which were near several packing houses. Cattle were not selling; the packing houses were down. People could not even sell milk; no one could afford to buy it. The producers were pouring it out on the streets. Joe and Ted, who drove the second truck, were in a quandary. If they brought the cattle home Joe could not afford to feed them. The cattle were turned out on the streets of Kansas City.

Joe's First Hay Baler

Joe could not pay for the cattle; he had mortgaged his farm machinery and stock cattle to buy them. The bank foreclosed, and Joe had to take bankruptcy. The sheriff held an auction selling the farm equipment. Neighbors bought some of his equipment, including a stationary hay baler, and loaned the equipment back to Joe. Joe jacked up one side of a truck and belted a back wheel to the baler, it wore out the differential gears often, but Joe bought new ones and installed them himself. He was able to bale lots of hay that way. It worked until Joe could acquire a tractor. The hay kept Joe going. The bank took his cattle except seven calves he hid in an old abandoned dug well. This was the start of his new herd.

The bankruptcy incident irritated Joe so much that one day he put a .32- caliber pistol in his pocket and went looking for the bank president. Apparently, someone told the president Joe was looking for him because he hid out. After walking around looking for the bank man, Joe asked himself, What am I doing? He took his hand off the gun in his pocket and went home. Needless to say, he did no more business with that bank.

When he could, Joe bought another stationary baler to replace his first one. It was an Eli baler with an elevator that two men could pitch hay onto. That enabled the hay crew to bale faster. Joe also was able to acquire a steel wheel 15- 30 McCormick Deering tractor to run the baler. It was a hard way to go, but the hay baling kept Joe in business as a farmer.

Eli Hay Baler with 15-30 McCormick Deering Tractor

In the photo above, Ted is the second from the left, and Joe is the first at the right as the viewer sees the picture. The tractor relieved the truck that was used to run the baler with its back wheel; the truck could then be used to haul hay. Farmers are innovative and do what they have to for getting jobs done.

Carol's Kodak Camera

Behind Joe is a hay rake used to rake the mowed hay into windrows for the sweep rake. A windrow is visible alongside the tractor and baler. No doubt, many of the photographs in this book were taken on Carol's Kodak Browning box camera with 120 film, especially the balers.

1936 1½ Ton International Truck1

Joe, who was no stranger to tragedy after losing three children and a wife and taking bankruptcy, gritted his teeth and dug in. He was able to buy the one-and-a-half-ton-rated 1936 red International truck that was lengthened and used to haul everything for the farm. The photographs at the right are of 1936 International trucks. Joe used his to haul grain or hay to Arkansas over the Boston Mountains in the winter and return with oak lumber. He used it regularly until 1951. The truck was a blessing. It is the one thing that kept Joe going during the hard times. On one trip to Arkansas, he took Jay, who was not yet school age, along. It was quite an experience for Jay; he remembered it always.

Joe and his 1936 International Truck (With Dog on Top)

Once, Joe took some of his hired help. Bob, the brother of Ted, ordered a steak rare at a restaurant they stopped at. When a cool, raw piece of meat was brought out, Bob exclaimed, "I wanted this rare not raw. Go back and cook it done!" Another time Joe stopped at a place that had a shooting gallery. He decided to shoot a .45 automatic pistol, his first time ever. When he pulled the trigger the recoil caught him by surprise. The gun kicked straight up and fired again. The establishment owner ran up the stairs, came back and said all was quiet up there. He told Joe he had better go.

On another trip in the winter, Joe came across a bunch of hogs huddled together on the road to keep warm in light snow. The area was open range on the Boston Mountains. Joe took the truck crank and punched a hog to get it to move off the road. It was a cranky sow, and it ran Joe back into the cab of his truck.

Close to the end of the Arkansas trips Joe collided with a pickup truck. The pickup was destroyed, and Joe's truck wound up upside down. The cab was damaged and its glass was broken. The windshield was ordinary window glass as was the door glasses. Fortunately, Joe was not hurt. Windshields now are made of safety glass with a layer of plastic between two layers of glass to keep the glass from breaking into sharp shards that become daggers. Door glasses were changed to tempered safety glass, which is prestressed glass that crumbles into small, diced pieces when broken.

Joe overhauled the truck many times during its lifetime on the farm. He and hired hands did it themselves. One time a hammer came off the handle and hit Joe on the side of the face. It broke some teeth. He had to have medical attention to repair the damage.

In April 1934, Ted, Joe's steady farm hand, was at his twenty-acre home west of Commerce, Oklahoma, in the morning drawing water from his dug well. He heard a strange chatter about three or four miles away. The chatter grew faster and lasted three or four seconds. A short time later, cars ran up and down his road at a high rate of speed; they continued into the night. What had happened was that Bonnie Parker and Clyde Barrow had come to Commerce, and speculation was that they were planning to rob the bank there the next morning. They were parked near a tailings pile, called a chat pile, about a mile south of Commerce and less than a mile west on the south side of the road. As the story goes, a farmer came by going to town the next morning. He told the constable in Commerce that there was a bunch of drunks at a chat pile south of town. The constable and the Commerce City marshal went out in their model A to see what was going on. Henry Methvin, Bonnie and Clyde's driver, was asleep in the car. What happened next was summarized by Jay for a Toast Master's Club meeting. He gave a copy of it to the Joplin Library. Some of the information came from the Tulsa Tribune[3] and some from the Pacific Reporter[4] of the law library in the Oklahoma City University. Jay used the information that he wrote in his Toastmasters presentation. Jay went to Commerce and talked to some of the witnesses who were there during that time. They were fuzzy about the details. Jay also checked with the Miami, Oklahoma, newspaper, but no information was found there. The library at Joplin, Missouri, did have some information on Bonnie and Clyde. The paper Jay wrote is shown below:

Bonnie and Clyde Came to Commerce[3]

April 6, 1934, was a cool, rainy Friday. At midmorning, a man stopped by the Commerce police station to report a car load of "drunks" parked on a county road just outside of town. Two lawmen drove to the site. When they saw the parked car, their suspicions mounted. The car in question had a bullet hole in the windshield. It began to back up when the lawmen arrived and

Bonnie Parker jokingly pointing a gun at Clyde Barrow.

Picture courtesy of the FBI.

Bonnie and Clyde[2]

stepped from their car. The retreating vehicle backed into a ditch, and the fireworks began.

This is how it all came about. Thursday Bonnie Parker, Clyde Barrow, and Henry Methvin left the home of Henry's parents near Caster, Louisiana, and drove to Fayetteville, Arkansas. From there, they drove into Oklahoma arriving near Commerce at 2:30 a.m., Friday morning.

Commerce (the home of Mickey Mantle) was a small mining (lead and zinc) town in extreme northeast corner of Oklahoma. Local residents think that the trio was there with the intention of robbing the Commerce Bank. The mines were still going at that time. Incidentally, Clyde and Bonnie's car was parked between two mines, the Crabapple on the north and the Lost Trail on the south.

The two lawmen, Percy Boyd, who was the Commerce City marshal and Cal Campbell who was the Commerce constable, drove to the scene of the action in Percy's Model A. When the parked car, a late model Ford, began to back up, Cal followed a few steps on foot before returning toward the Model A. Gunfire commenced from inside the retreating vehicle after it had backed approximately one hundred yards into a ditch. The lawmen returned fire. Clyde, a small man (five feet seven inches, 150 pounds), jumped from his car with a Browning automatic rifle and trained it on the officers armed with pistols. Clyde was a good marksman and had won several gun battles already. Cal Campbell was shot in the chest and fell dead in the road. Percy was grazed along one side of his head and fell to the ground.

Henry Methvin, who was asleep in the back seat, was ordered to bring up the injured man. Henry walked up to Percy, pointed a rifle at him, relieved him of his pistol, and told the marshal, "Get up and come with me.." Percy stood up, put his hands over his head, and walked toward the car stuck in the ditch. Henry was right behind him. On the way Henry prodded Percy saying, "Hurry up! We're taking you with us."

At the car, Bonnie was still behind the wheel. Clyde had gone to a place across the road for a car to pull his car from the ditch. For tow a rope was used, but it broke. Several people were stopped and ordered to help get the Ford out of the ditch. Henry was in the road stopping the cars that came along. After seven or eight people were gathered, Clyde said, "Boys, one good man has already been killed, and if you don't obey orders, others are liable to be."

Charley Dobson, coming from Commerce, drove up in his truck. He was ordered by Clyde to fasten a chain to his truck and pull the car from the ditch. When this was done, Clyde turned the car around. Percy was ordered aboard, and the fugitives drove west on the county road they were on. They crossed the Stepp's Ford Bridge across the Neosho River and into the next county. They were seen in Welch, a small town twenty miles west and slightly south of Commerce.

Lawmen and newsmen searching for Bonnie and Clyde did not know who the third person, Henry Methvin, was. They thought he was Raymond Hamilton, who at one time was Bonnie's suitor. A picture of Bonnie, Clyde and Raymond appeared as the three being sought in the Tulsa World newspaper.

Clyde met Bonnie at the place where she worked. Bonnie, whose husband was in prison, had met Raymond in a café in Dallas where she was employed. When Clyde entered the picture, Bonnie was attracted to him. After a short while Raymond had his fill and parted company with Bonnie and Clyde. Henry's involvement with Bonnie and Clyde came about in Texas where Henry was an inmate at the Texas Prison Farm. During a gun battle between the prison guard and Bonnie and Clyde, Henry and some other prisoners escaped. The date was January 16, 1934. Henry ran across Bonnie and Clyde's car and rode to Dallas with them. He stayed there three days before going to Hasland, Texas, where he found a job in a lumber camp. After about three weeks Clyde and Bonnie found Henry at Hasland and took him with them. They went to the home of Henry's parents. There Henry and his parents made plans for Henry to help capture Bonnie and Clyde in return for Henry's exoneration by the state of Texas. This happened just prior to the incident at Commerce.

After the shooting at Commerce, Bonnie, Clyde, Henry and their captive drove back roads and escaped into Kansas. They stopped in the vicinity of Fort Scott. Later they entered Fort Scott where Henry left the car several times to get road maps, a newspaper at a drug store, food at a grocery store, and twice to look at cars that Clyde pointed out for Henry to steal. They did not steal the cars because Henry said they were locked. Later, Henry testified at his trial that the cars were not locked, but he just did not want to steal them.

After Clyde read that Cal Campbell was dead, he said to Percy, "I'm sorry I had to kill that old man." Bonnie told Percy that she was not a cigar smoker, and that the picture of her with a cigar was actually with Clyde's cigar. Cal Campbell was nearly sixty years old, Bonnie was twenty, Clyde was twenty-four, and Henry was twenty- two. Percy was in his thirties.

Around ten o'clock Friday evening, Percy was released eight miles from Fort Scott. He was given a coat and offered some money for his trip home. He walked to a farm house, explained the situation, but was turned away. He walked to another farm house. This time the farmer was willing to help. The local sheriff came out, picked up Percy and took him to a hospital in Fort Scott.

Meanwhile the Barrow gang headed for the home of Henry Methvin's parents. Here the plan for the capture of Bonnie and Clyde was put into action. Henry—cooperating with Federal, Texas, and Louisiana officers of the law—parted company with Bonnie and Clyde in Shreveport. The next morning the couple went back toward the home of Henry's parents. They were ambushed and killed a short distance from their destination.

Texas pardoned Henry for his help. However, he was brought back to Oklahoma and tried for the death of Cal Campbell. The first trial at Miami, Oklahoma, the Ottawa county seat, ended in a mistrial; the jury could not reach a verdict. He was convicted of first degree murder in the second trial and sentenced to death in the electric chair. On appeal in 1938, Henry's sentence was changed to life in prison. He was released about eight years later.

Henry's father had made the deal for Henry to be excused from his crimes in Texas for helping to catch Bonnie and Clyde, but the state of Oklahoma was not willing to forgive him for the Commerce incident[4].

Carol's 4th child, Jay

In 1935, Joe and Carol were in town buying supplies. When they returned home, they found their house burned. There was a truck near the house that burned, also. They moved into their barn with the three small children and the two younger ones from Joe's first marriage. The two from Joe's first marriage were at a one-room country school, called Yellow Dog School, one and one-fourth miles away; they saw the smoke.

Carol gave birth of her fourth child in August. The loft of the barn served as the master bedroom. Vera, the youngest living child from Joe's first marriage, said she wondered how Carol ever was able to climb the ladder, made of two-by-fours nailed to the side of the barn, the night Jay was born. He was bottle fed and was allergic to cow's milk; he was given goat's milk.

With the clothing and other things given by neighbors, they survived. Dr. Duembler from Seneca, Missouri, delivered the child in the barn. All of Carol's children were delivered at home. Times have sure changed from 1935. Doctors will not make house calls now, let alone barn calls.

When people told Jay to, "shut the door; were you born in a barn?" Jay just grinned. Jay thought that being born in a barn was not so bad; after all, Jesus was born in a stable.

Top: barn. Upper right and right: barn and milk shed (cook shed). Lower right: milk shed. This was living space until mid-winter when a house was made available. Temporary Barn Home

The barn was home to the family for the next five months after Jay was born. January 1, 1936, Joe was able to rent a house and land nearly a mile away. It had a huge horse barn with the house and nearly one hundred acres of land around it. The old house was probably built before Oklahoma became a state. It had a two-story section with two single-story rooms attached. Joe and his family lived there for approximately twenty-five years.

The barn still standing in October 2013

While Carol was still alive, Jay remembers a huge dust storm. The sky to the west was black from the ground to the heavens. Carol took towels and rags to stop up cracks in the doors and windows to keep the dust out. Jay remembers it was difficult to breathe during the storm. Jay's family talked about life being hard during those times. There had been a lingering drought, and with the drought came the dust storms; many farmers abandoned their farms in Oklahoma and moved to California according to the talk Jay heard.

During the twentieth century there were several droughts5. The year 1934 was the worst ever in the 1900s. Almost the entire country was under a severe drought. The 1936 and 1937 years were bad drought years for the central United States. Other years with drought covering more than half of the country were 1911, 1918, 1931, 1940, 1954, 1955, 1956, 1977, and 1988. In the twenty-first century, 2012 was almost as bad as 1934.

Carol was not unhappy with the house her family had moved into. In the lower floors of the two-story part was the master bedroom and living room. The two added rooms were the kitchen and a bedroom for the girls; it later became the dining room. The kitchen had a wood-burning cook stove and a table. The wooden ice-box was on the screened-in back porch. Carol had a square sign for ice delivery she put on the

Ice Delivery Card

living room screen door which faced the road. The sign had 25, 50, 75, and 100 pounds, one number on each edge. When the ice man came by, he knew how much ice to bring to the house from the position of the card.

The upper room was a dormer with a bed at each end. One of the beds was for J R, the son of Joe's first family. J R did not stay long. As soon as he could he moved away. He went to live with his sister, Lou and her husband. Jay wanted him to stay. He did not much like the younger kids playing with his possessions. The other bed was for Carol's two young boys. After J R left, the bed at his end became the two young girl's area; not a real good arrangement.

Joe and Carol's Home after theirs Burned. Some Family members are shown in photo taken in late 1950s.

J R was drafted into the Army during WWII. He was sent to the army base at Camp Chaffee. Not long after he had been there he wrote Joe that he would be home soon, that he could not get along with those people down there. Joe wrote back and told J R that he had better stay there because deserters are shot during war time. A few days later J R wrote Joe that things were not so bad. He was on KP and that he and the cooks would cook up big steaks for a feast after everyone had gone to bed. Later J R was released; he had a hole in his knee cap. It may have been caused by bucking baled hay with his knees.

When J R came home he told Ted what happened in camp. J R, the rounder, had gone on a pass into town. When he came back he was inebriated. At the base, a "shave tail" lieutenant was at the gate watching the security people and returning soldiers. J R gave a sloppy salute. The lieutenant told J R to come back and give a salute. J R slopped him another salute. The lieutenant told him to give a military salute. J R said, "How would you like to kiss my military ass?" J R was thrown into the guard house and later assigned to KP for a long time.

Joe continually leased some of the land he farmed from Indians. He had to go through the Indian Agency because the Indians were restricted on what they could do with their land, according to Joe. There were many heirs to each piece of land. Sometimes one would come to Joe with a sob story like "the wife is sick and needs money for medical help," etc. It was against the rules, but Joe sometimes gave them an advance on their lease. All heirs had to sign the lease before it was finalized. Joe had to go to each one and get his or her signature. Once, Joe was at an Indian stomp-dance near a stomping ground by Spring River near Quapaw, Oklahoma. He was there to get signatures. Joe was invited to eat with them. Indians poured everything they had to eat into a big pot over a fire and cooked it. Joe dipped himself a bowl of the soup (which tasted awful to him). An old Indian nearby said, "Dig deeper white man, dog in bottom."

Even though the youngest girl, Vera, of the first family was seven when Carol married Joe, Carol treated her as her own; they bonded well.

Carol painted the living room floor redish brown around the edges. Color- blind Jay, though he did not know he was color-blind at the time, saw the edge trim as brown. She put linoleum over the rest. She papered the walls with a border around the top. She also papered the ceiling. The walls and ceiling were plastered laths. Carol cut a window in the kitchen to the consternation of the owner. She also had glass installed in the solid kitchen door.

West of the house there was a wooden chicken house that was no longer useful. Also, there was an old smoke house by the cellar near the West side of the house. Both were dragged to the forty-acre hog lot some one hundred and fifty yards away and used for hog sheds. Carol managed to get the owners to build her a modern chicken house with rock walls, a metal roof and bars on the windows. The inside had a roost of rails two feet apart with chicken wire attached beneath the rails to keep the chickens out of the droppings. The floor of the roost was approximately four feet above the ground and two feet below the roost rails. Chickens flew upon the roost. The roost area covered approximately half of the chicken house. Along the edge of the roost was chicken wire hanging down with poles attached to hold the wire down on the sides. The poles could be raised for cleaning the floor beneath the roost. Below the roost at the outer edge was a row of nests for the chickens to lay eggs. The front of the nests had hinged doors for access to the eggs. The chicken house had a dirt floor. There was a front and a back door in the chicken house and a door at each end of the attic. One of Jay's jobs was to clean out the chicken house; he hated the job. The ammonia from the chicken droppings kept Jay alert!

One Saturday morning in the summer, Wes and Jay caught a rooster they wanted to take to town and sell that Saturday night. They put him in the attic of the chicken house. The metal roof caused the rooster to suffocate from the heat.

Shortly after Carol and Joe moved into the old house, Carol had the carpenter who built the chicken house build a two-hole toilet with an access door in back for clean out. Each hole had a pan under it. One hole was smaller with a step up. According to Carol, the WPA built semi-modern outdoor toilets for counties. One was built for Joe, Carol and family. It had a concrete floor with the stool built as an integral part of the concrete floor. The stool had a smooth wooden seat on it with a cover. Under the floor was a large hole approximately four feet in diameter and perhaps five feet deep. A vent pipe (made of wood with a square cross section) was behind the seat. At nearly four feet above the stool, the pipe teed to a horizontal pipe of similar construction and was vented to the sides of the structure. The exits were screened. This outhouse was painted; the carpenter's outhouse was not. Kids did not like to use the outhouses because wasps and spiders made their homes there; needless to say the smell was somewhat offensive. Sears and Roebuck and Montgomery Ward catalogs provided necessary cleanup equipment. Sometimes a Penny's catalog did the honors. The writer was reminded of the story of a lady who wrote Sears, asking how to order toilet paper. The answer came in the mail stating that the material was located on page 358 (or there about). The lady wrote back that if she had 358 pages of the Sears catalog, she would not need toilet paper.

Before the outhouses were placed in their location behind the new brooder house, which was built in place of the old chicken house that was moved to the hog lot, Joe's beehives were there. Joe loved to tell about a goat that hopped upon one of the hives. He made the mistake of raising his tail and a bee found its mark. The goat had a lot to say about his discomfort.

Shower House

Before the new brooder house, there was an old, small one south of the house (not the chicken house moved to the hog lot). Carol had trouble with rats killing her little chickens. They did not eat the chicks; they just sucked their blood and killed them. She found the rats' burrows in the ground and poured salt water into them. The rats came out and Carol drove stakes through them.

Carol had the carpenter screen the back porch and each window. The carpenter hung a hinged screen over each window to enhance cleaning.

Always the innovator, Carol built a shower house. It was pyramid shaped with a metal fifty-five-gallon drum on top. The drum was filled with water in the summer time and the sun heated the water. It worked, but getting the water from the hand-pump well and carried in buckets to the drum was a lot of work.

Wash Board in Wash Tub

Now Carol washed clothes by hand under a large cotton wood tree near the well. She boiled water in a cauldron over an open fire. She put clothes in the cauldron, and after they boiled awhile, she pulled them out with a large stick and washed them with soap on a scrub board (washboard). The boards had a rough side for ordinary clothes and a smoother side for finer materials. She wrung them out by hand, rinsed them, wrung them by hand again and placed them on a clothes line; a hard way to go.

Later, she built a washing machine by cutting a steel drum in two and cutting a door and vent holes in the bottom half used for a fire box. Then she set the other half on top. She rolled the edges of the top half. She cut a hole on each side near the top and put a steel pipe through it. Attached to the steel pipe in the center was a wooden paddle with holes in it for the wash area. Now, she could pull the top part of the

Hand-cranked Washing Machine with Wringer[6]

paddle back and forth to wash the clothes. She still wrung them out by hand.

Later yet, Carol's mother gave Carol a hand-operated washing machine that was made commercially. Hand-cranked wringers were available. The agitator was driven by gears activated by a handle pulled back and forth (the wheel acted as a flywheel). The agitator would go up and down and twist some in the process. It was discarded and wound up in the trash heap in the hog lot when Lou, from Joe's first family, learned to drive.

Lou would pick up Carol and her laundry once a week and take her to town nearby to a public laundry. It consisted of several electrically driven washing machines with wringers attached. Each machine had two tubs on legs for rinsing. The machines were supplied with hot and cold running water. The rental fees were reasonable. The clothes were taken home and hung out to dry. On one occasion, Lou, the new driver, stopped to fill her car with gasoline. Not yet fully familiar with cars, Lou poured the gasoline into the radiator instead of the gas tank filler in front of the windshield. The fix was minor.

Gas Cap

Early Ford with Gas Cap in Front of Windshield

Milk Can

Carol bought a mechanically operated barber outfit for her boys. She cut a wooden barrel down in the shape of a chair. A board across the arm rests put the young boys at the right height. The boys did not like her haircuts much; her clipper pulled hair each time it stopped in each direction.

For extra money and milk for home use, Carol milked a couple of cows. She had two ten-gallon milk cans and a five-gallon cream can. When the cans were no longer needed for milk, the larger two served as gasoline cans to carry gasoline to the fields for farm machinery, and the smaller was used for coal oil for kerosene lamps. The lids were held on by friction.

Strainer

Carol sent her milk to the cheese factory in town by a nearby neighbor. He returned the cans with whey, the liquid left after most of the food stuff was removed. Joe mixed shorts (wheat hulls) from the flour mills with the whey. He fed the mix to the hogs; they were nuts about it. Carol later bought a cream separator at a farm sale and was able to separate cream for coffee, making butter, etc. The separator had a bell in the crank handle. When the bell stopped ringing the system was turning

Cream Separator

fast enough to pour in the milk to the system. The milk was first strained through a metal bowl strainer with a cotton filter pad held in place with a perforated plate and locking ring.

Carol also raised chickens. She would take eggs and chickens to a poultry house in town. In the back of the poultry house was a parrot that talked; it scared the kids when he talked. With her egg and cream money, she managed to buy a Coleman gasoline-heated iron for clothes. The iron had a gasoline tank on it that held approximately a cup of white gasoline. The gasoline tank was

Coleman Gasoline Iron Kit[6]

pressurized with an included pump, and the flame was controlled by the valve with the black knob at the rear along with a wire handle valve at the back end of the iron body. The fire was lit with a match through the hole near the back of the iron body.

The iron in the photograph at right is owned by the author of this book. The kit shown was more like the one owned by Carol. It came with a measuring can, a pump, a rack for use when iron is hot and a screened funnel (not shown).

Coleman Gasoline Iron

Before Carol bought the gasoline iron she had flat irons. Her kids often wrapped hot irons in news papers, and put them at the foot of the bed as foot warmers in the winter time.

When Carol cut the window in the kitchen of the old house so she could see out and had glass put into the kitchen door with the idea that the glass in the door and the window would add light to the kitchen as well as the view, she drew scorn from the owner.

The place was a rental house, and the older lady who owned the house came out from a small town in Kansas where she lived to see her property from time to time. She and Carol had a discussion about the modifications. During the discussion, the old lady noticed Ellen, Carol's older daughter, had dark eyes. She knew Joe had blue eyes. She noticed that Carol had dark eyes and said that she guessed that Ellen came by her dark eyes honestly though the other kids had blue eyes like their dad. Carol became so angry she wanted to thrash the old lady had she not been the owner of the place.

Before WWII scrap metal was sold to Japan. After the war started Carol complained about the scrap steel the USA sent there. During the war she sang "There is a Star Spangled Banner Waving Somewhere." She liked to sing. Her favorites were "I will Fly Away" and "Will There Be Any Stars in My Crown."

When Carol and Joe were first married, Joe did things for her like taking her and the kids to the local Baptist church about two and a half miles away. He would kill chickens for dinner, etc. Later he was "too busy." Carol walked and took the kids to church. To the kids, the trek seemed like what ten miles would be to an adult. Boy, when the kids reached home after church, they could not wait to pump some cool water to quell their thirst. If the kids had dirt on their faces when they reached church, Carol would wet her handkerchief with her tongue and wash off the spots on the kids' faces with it. One day Carol's sister, Alice, from nearby Kansas came to see Carol. With her was her three-year-old daughter. Carol asked Joe to go by the bus stop in town and pick her up. Joe would not do it. Alice and her daughter walked all of the way to Carol's house. It was a very hot day and part way was over dusty roads. It seemed that both Carol and Alice never forgave Joe for that. Later when Alice became a widow and Carol had died, Joe offered to become friends with Alice; he may have been interested in Alice. Alice was supporting herself, her daughter and Joe's youngest daughter with some help from Joe, someone said. However, Alice shunned Joe. He never tried again.

Flat Irons

People walked around the neighborhood, which was about six miles from town. They did not have money to buy transportation. After the war began in earnest in 1942, people had money, but they could not buy things; goods and materials were rationed and poor quality. Everything went to the war effort. People still walked. Jay bought a flashlight made of pressed paper; the ends would not stay on.

Money was hard to come by before WWII started, and each penny was divided into ten mils by some states for tax purposes. One-mil pieces were of thin metal, probably aluminum, with a hole in the center and five mil pieces were

Oklahoma Mils

of thin Brass. Some were made of wood and some of paper. They were used extensively at that time. In the photograph right, the five mil piece is of brass, the silver ones are of aluminum and the one on the right as seen by viewer, is of paper. Some were marked "Tax Token." On the back side of some were markings "For Old Age Pension."

Collapsible Drinking Cup

Stores stayed open late on Saturday nights. The town was busy then. When Joe, Carol and kids went to town the streets were filled with noisy cars honking everywhere. After the war started the streets were quiet; the young men parked their cars on blocks while they were away. The kids' favorite stores were Woolworth 5¢ and 10¢ store and the ice cream store. To give her kids a drink, as they were eternally thirsty, Carol carried a collapsible cup for water.

Carol bought Folgers coffee in fat, round cans with sailing ship pictures painted on the side. The cans had a key to open them by rolling a strip of the metal along the side with the key. The photograph at right shows a key used to open the can somewhat similar to the Folgers cans. The key is removed from the can and the tab shown under the key is inserted in the slot in the key for winding.

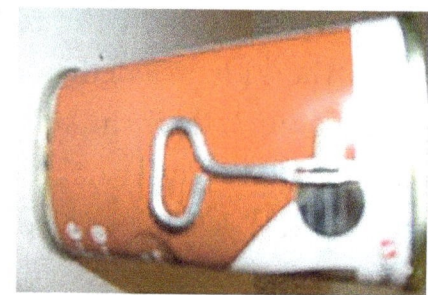
Can with Key Opener

The band of metal wound on the key was sharp, but Jay, as a child, enjoyed playing with it anyhow despite the minor cuts.

Two Federal highways and a state highway ran through the town located on the edge of a river that flooded the town from time to time. There was an A&M junior college there. Nearby were lead and zinc mines and mills. Later a tire plant was located in the town.

During the war (WWII) a British flight training school was located there. The British student flyers were extremely bold. One day when Carol and Jay were outside feeding chickens, two AT6s came chasing each other. They dropped down over the tall trees in the hog lot into a two-acre clearing behind the chicken house and under the power lines just barely clearing the fence and the high line. There could not have been much more than two feet total clearance between the high line, fence and aircraft. That kind of guts was needed for fighter pilots. The trainees would roll their main gear along the cat walks on top of moving boxcars, changing from side to side of the main gears. They flew under a bridge, called the Sailboat Bridge on a large lake known as Grand Lake. Pieces of aircraft were found near the bridge, but none of Joe's family mentioned whether any aircraft were lost there.

Joe and Carol's children liked to tease Carol's roosters, which were aggressive. The youngsters would go into the barnyard or chicken yard where the roosters were and, when the roosters charged, the tots would get under a tablecloth. The rooster, or roosters, would dance around on top.

Carol froze homemade ice cream and put it into cones for the children. They liked that tremendously. Also, she made Kool-Aid for them, which was considered a great treat.

A Singer foot-treadle sewing machine was Carol's pride and joy. She made clothes for her young and herself. She made a quilting frame and hung it from the ceiling of the dining room. Every once in a while she invited the neighborhood ladies over. They would stretch cloth over the top and another over the bottom of the frame. Cotton filler was placed in between. The women would sit around the frame and gossip while sewing the quilt by hand. Likely they

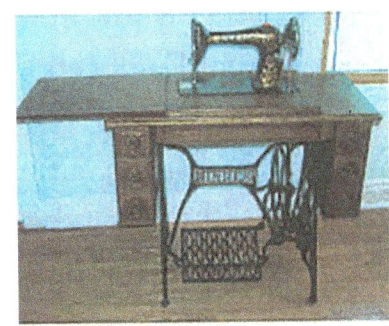

Singer Sewing Machine[8]

helped each other make quilts. Jay, not yet school age and who was shy, hid out while the quilting parties were in full swing.

Raising gardens was a yearly event for Carol. She canned several different kinds of produce from her garden. She bought sweetened vinegar for her sliced beet pickles; sugar was rationed. She would go to Joe's corn fields when the corn was roasting-ear-ready, and, with a neighbor, pick a pickup load of the green corn. She cut the corn off the cobs for canning. She had a hand-crank pea- sheller that would also slice green beans. Her pressure cooker got a good workout every year. There was a concrete cellar with a vertical door at the bottom of the concrete stairs and a slanted door on the outside of the cellar. There the canned goods were stored. Since there were no air conditioners or electric fans, canning was hot business.

The garden also produced pie squash (they actually looked like pies). Carol scooped out the middle, placed in sugar and spices and baked them. Jay remembers that they tasted pretty good. She also made sassafras tea by digging up roots from sassafras trees and boiling them. It was said to thin the blood; whether it did or not, it tasted good as Jay remembers.

Blackberries were plentiful around the house and surrounding area. Carol and all of the kids picked blackberries. For every berry there must have been two chiggers. That did not bother Carol; she donned her bonnet and loose clothes and charged ahead. She said she could actually see the little red chigger spiders. She canned a lot of blackberries. In the lane from the barn yard to the hog lot was a dewberry bush. The dewberries were like blackberries but were much larger and very sweet. Everyone who passed by that bush when the berries were ripe enjoyed them immensely.

There was a river about a mile from the house and bordering the property on which the house was part of. It was a muddy river with tall weeds all around and plenty of water moccasin snakes. At one time, there was a dead horse near the mouth of a slough where Carol liked to fish. She fished the river often and caught enough fish to feed the whole family from time to time. The river was close to the new lake that was built by the Corps of Engineers. The big trees that would be in the river when the lake was filled were bulldozed.

One morning, Carol cooked some fish she caught. She told Jay, her youngest child, to wait until she could pick out the bones before he ate. Jay was hungry; he ate any way. Sure enough, Jay of preschool age, wound up with a bone lodged in his throat. He was told to eat bread, but that did not work. Jay was in misery. Joe did not have time to be bothered with kids; he had farming to do. When Ray, the husband of Joe's oldest daughter, came by to take Carol's milk to town, Carol asked him to take her and Jay to the doctor in Seneca, Missouri, some eighteen miles away to get the bone out. The doctor, the same one who delivered Jay, removed the bone with a pair of long nose hemostats. Jay was the baby of Carol's family at the time, and she coddled him. She cut the corn off the cobs for him, and always saw to it that Jay got the pulley (wish) bone when she fried chicken. Joe liked the breast. Carol would wring a chicken's neck or pull the head off by placing a board on the neck and pull the feet. When the chicken quit flopping, she would scald it in a bucket of hot water and pick off the feathers. Then she would roll up a newspaper, light it and burn off the pin feathers.

Wood Burning Cook Stove

The nearby river and another river three miles away came together about six miles from where Joe and Carol lived with their family. They formed the large lake that was dammed by the Corp of Engineers just before the United States entered WWII. The lake was called Grand Lake of the Cherokees, or just Grand Lake. Carol once drove J R's 1930 model Chevrolet car to the river to fish. The car died and would not start. J R found that it was out of gas and carried fuel to it grumbling all the way. Carol never used J R's car again. She would sometimes hook up a team of horses to a wooden-wheel wagon to go to the river to fish, gather cook wood, etc. The wooden wheels would shrink when they dried out. The steel tires would come off. Carol sometimes soaked the wheels in the creek running through the hog lot to secure the tires. Other times she wired the steel tires (rims) on with baling wire, which wore out quickly.

One day Joe found one of his cows with a broken leg. A tree root looping out from the bank of a creek in the cow path trapped the cow's leg as she started down the bank. It broke her leg as she moved forward. Joe brought her to the house tied on a sled. He had the leg splinted. Then he put a belt around the cow's breast area and suspended the cow to a rafter in the shed on the south side of the barn. There he kept the cow for some time, but the cow did not improve. Joe shot her and dragged her into the hog lot for the hogs to eat and skinned her. He sold the hide.

During WWII, Carol managed to get to town with her youngest son one afternoon and see a morale-boosting news reel at the Glory B Theater in town. It was about Jimmy Doolittle's raid on Japan soon after it happened. The film showed Doolittle's planes, or some similar to Doolittle's planes, dropping bombs. Jay said later it looked like a long stream of bombs being dropped.

Tractor Mounted Buzz Saw

In the fall, Joe, with his farm help, would mount his buzz saw on the front of one of his tractors and cut cook wood and heater wood. They then stacked it on one of the three porches. Carol cooked and heated the house with wood.

Every year, Joe bought a King Heater. It was made of very thin metal like stove pipe material. It had to maintain a thick layer of ashes in the bottom to keep the fire from burning through. Stiffening rings were pressed into the sides for rigidity, as seen in the lower photograph at right. It sat on a fireproof pad to keep the stove from burning the floor. The sides glowed red hot when the fire was burning hot. Sometimes when the fire was burning too fast the stove would jump up and down. One cold evening, Jay was sitting close to the heater facing it in a wobbly chair.

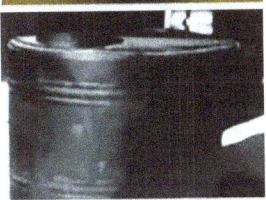

King Heater

The chair leaned forward pinning Jay's knees against the red hot stove. Jay yelled and someone pulled the chair away. Jay had the scars for the rest of his life. When sawing wood, Joe carried a gun in his truck, and, if a dog scared up a rabbit, rabbit was on the menu. Joe sometimes cut the wood extra-long and sold it for fireplace wood in town.

Carol had a wooden rain barrel (a former vinegar barrel) at the intersection of the roof of the two-story part of the house and the single story part. It was always full of wiggle-tails (mosquito larva). However it was soft water good for washing hair. Kids played in the barrel a lot. Actually, Carol's kids had a cellar door and the rain barrel that the song "Playmate9" was written around. The song started by asking a playmate to come out and play and to bring her three dolls. Then it mentioned climbing up an apple tree, look or shout down the rain barrel and slide down the cellar door. But then it said the playmate could not come out because her dolls had the flu. Joe and Carol planted an orchard behind the chicken houses, and there was a large apple tree in it. Jay's sisters had several dolls. They sang the "Playmate" song often.

Now, Carol liked her kids, probably more than Joe. Joe did not like kids playing around the barns and getting into things. When grand kids came with their parents to visit, Joe grumbled a lot. Joe intercepted a letter from his oldest living daughter from his first family, Olla, to the next oldest daughter, Lou, living at home. Olla was already married at that time. The letter told Lou to take some money from their dad's pocket when he was asleep and come for a visit. Now Joe's money was dear to him. He became very angry and griped about that letter for many years. He said he did not care for the

Sherry, the Fifth Child

older daughter much after that. He finally got over being angry with the younger daughter of the two. Carol tried to calm Joe the best she could after the incident.

January 29, 1943, Carol gave birth at home to her fifth child, Sherry. Just before she gave birth, the four other children watched a female cat give birth to kittens. They went running to Carol yelling, "Mama, mama, we just saw some kittens born." Carol spanked all four.

Jay liked to sit on his mother's lap. The evening of the fifth child's birth, she put Jay down and told him to stay down. Jay's feelings were hurt. Then, Carol told her four kids to go to the closest neighbor some three hundred yards down the road and ask the neighbor lady to come up. When they came back a few hours later Joe was sitting in the dining room reading by a new battery powered lantern he had bought for the occasion. Carol had

Carol's Mother

a bed in the living room where there was a wood-burning stove. She showed the kids the new baby sister. Dr. Duembler from Seneca, MO, made the delivery.

Carol was sick after the new baby was born. The old drafty house along with her frequent need to go onto the cold porch for wood did not help any. Carol's mother came to help a few days later. She told Joe that Carol was bad sick. Joe had an ambulance come to the front door and take Carol to the hospital.

Two weeks after the birth of the fifth child, Carol died of pneumonia. Carol's mother told Wes, Carol's oldest son, "You did not even cry when your mother was taken to the hospital," Wes said, "I did too." Jay, who was not sure of what was happening, said, "I didn't." His grandmother scolded, "Shame on you!"

Carol was kept at the funeral home. When Jay saw his mother for the first time after she expired, he reached into the coffin. That is the first time he realized his mother was dead. At the funeral in the First Baptist Church in town, Jay saw his dad cry for the first time.

The new baby was taken to Wichita to live with her aunt, her mother's sister. The aunt, Alice, went to Wichita to work in the aircraft factories during WWII. Carol's mother went along to take care of the newborn and Alice's three-year-old daughter. Joe moved them with his truck. The morning of the move, Joe was up early and milked Carol's cows. J R, Joe's son from his first family, and J R's wife were there with their kids to help get ready. Someone built a fire in the wood cook stove. All at once there was a fire in the ceiling

Alice

and in the attic at the flue. J R and Joe grabbed the milk Joe brought in and ran upstairs into the attic with the milk. They knocked down the flames with the milk in the smoky attic. The attic was not floored, so the men had to be careful to step on rafters. J R then ran down the stairs, and he and Wes pumped water into a tub and carried it to the attic. The fire was extinguished. It was determined that Carol had papered the flue too close to the pipe entrance. Joe later concreted the flue around the entrance to the flue and left it bare. He did the same to the other side in the dining room where the wood heater was. Wes went to Wichita with the move to help out. When he returned he told his young brother, Jay, that he saw bunches of oil derricks around Wichita.

Alice's husband was in a sanatorium with tuberculosis (TB). Alice made enough money working two jobs in Wichita to buy a small farm after the war. The farm was in SE Kansas where she earned her living milking cows. She milked somewhere around eighteen cows by hand. She was now a widow. After a few years Alice married her childhood sweetheart. She continued to milk the cows, but later bought a couple of milking machines. She milked two cows at a time. When she let one out, she called another by name. That cow was the only one that moved; she took her place without any coaching. The cows gathered around the door to the barn waiting their turn. It was a sight to see. A large- volume milk truck came by every morning for the milk. The milk was cooled in a tank of water at night. Alice was a remarkable woman.

Chapter 3

Sarah

Sarah

Joe's sister, Sarah, came to live with Joe and take care of his youngster. She had been a widow for a few years. Ellen was told that Carol's four children were destined for an orphan's home in Tulsa. Sarah was hired by Joe to keep that from happening, according to Ellen.

Now Sarah was nearly seventeen years older than Joe, and there had been some sibling rivalry. Joe paid her forty dollars per month and let her sleep in the living room. Joe was irritated that Sarah gave her two middle-age, married daughters her money each month. It was assumed that it was Sarah's way of getting her daughters from a nearby Kansas town to come to see her. Sarah was in her sixties; Joe was in his early fifties.

Rummage sales Sarah went to were a source of clothes for the young girls, Ellen and Bonny. She brought clothes home for Joe's approval and payment. Joe was not overjoyed about the rummage clothes, but he was not eager to buy the girls any other clothes either.

Then (~1945)   Recent (~2009)
Vera and husband

Sarah sold eggs from the chickens she raised, butter from the cow she milked and Christmas cards she sold locally. She was industrious.

Sarah was hard of hearing. When Vera, the youngest living of Joe's first family, told Sarah that she and her fiancé were planning to get married, Sarah said, "It does look like rain."

Sara raised a large garden and canned vegetables. She liked rhubarb. She raised it along the edge of the garden. It was a there every year. It made good pies, though it was tart. With ice cream on it, it tasted really good.

Sarah liked sour kraut. She cut up cabbage she raised and put it in a cloth-covered crock jar in the old cellar to process. Then she cooked it and canned it. It was potent. She made hominy by soaking corn in lye she made of wood ashes. Then she boiled the de-skinned corn she presented as hominy. It was always a medium gray color.

The chickens Sarah raised were pampered. Cornbread was cooked in a large iron skillet just for them. They were crazy over it. Sometimes the kids would sneak some of the cornbread.

Often, dogs would suck Sarah's eggs in the henhouse. Some of the eggs were "doctored" with cayenne pepper or ipecac by Sarah. These were old remedies that were supposed to make the dogs sick and break them from sucking eggs. They were not all that effective; dogs were always hungry and liked eggs. It is very difficult to break dogs from sucking eggs or chasing cars.

One day Wes and Alex, Ted's oldest son, decided to turpentine a worthless, egg-sucking, and car-chasing dog that hung around. Corn cobs were used to make the dog's rear end raw. Then the applied turpentine did its thing. The dog ran from porch to porch scooting across each as fast as he could. Sarah stopped the dog, grabbed his tail and soused his tender part with a pan of water. This episode was repeated a few times.

Sarah was a scrounger to get things done. Sometimes, when she ran out of wood for cooking, she would use fence post or other wood poles she found around the barnyard. She would leave the fire box open with the post sticking out propped up on a chair. Sometimes Sarah would put in a pole so long that it was into the stairway across the room. She would prop the stairway door open and lay the pole on the stairs. The children complained, and Joe grumbled. It made no difference; the meals got cooked.

Joe let Sarah sell eggs beyond the needs of the family and the same for butter from the milk she milked from the cow. She skimmed all of the cream off the milk and made butter to sell.

She had a box mold with a false bottom attached to a round handle through a hole in the bottom of the box. The false bottom pushed the butter, which weighed approximately a pound, out of the mold.

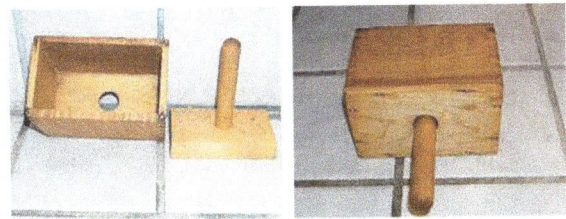

Butter Mold

Sarah became a little greedy with the milk. To make the milk stretch for cooking, she added water to what she used for cooking. When she made gravy it was brown and looked clabbered. It should have been a smooth white sauce. Ellen challenged Sarah at the breakfast table stating in the presence of Joe that Sarah had watered the gravy. Sarah said, "Why, Ellen! I didn't put water in the gravy. You should be ashamed." Joe became irritated and left the table.

Sometimes Joe would take a hog to the lockers in town to have it butchered. The meat was wrapped and placed in Joe's rented cold storage locker. Sometimes when he passed through town on his way home he would stop and get some meat from his locker. One time, Joe was feeding the pigs from the truck. One shoat had his head in front of the back wheels eating corn that fell there. When Joe drove off he ran over the one-hundred-fifty-pound pig's head and killed it. It was in the winter time (farmers usually butchered in the winter time on a cold day). Joe and the hired hand, Ted, hung the hog up by the back feet in a tree and dressed it. Sarah took the fat from the hog and cut it into approximately two inch cubes. She rendered it into lard in an oblong iron kettle. The kettle sat across two holes in the top of the cook stove. With a tea towel, she strained out the 'cracklings' from the lard and gave them to the kids. Ted got the pig's feet; he loved pickled pig's feet.

Cow Bell

One of Jay's chores after he came home from school (around 5:30 p.m.) was to find and bring in the milk cow. She would hide among the brush in the hog lot. She had a bell, but the ornery cow would stand perfectly still so the bell did not ring. She sure was aggravating. Some men would say that sort of thing was hard on one's religion.

Sarah kept her purse in Joe's bedroom. The kids found it and took some money to buy candy, especially Baby Ruth bars which cost a nickel for the one- fourth-pound bar. Sarah complained to Joe. The old sibling rivalry kicked in. Joe sent Sarah packing. She went to live with one of her daughters in a nearby Kansas town.

One of Sarah's sons-in-law ran for sheriff of the county where he lived, and he won the election. In fun, Joe told him that he should file the front sight off his pistol because someone might take it away from him and shove it where it would not feel so good.

Joe's kids had no adult woman running the house until the kids were grown. Since Joe was gone a lot tending his cattle and fields, the kids had it rough. The girls did not cook very well. Actually, they did not have much to cook with or anyone to teach them. Fortunately, the girls turned out good. The boys did not fare so well. Two of the sisters from Joe's first family, both married, helped out all they could. Their help was considerable.

The school that the kids attended had a primary grade before the first grade. Students had to be six before they could enter. After Jay finished the primary, it was abolished.

Jay was miffed about that because half of his class was a year younger than he. He was always sensitive about that.

Jay liked a pretty girl, Nancy, in his class. She was one of the younger ones that did not have to go through primary. She was not even six years old when school started (her birthday was in October). He chased her around the merry-go-round and around the slide. He was intrigued with her all through their school years. However, he knew he could never qualify to be her beau. She lived on a modern farm in a modern house. Jay always wanted to impress Nancy, but he was living 1800s lifestyle while she was living modern with both good parents that looked after their two kids. In other words, Jay was on the "wrong side of the tracks." Nancy lived some two miles away in Jay's neighborhood. She rode a different school bus. The bus on her route and the one on Jay's route were wooden with one-fourth inch bolts protruding down from the bows supporting the roofs; seats were lengthwise along the sides and a double down the middle where students sat back-to-back. Rollup curtains along each side sufficed for windows. Her dad was president of the school board. She was the prettiest girl in the school and became prettier as she grew older. She had her pick of any of the boys around her age if she wanted them. Many of Jay's friends fantasized about winning Nancy's heart, but they, like Jay, knew they could not qualify. She was a jewel that only the privileged could hope to win.

If Nancy felt not liked or not popular, that was not the case. The other students felt that they could not measure up. She unwittingly had set the bar too high. She had a good personality and made excellent grades. Jay shied away because he knew he had no chance with her. Boys stayed away because they did not want to be rejected and then teased by the other boys. She was a prize that would not be won until she was past college.

In the class photographs, Nancy is on the second row next to the teacher in the top photograph.

In the second photograph, she is on the second row and between the second and third boys on the front row from the viewer's right. She stood out as the most attractive girl in both pictures.

Jay's 4th and 6th Grade Class Photos

Wes was sweet on a girl when he was in the lower grades. He confided in Jay.

Who else could he talk to about it?

Classes were around twenty-fve students. The town the school was in was small. The only industry in the town was the school complex, grades 1 through

12. Grand Lake was nearby and the school sometimes flooded even though there was a dike around the school. Jay was as poor as most other students in the school's back-woods area. His clothes were not good, and usually he and Wes had no underwear. Joe had long johns and when the boys were younger, he had bought them long johns. Otherwise, they did without. Vera, their half-sister, bought the boys bathing suits; they wore them for underwear until they worn out.

Grade School

The grade school building had been built by the WPA, the Works Progress Administration (renamed in 1939 as The Works Projects Administration). The photograph below was taken of the building in 2014. It was a modern rock-wall building with boy's and girl's bathrooms in it when it was built. However, outside toilets with several stools in them were used instead of the bathrooms. The boy's outside toilet had a sloping concrete trough the length of the toilet. It smelled terrible. Jay would wait until he was home to go to the toilet each day, even though it meant lots of misery.

Both Wes and Jay were infatuated with Dale Evans. They went to the cowboy movies on Saturday evening every chance they got. The boys saw a movie in which Gene Autry sang "Red River Valley." That became Wes's favorite song. Also, serials such as Batman, were being shown during that time. The boys tried hard to catch as many episodes of each serial as they could.

Wes had begun to read books in grade school. He read Treasure Island and told the whole story to Jay. Wes was a fair storyteller.

Wes was ornery. He knew that Ted, the hired hand, was goosy, especially around snakes. He and his siblings put a dead black snake in Ted's Model A Ford car. The driver's seat back folded onto the seat hiding the snake. Ted nearly ruined his door and its frame when he almost sat on the snake. The kids thought that was funny. Ted could have hurt himself.

The chicken house was opposite Joe's bedroom window. One night, Joe let Ted use his 1939 Ford to go home; Ted's vehicle was in the shop. There was a pie supper at the country school house diagonally across the section (one mile by one mile). The school was still in use. No doubt neighbors thought Joe and family were at the pie supper; they were not. Some neighborhood boys decided to steal Joe's chickens. They had big sacks that they put the chickens in. Joe heard the commotion of the thieves gathering the chickens, threw open his window and fired his double barrel shotgun toward the thieves. He then reloaded and ran to the outside southwest corner of the house where he fired again striking one of the thieves who ran southwest across a freshly plowed patch of ground between the house and hog lot. There was blood on a post along the hog lot fence. Footsteps in the plowed ground were extremely long. Joe called the sheriff on his recently-installed eight-party-line telephone. The sheriff stopped a young boy in a Model A Ford coup heading home from a date in the area. As the sheriff searched the car, the boy was scared stiff. The sheriff sampled the blood on the post and found it was human. Sometime later it was learned that a neighbor had gone to his doctor with a shotgun injury that "occurred during a hunting accident with a friend."

Someone dumped a female dog and four pups out near Joe's house. The kids wanted to keep the dogs, but Joe allowed them to keep only two, both females. As pups the dogs were taken squirrel hunting in the forty-acre hog lot. An older dog treed a squirrel, and someone shot it. The pups started to the house frightened by the gunshot. But then they saw how the old dog was so excited waiting for the squirrel to fall that they returned and jumped into the middle of the fray when the squirrel fell. From then on the pups were squirrel dogs. They became so good at it that, when they were grown, they would rush to the hog lot and tree a squirrel any time anyone stepped out on the porch with a gun. They seldom barked up an empty tree. Squirrels could hide from hunters by moving to the opposite side of tree limbs; however, the hunter could stand close to the trunk of the tree and usually see the squirrel.

In grade school the boys all played with marbles. They called them doogies. Most marbles were standard size, but some were considerably larger. The larger ones were called stoogies. During recess and noon hour, the boys would draw a circle about three feet across in the dirt, and each would place a marble in the middle of the circle. Who shot first was usually the largest boy at the circle. He would use his large marble and flip it with his thumb. If he did not have a large marble he could use a standard size one. If he knocked out a marble it was his and he could shoot again. Then the next boy beside the shooter would shoot. Any marbles he knocked out was his. This went on until all marbles were knocked out of the ring or the bell rang signifying that school was back in session. Sometimes, someone used a steel ball bearing. The steel sometimes chipped the glass marbles. This game was a bit like pool. A sack of marbles was an acceptable Christmas gift for the boys. The classes drew names so that each student would have to buy only one gift. Marbles were economical, too.

Another game the boys loved to play was mumbly peg. They would use a pocket knife with two blades. They opened the long blade out straight. The other was opened halfway. They had a procedure to follow; they would start with the short blade stuck into the ground. They would flip the back end with a finger. If a blade stuck in the ground, they would go to the next step. They set the long blade on their wrist and flipped it in a circular motion toward the ground. If it stuck the elbow was next followed by the shoulder, then the chin by holding the tip of the blade with two fingers at the chin. Last was "over the world" by throwing the knife over a shoulder. Kids know how to entertain themselves even if their games are a bit weird.

Jay was in the first grade when his mother died. He was shy and did not ask his dad for things. The class students each bought a tonett, an oboe type wind instrument. Jay really wanted one, but he knew there was no way he could have one. He missed his mother. He listened and enjoyed the music from the next room where the students were taking lessons on their tonetts. He liked his second grade teacher. She was young, pretty and pleasant. She was a single lady. All of the kids enjoyed her class. The grade school building is still there, but there are buildings attached on each end now.

In the fourth grade all of the kids exchanged valentines. Nancy gave all of the kids in class a valentine. Jay was so ashamed that he had none to give her in exchange. Jay had no way to get any valentines. He had no money and no way to get to town to buy any. Besides, Joe, Jay's dad, was not about to spend money or time on such things.

Jay was not athletic. He was small through grade school. He did not eat well, as was the same for the other three siblings. The fifth grade teacher was a softball fan. He picked a good team from the class boys and took them around the county to play other schools. They were well coached and won most of their games. But Jay did not make the team, no matter how hard he tried. He was deeply disappointed.

Jay was in the fifth grade when his brother, Wes, was killed on a Boy Scout trip camping for his eagle badge. It was a down time for Jay. Wes was buried next to his mother. Wes excelled at handling farm machinery.

Jay was not close friends with his sisters; they were close friends with each other. His dad was aloof. Jay became introverted. He was not a happy lad. The highlights of his life then were the Sundays and holidays when Lou and her family and Vera and her family came out for the mid-day meals and socializing. The family's two dogs were a lot of company. They chased squirrels through the tree tops together. The dogs seemed to know where all of the squirrels were in the forty-acre hog lot which had lots of big trees and a spring-fed creek running through it.

The seventh grade was considerably better. It was junior high and each class had a different teacher. Teachers graded on the curve. The math teacher had a ciphering match on Fridays in his class. This type of schooling began to click with Jay. He figured that if he just simply paid attention in class and did his homework as it was assigned, he would make good grades. It worked. There was an ulterior motive; impress the pretty girl, Nancy. Also, he became good at horse shoes and table tennis. The classes were held in second story class rooms around the gymnasium with a basketball court and a stage area for assemblies and plays. This was the time when President Truman fired Jay's hero, General McArthur. When Roosevelt died, Jay was not happy, but he was relieved; he did not really know why except Roosevelt was in office for his fourth term. A dictator?

Key Signature Sample
[(E♭) → E flat]

Good Debts Are Everlasting, But Few Collect." The last two are sharp.

In the eighth grade, things began to gel. Good grades were the order of the day. Jay began to feel better about himself. He was still a loner but not by design. He did have friends. The school had picnics at Shiffindecker Park in Joplin. Each student was to bring something to put on the table to share for lunch. Jay did not have anything worthy to share; he brought what he could scrape up, put it in a sack and went off down by the river by himself during lunch. When playing volley ball, Nancy hit him on the nose, by accident, causing it to bleed. He did not mind because he had been touched by her; he felt privileged. She probably thought, Clumsy oaf, he should have stayed out of the way.

In the ninth grade Jay had gained respect as a straight A student. Some of the lazy guys sat as close to Jay as they could to copy on tests. Nancy sat in a desk next to Jay in a class. He was elated. Jay tried to strike up a conversation with her. Being shy, he was awkward. He was embarrassed by a remark by one of the guys that liked to sit close to Jay and ruining it for Jay. Jay got up and moved to the back of the room where the guys could not gather around. He secretly hoped she would move back, too; she did not. Jay saw that as his last and only chance with her. What a shame; he worshiped her.

In the tenth grade, Jay was sixteen. He enrolled in a class that he did not like and he did not like the teacher's methods. He dropped out and the teacher gave him an F for the course. He made good grades in the other courses because he had developed good study habits. He met an attractive girl in a lower grade and courted her. That was his undoing. She was a sweet girl and was good to him, but he did not know anything about courting or how to treat a girl.

At the end of the school year they ran off together. It was a dumb Idea. She was having her period and needed things including food. They stayed overnight courted her. That was his undoing. She was a sweet girl and was good to him, but he did not know anything about courting or how to treat a girl.

At the end of the school year they ran off together. It was a dumb Idea. She was having her period and needed things including food. They stayed overnight in a tree house that Jay and Carl built. The sheriff's deputies came out and took the girl home. Someone had seen them walking that way.

Young people need parental guidance; otherwise, they dream up dumb ideas and try to make them work. It was a desperate situation for Jay, or so it seemed at the time. With school out he would not be able to see her except on a weekend, sometimes, maybe. He never saw her again. After she was married she called Jay once for a short conversation.

Many years later when Jay was working as an engineer in the nuclear weapons complex, he saw young men become desperate when they thought they were losing their sweethearts. One of Jay's close friends, a fellow engineer who had been valedictorian of his entire graduating class at Kansas State University in both undergraduate and graduate classes, nearly go nuts when he thought he was losing his sweetheart. He had met her in a class in college and helped her get passing grades. They were now graduated and working at good jobs. She decided to date other guys; she did not want to change her name because her doctorate degree was in her maiden name. The young man was at her apartment once when another suitor called; he said he felt like shouting, "Hang up the phone and come back to bed." He did not. He fretted a lot about his predicament until he got the romance back on track after much effort. They were married a short time later. Jay remembered his situation.

Then, a young fresh out of school engineer who was in Jay's group at the same facility, lost his sweetheart. Jay saw her at a department picnic; she was a beauty. This fellow was living with her and her five-year-old son. One day she ask him what his intentions were. He said he liked things the way they were.

completely. He worked on Jay's project and needed help until he recovered enough to perform his duties well.

The following Fall Jay now in the eleventh grade, refused to go back to the school he was in. Lou encouraged him to go back to school. He had a driver's license and Joe let him use the old International truck for transportation. Jay went to the high school nearby and asked the superintendent if he could go to school there. The superintendent gave Jay paperwork for release from the other school. Jay took it to his former school's superintendent for his signature. A signature was reluctantly given; Jay convinced the superintendent that he was not coming back to that school no matter what.

Starting in the eleventh grade late in the first semester, Jay made good grades including the school's honor roll. He fit in well and enjoyed school. He parked the old truck a few blocks away and ate lunch in it. Since he never had much money, his lunch usually was a small can of pork and beans, a small bottle of milk and a package of potato chips. A few students harassed him about the girl incident, but it did not amount to much. He made friends and got along well with the other students. He saw Carl, his nephew, there sometimes. Jay was told that he finished sixth of 132 students with his grade point average at the high school. He enrolled in a local junior college the following fall.

The high school had driver's training classes. Jay took the course to finish the required number of credits he needed even though he had been driving farm equipment, including trucks, since pre-teen age. He got his driver's license as soon as he was old enough. Jay joined the high school driver's team and became their top driver. He made top scorer of all of the schools in the local area contest and the regional meet. He was last of the team to drive each time. On the team were two girls. He liked both, but one seemed to like him. The team did well in all of its contests. He began dating one of the girls after high school graduation. The girl was a year behind Jay.

He asked for the opportunity to drive first at the semi-state contest because the "butter flies" in his stomach bothered him while waiting his turn to drive. It was granted. He did not do as well on driving this time but he made a perfect score on the written test part of the contest.

The driver's team consisted of three primary drivers and two alternates. The primary drivers were Jay and the two girls. The alternates were guys. The regional contest was held at Claremore, OK. There Jay saw the Davis gun

The Davis Gun Collection

collection. It was in an old wooden hotel at that time, and was running over with guns of all types and ages. Today the collection has its own museum located on the old US 66 highway in Claremore. It has approximately fifty thousand guns in the museum.

Speaking of the old US 66 highway, the original paved highway 66 ran from near the Kansas border for a short distance toward Tulsa (to Afton) as a single lane9. When two cars met, each had to get two wheels off onto the shoulder. It was sometimes called the Sidewalk Highway. It ran through Miami, OK, down Main Street south by the Fair Grounds, south a few miles, west a few more miles, south again a few miles and west again to the present US 66 highway near Narcissa. The marker in the photograph at right is Jay helped his dad, Joe, farm an eighty-acre field alongside this road. As Jay was

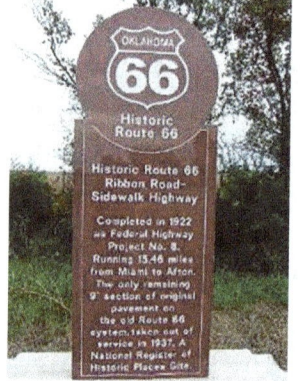

Highway 66 marker

opening up the field with a self-propelled combine, Joe was standing on the platform with Jay, who was driving. Joe wanted the combine going to the right around the field for unloading the bin; a mistake. The bin auger hung out over the left side. Joe was blocking Jay's view of the auger as they approached a telephone pole. The auger was bent severely. Joe took it to the local blacksmith shop in town and had it straightened. It worked OK after that.

Jay liked working the 80 acres field along the old highway. It had a pond at one end with clear water. An old abandoned John Deer tractor was near the pond. Sometimes Jay and Wes worked some parts off the old steel wheel tractor. Jay liked swimming in the clear water of the pond there. There may have been some varmints in the pond, such as snakes, but that did not bother Jay.

Jay normally bathed after a hard day's work in a local pond or stream. Bath facilities at the old farm house at home were 1800s style (#3 wash tub). The livestock ponds were usually muddy and not too sanitary. Jay swam in them anyhow. He was always wondering if he got more on than off. He did not dwell on that, though. The water was inviting. There was a time when he and his nephew seined a water moccasin out of a creek. The snake went back in the water and the boys continued to seine for minnows for fish bait. It is a wonder that farm boys ever reached maturity.

Old 66 Highway

Livestock Pond

Clear Water Pond

The government built ponds for farmers shortly after WWII as a conservation measure for farmers. Joe had several.

Chapter 4

Hard Times

The four semi-orphans are now more than one half orphaned. Joe was gone farming a lot, and the four were on their own most of the time. Ellen told Jay that there was a rumor indicating the four kids were destined for an orphanage in Tulsa before Sarah came to care for the kids and keep house. Also, there was a rumor that Joe's sister nearest Joe's age, Anita, wanted to take Jay. She and her husband lived on a farm near Jasper, Missouri. She was Jay's favorite aunt on his dad's side of the family. The sister and her husband had no children of their own and had a nice, modern, three story farm house. She was one of two favorite aunts, one on each side of the family.

Since the girls did not know how to cook or have much food to cook, they did not have much interest in the same. Ellen called Wes "Big Shot" because he bullied the younger three.

The boys were not much interested in house work. When Sarah was with them, she cooked such things as cornbread and pinto beans. The kids grew to like them. She also cooked a good custard pie. One time she cooked a custard pie and gave it to the boys. They ate it all in one sitting. The rhubarb pies she cooked were a bit too tart for the boys to enjoy.

Once, Wes decided to make egg custard after Sarah was gone. Sugar was rationed and scarce, but his mother, Carol, had bought a large box of saccharin, which is about four hundred times sweeter than sugar, because she could buy only a small amount of sugar with ration stamps. Wes used the same amount of saccharin that the recipe required of sugar. Wes and Jay tried to eat the "custard" and became very sick. Jay reacted to saccharin for years after that (it is a common sweetener in toothpaste).

During the war such things as ice cream was not always available. Joe and his two boys went to Joplin on farm business one day. On the way back they stopped at a store along the road and Joe bought each a pint of orange ice cream, the only ice cream that the store had available during that war time. They immediately realized why the treat was available; it had grated orange peel in it. The peel was bitter, but they ate the ice cream anyhow sitting on the flat bed of the truck. Of course they spit the orange peel out as they went; it was better than nothing.

Sarah was born around 1873 and was comfortable living the old 1800s lifestyle. Now the kids had to scrounge without a woman in the house after Sarah left. Joe and his "lack-of-creature-comforts" attitude did not help much. His philosophy was to "put your money in livestock and farm machinery rather than the home." He said, "the home won't make you any money."

For lighting in the house Carol had two ordinary coal oil [kerosene] lamps and an Aladdin lamp that gave light equal to a sixty- watt electric light bulb. Joe used the Aladdin lamp; the kids studied with the other two, which gave a dim light, for studying.

Coal Oil Lamp   Aladdin Coal Oil Lamp

During the WWII years, almost everything was rationed. Materials available were poor quality. As stated earlier, Jay bought a flash light made of pressed paper; the ends would not stay on.

Kids were rationed to three pairs of shoes per year; however, for kids on the farm the poor quality shoes would hardly last four months. Joe would only buy his boys high top work shoes, along with overalls for clothes. The shoes would break loose in the back. Jay wired his together; this hurt his feet and ruined his socks (when he had a pair). His heels looked like rusty metal. Sometimes Jay wore overshoes, if he had a workable pair, to school on good days to hide his broken shoes and dirty, rusty heels. It took about three weeks of begging Joe to get a new pair of shoes. Jay would sometimes fry an egg and put it between two pieces of hard bread. If a trip to the grocery store was made on Saturday night, bread, which was wrapped in wax paper, would be hard as rocks by midweek. Sometimes the only pieces of bread left were the heels. Jay wrapped his egg sandwich in a newspaper and tied a string around it. It looked like he had a lunch; he threw it into the waste basket at school and went out to the playground at noon. There was a lunch room available in the basement of the Friends Church, but Joe did not give the kids money to buy lunch at that time. Later the school set up a lunch room with reasonable costs for lunch. The kids begged Joe for lunch money on Monday. Sometimes by Wednesday he gave them money for lunch. Usually, he said, "I ain't got it" and walked off. Jay and Ellen hated to ask Joe for money and would rather do without lunch. Bonnie continued to beg for the money with some success. Even though he did not have enough money with him, he would write a check when Bonnie asked. It was nice to have lunch and a hot lunch at that.

Once, when Jay was in the fourth grade, the kids were told to bring some money to see a puppet show the school sponsored. All students had the money except Jay, who refused to ask his dad for it. He was left in the room by himself. One of the teachers came back to see what he was doing and reported that he was crying; that was not the case for he had borrowed a large-part puzzle from the desk of another student and was working it. The teacher took Jay to the gym where the show was and let him watch from the balcony. Due to the circumstances, Jay was developing a thick skin. He became used to living like a pauper.

Ellen and Bonnie slept together in the East end of the upstairs dormer. The boys slept on the other end. Ellen sucked her thumb well into her teenage years. She held a piece of cotton in her index finger and tickled her nose with it. The cotton came from the mattress on Bonny's side of the bed. Over a period of time, Bonnie found herself sleeping on the "bare" springs.

There was a cat on the farm named faucet by the kids. It would stand at the door and come into the house when someone went out. He invariably did his daily toiletry on the living room floor. One day the kids took the cat to the creek that ran through the hog lot to drown him. Every time he came out, the kids threw him back in. The cat finally got so tired that he could not swim any more. The kids felt sorry for him, dried him off and took him back to the house.

It was tough sledding in those years. Joe owned several head of beef cows. He felt that the kids were not old enough to take care of a milk cow and milk it. Joe bought milk when he came through town or by a country store. When he did not, they all did without. When he did, he bought four quarts in glass bottles; he drank a quart for supper and one for breakfast. The kids divided the other two.

The kids had chores when they came home from school. One of their responsibilities was taking water to brood sows with small pigs. They had to pump the water and take it to the pig pens. From time to time Joe stepped into the pens with the sows to straighten and clean their troughs. The sows with small pigs were cranky and aggressive toward anyone in their pens. Joe normally was able to keep them at bay by

Joe with his Yorkshire Sows with Piglets

yelling and kicking at them. He did get bitten once but not serious. The photograph at right shows Joe in the pig pen wearing his Makenaw coat.

Joe had a stern attitude with his animals. He broke his horses by putting the horse to be broken to work in between two other horses on a gang pulling a

wagon. He would drive them onto the county road in front of the house with the middle horse bucking and snorting. Then, with his lines, he slapped each horse on the back side: whap, whap, whap!

The horses took off down the road at a dead run. When they came back from going around the mile section (four miles), the new horse was broke and dead tired. Draft animals cannot run very far, not like Arabian saddle horses that can run for miles at a time.

For some reason Joe favored the oldest son, Wes. Maybe it was because he looked to Wes to help with the family. Wes sometimes went to the field with Joe. The other three found canned tomatoes in the cellar where Sarah had put them or dug potatoes when they were available in the summers. That was better than nothing. One time the three came up with some money among them. It was somewhat less than a dollar. They walked to a country store nearly two miles away and bought a brick of chili and a small, single-stack box of crackers. They had a feast, or it seemed. They were hungry and did not mind that the chili had windpipes, eye balls, etc., in cow fat (tallow).

Jay and Siblings as Adults

Joe insisted that the kids raise a garden. He plowed it with an old mare and a walking plow. The kids did not like pulling weeds much; the weeds were heartier than the vegetables. However, the three sure were glad to have something to eat when the garden did produce. Fried new-potatoes in lard did not taste all that great but they are fantastic when you are hungry.

The photograph at right shows the three after they were grown. They had plenty to eat when they were adults, according the picture.

When Jay was eight years old, he too went to the fields. Joe always bought a good dinner (lunch) for the three consisting of a quart of milk apiece, a loaf of bread, bologna, bananas or other fruit, potato chips sometimes and cookies. The boys loved to go to the fields just for that. Wes raked hay scraps in the summers with the mule named Jude. The scraps were left by the sweep rake and, also, the baler when it moved to a new site. Jay played with other kids of hay hands; they came to the field with their dads. By the age of thirteen, Wes was running the sweep rake mounted on a tractor and Jay was raking hay with Jude.

A carnival came to town one weekend, and Wes and Jay walked the seven miles to town and across the river to the fairgrounds where the carnival was. A fair was going on, too. They took in the sights, spent the few coins they scraped up and were too tired to walk home. They walked to J R's house at the east end of Central in the town and spent the night. J R's wife cooked some store-bought bacon the next morning; boy, was that good for boys used to eating whatever they could get. J R's wife was a good cook though J R once told her that if he wanted to eat slop, he would eat with the hogs. It hurt her feelings.

One day a circus came to town. Ted and Joe were working the twenty-acre field behind the fairgrounds. The circus set up across the road north of the field. The circus's setup-foreman asked Ted's two boys and Joe's two boys if they would like to earn some money. They all four worked all day helping set up the big tent and the seats. At the end of the day the boys found that the pay was a pass to the circus. Ted's younger boy and Jay slipped out under the tent to catch their dads to go home. The two older boys stayed. Ted waited for the boys until the circus was over. He took Wes home with him. Joe was a stern man and did not wait. That is not the only time he ran off and left his kids in town to walk home. He let it be known that he did not much like kids.

Another time, J R's family and the two older sisters of Joe's first family, with their families, had a picnic near Stepp's Ford Bridge. Until recently it was the oldest in-use bridge of its kind in its area. It is located directly west of Commerce, OK. Wes and the daughter of Lou were swimming in the Neosho River that ran under the bridge. They stepped off in a hole and both were being swept down the river with just their heads bobbing out of the water.

Stepp's Ford Bridge

A Good Samaritan nearby saw the plight and jumped into the river with his clothes on; he rescued both. Jay never knew who the Good Samaritan was, and probably none of the others there found out who he was either. They were swimming in the area shown in the lower photograph of the bridge.

Wes was old enough to handle a tractor and drove one, usually plowing or disc harrowing. He had his pick of the tractors when they were doing a job he could handle. Wes was mischievous. He was driving a steel wheel Case tractor from the cow barns, a half mile away, to the house. He asked Jay, seven years old, who was riding with him, if Jay wanted to drive. Of course he did, and Wes stepped off after putting the tractor in motion. When Jay looked around and saw he was alone he panicked because he did not know how to stop the tractor. It ran into a deep ditch and out the other side

through a fence before it came to a stop with one wheel in the ditch still driving. Joe came up in his truck, was mad as a hornet, and stopped the tractor. He gave the boys a lecture with a few expletives thrown in.

This was not the only time that Wes got the boys in trouble. He found some dynamite caps and some fuse in the shed portion of the big barn at the house. He clinched the fuse in some caps and stuck the caps in some cracks in rocks along a cliff at the creek in the hog lot. The idea was to blast a "cave" in the hillside. Fortunately, there was no dynamite available. Joe had the caps and fuse for dynamite to remove stumps. That was a

Tandem Disc Harrow

This was not the only time that Wes got the boys in trouble. He found some dynamite caps and some fuse in the shed portion of the big barn at the house. He clinched the fuse in some caps and stuck the caps in some cracks in rocks along a cliff at the creek in the hog lot. The idea was to blast a "cave" in the hillside. Fortunately, there was no dynamite available. Joe had the caps and fuse for dynamite to remove stumps. That was a close call for the boys.

Another time the kids were helping paint the corral. It was made of full two by eight inches cross-section oak boards attached to large hedge posts. The fences were about six feet high. A worthless dog that Joe picked up at the city animal shelter came around where the kids were painting with red paint. Wes grabbed the dog by the tail and painted his private area. It could not be seen with the dog's tail in its normal position. However, when the dog was chasing a car, he ran with his tail up. The kids noticed that the people in the cars driving by were smiling and laughing. One afternoon the dog came out to chase the school bus. The kids discovered the amusement the dog was causing. They gave the dog to the school bus driver. The driver did not keep him long.

Wes "borrowed" Joe's single shot 20-gauge shotgun from Joe's bedroom. When Joe came home, he immediately realized the gun was missing. He challenged the boys for the gun and gave them another stern word or two about messing with things they should leave alone.

The boys were plowing a field on what was called "the prairie" because of lack of trees. Wes was driving a new

VAC Case Tractor

VAC model Case tractor that drove like a car. It had a hydraulic lift for the tractor-mounted, two fourteen-inch plows. The tractor that Jay was driving was a fairly new SC Case pulling a two bottom, fourteen-inch drag plow mounted on wheels. Wes asked Jay if he wanted to drive the VAC. He did, and Wes started off ahead. For some reason Wes decided to throw the broken parts into the furrow and plow them under. Joe was puzzled as to how the plow was broken. Of course the boys "did not know how it happened." Joe went to town and bought replacement parts. The plow could be used with the broken parts, but it could run somewhat sideways at times.

The SC Case tractor that Jay was driving was a 1946 unit. The one Wes was driving was newer. The VAC Case tractor was a new model after the war. The boys were around eleven and fourteen years old at the time. They were both experienced tractor operators and the accident should not have happened.

These tractors seemed like toys in the 1990s, but in the 1940s and 1950s they were medium-size tractors since both pulled two fourteen-inch bottom plows (moldboard plows with fourteen-inch-cut shears). Jay thought the SC model was awkward with its hand clutch, steering rod sticking out to one side, seat down between the wheels and tiny disc brakes that did not work. All

SC Case Tractor

of that was not as much of a problem on the VAC model. The steering rod on the SC was bent several times when plowing because the tractor would not turn well at the end of the field because the tiny disc brakes did not hold, and the rod struck fence posts when turning to the right.

On a Sunday evening, Joe was away. Wes and Jay caught the worthless, suck-egg, car-chasing dog, tied baling wire to his tail and tied the other end to all of the new SC Case tractor's spark plugs. The spark plug wires had no boots at the plugs, and the connectors were bare where the baling wire was tied. Wes hit the starter button with the magneto ground switch open. The electrical jolt gave the dog a kick start. He ran off with all of the spark plug wires, including a grommet holding the wires in a bundle, through the weeds. Wes and Jay found all of the wires but no grommet. The boys knew nothing about firing order of the engine

plugs, and the connectors were bare where the baling wire was tied. Wes hit the starter button with the magneto ground switch open. The electrical jolt gave the dog a kick start. He ran off with all of the spark plug wires, including a grommet holding the wires in a bundle, through the weeds. Wes and Jay found all of the wires but no grommet. The boys knew nothing about firing order of the engine cylinders. They put the shortest wire onto the spark plug nearest the closest port on the magneto. The other wires were installed with the same pattern in mind.

The next morning when Ted came to work he needed the SC tractor. He tried to start it, but it sounded like the Fourth of July. It popped and cracked because it was firing with the valves open. The firing order was wrong. Joe came to see what was wrong. Neither could figure the problem out. Joe backed his truck up to the tractor and Ted tied a log chain to it. They drug the tractor down the rough country road at a high rate of speed. Ted, a very conservative man in all he did, was challenged to hang on the tractor, especially since the brakes were nearly useless; he could not keep the chain tight. Ted remarked later, "It ain't no need of a man driving that way." Less than an hour later, the boys could hear Joe's truck coming more than a mile away. The truck had no muffler, and they could tell that it was coming at a high rate of speed; they knew they were in a heap of trouble. They hid out for about three days until Joe got over his mad. Town was around six miles away, and when Ted came driving the tractor back he grumbled loudly. The boys avoided him, too. Ted had another favorite saying for someone driving too fast: "skinning it back." That is vulgar but no worse than "pissed off" which is in the dictionary. Sometime later as Jay was plowing with the SC Case tractor the rear axle on the right side broke placing the tire in Jay's lap. The axel was approximately four inches in diameter. It was replaced in the field where it broke. Jay never did like the Case tractors much.

1939 Ford Sedan

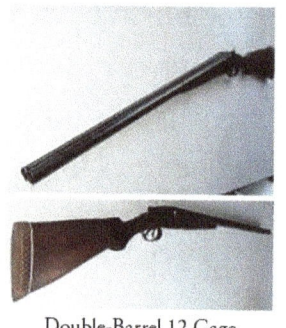

Double-Barrel 12 Gage
Shotgun

One spring Joe decided to take a look at one of his large hay meadows. The grass for the hay was native blue stem, a medium fine grass ideal for hay. Wes and Jay were with him in Joe's black 1939 Ford car. The meadow was wet from a recent rain, and the car became stuck in the mud. Joe decided to walk home for a tractor some thirteen miles away. Why he did not go to Ted's place that bordered the hay meadow is not known. Joe had his double barrel twelve-gauge shotgun in the car. He usually carried a shotgun when he went to his fields or pastures. Wes decided to cut off the lead-shot end of shells and fire the gun. He fired both barrels; nothing came out. The wadding was stuck about ½ way down each barrel. Wes tried to poke the wadding out with a coat hanger. It did not budge. He knew they were in trouble with their dad again. Wes put two live rounds in the gun and fired them. Each barrel had two bulges about half way down. Years later

Jay noticed the bulges were gone when he and Joe were walking through the hog lot during a visit by Jay. He asked about the bulges; Joe said he had the bulges rolled out at the machine shop. When asked if he knew what caused the bulges, he said he thought he stuck the gun in the mud sometime or another. When told what really happened, Joe made no comment.

Joe thought well of Wes. Wes asked for a saddle and pony. Joe had a young work-type horse broken for Wes. It was broken by rodeo men, and it was temperamental. Wes got along OK with it, but Jay did not care much for it. The saddle was brand new and had protrusions on each side of

Wes and Horse   Wes, Horse and Niece

the saddle horn to lock the rider's knees under. It was called a bucking saddle. Wes rode the horse around the farm a lot. Jay never had any desire to ride. The work horse rode like a lumber wagon plodding along at a work horse gait. Too, the stirrups were too long for Jay; it was uncomfortable to ride without feet in the stirrups. Jay was content to leave the horse alone. By the way, the niece in the photograph above was the one with Wes when they nearly drowned during the picnic at Stepp's Ford Bridge.

Wes asked Joe for high lace-up riding boots. Joe bought them for Wes. He also bought a pair of spurs with only a knob on the ends. Wes and Jay would have liked a smaller riding pony to help work cattle with. Joe had accumulated several head of cattle, and a pony would have been a big help.

When Wes was in junior high school he joined the boy scouts. Joe bought him the usual Boy Scout paraphernalia including camping gear. Wes did all the requirements for the badges up to the Eagle badge. He worked on that. His remaining step in the Boy Scout requirements was for the Eagle Badge. He reached that goal even though it cost him his life. Wes was a go-getter. He knew how to handle his dad to get much of what he wanted. He was successful in life. He already made the ultimate accomplishment: Acceptance of the Lord's salvation plan.

Joe had a 15-30 steel wheel tractor. He was not allowed to drive it on the highway, so he hauled it in the back of his truck. It was hard on the truck bed, which was made of full two inches by six inches oak planks. When Joe moved the tractor, he backed the truck up to a creek bank. He backed the tractor onto the truck. The tractor's brakes were not so too good. One Saturday afternoon Joe and Ted loaded the tractor onto the truck at the creek. Wes and Jay were standing in front of the left

McCormick Deering Farm Tractor

rear wheel. Joe started out of the creek with the International truck. The truck stalled after a few feet and Joe let it roll back into the creek. The tractor moved a couple of feet toward the boys as the truck came a sudden stop against the high bank used as a loading dock. Joe put the truck in low gear in the two-speed rear end, revved the engine, and with the transmission in compound low, lurched forward. The two boys had climbed upon the high sides after the tractor moved the first time. This time the tractor rolled and the front end fell into the creek. With big loading boards and house jacks, Ted and Joe were able to get the tractor back onto the truck after hours of effort. A log chain helped to keep the tractor on the truck.

 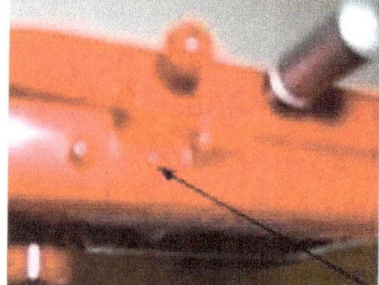 

Gasoline tank

Farmall M International Harvester Tractor

In the spring of 1942 Joe traded the 15- 30 for a Farmall M. Carol's brother, Hank, who was working for Joe at the time, brought the new tractor home. Joe put a sealed beam fog light on the front of the tractor, and he, Hank and Ted ran the tractor twenty-four hours a day. The tractor had a large kerosene tank and a small gasoline tank (center photograph above). The gasoline tank was for starting and warming the tractor.

Steam Engine and Stationary Thresher

The three ran the tractor on kerosene because gasoline was scarce due to high demand for the war effort. The dealer who traded the Farmall to Joe tried to start the 15-30; it had to be hand cranked. Instead of pulling the crank through so that the crank would be jerked out of his hand if the engine kicked backwards, the dealer tried spinning the engine. It kicked back and broke the dealer's arm.

The M at the time of purchase was a large tractor. It pulled a three-bottom moldboard plow with fourteen-inches cut for each bottom. The size of the plow a tractor could pull was the normal size-designation for tractors at the time. The M was a pleasure to drive. It had a foot clutch and brakes that worked. They were fitted with large brake-wheels with bands around them that held the wheel when the brake was applied. For road travel, the two brakes were locked together tractor twenty-four hours a day. The tractor had a large kerosene tank and a small gasoline tank (center photograph above). The gasoline tank was for starting and warming the tractor. The three ran the tractor on kerosene because gasoline was scarce due to high demand for the war effort. The dealer who traded the Farmall to Joe tried to start the 15-30; it had to be hand cranked. Instead of pulling the crank through so that the crank would be jerked out of his hand if the engine kicked backwards, the dealer tried spinning the engine. It kicked back and broke the dealer's arm.

The M at the time of purchase was a large tractor. It pulled a three-bottom moldboard plow with fourteen-inches cut for each bottom. The size of the plow a tractor could pull was the normal size-designation for tractors at the time. The M was a pleasure to drive. It had a foot clutch and brakes that worked. They were fitted with large brake-wheels with bands around them that held the wheel when the brake was applied. For road travel, the two brakes were locked together to prevent turning the tractor over at high speed with one wheel brake applied. Too, the driver sat up high out of the wheel dust.

Before the 1940s Joe owned a binder pulled by horses. The binder had wheels mounted to the two ends of the binder for moving the binder from one field to another. They were either removable for field operation or cranked up out of the way.

Grain Binders

In operation the platform gathered the stalks of grain. It was supported by a small wheel at the outer end. The other end was supported by a bull wheel, under the driver, which drove the binder operation.

The leading edge of the platform had a sickle bar that cut the stalks of grain close to the ground. The grain fell onto a canvas conveyor, encouraged by a reel, with slats to move the grain toward the bundling and tying apparatus. For tying,

The 6-Feet Cut Allis Chalmers Combine

In 1942, Joe bought a six-foot cut Allis Chalmers combine, tractor-powered. That sure made harvesting a lot easier. Jay was mesmerized by the steam engine and thresher, though. One day, a hired hand was pulling the combine with the Farmall M

Clutch   Stand
Allis Chalmers Combine Stand and Clutch
Position[10]

tractor. Jay was riding the combine standing on the small platform near the grain bin. His job was to rake down the oats being harvested in the bin. Oats did not settle well into the bin, not like wheat or beans. They would pile up under the grain elevator and plug the elevator if they were not raked down. Jay became fatigued and sat down on the platform. Beneath the platform was a spring-loaded clutch made of two surfaces of steel with their rippled surfaces held together by springs on long bolts. Castellated nuts held the springs in place and had cotter pins with protruding ends to hold the castellated nuts in place. The clutch was on the drive shaft from the tractor. It was a safety device to protect the combine if the combine locked up for some reason like picking up a rock.

Spring-loaded clutch

The clutch in the photograph at right is nearly the same design except the nuts were castellated as shown in the photo on the next page of a castellated nut. Cotter pins were inserted through the slots in the nut and through a hole in the bolts; the cotter pins grabbed anything near them. Later, locking nuts replaced the castellated nuts in most cases. Most farm machinery used square nuts for general purpose at that time.

Square Nut

Locking nut

Castellated Nut

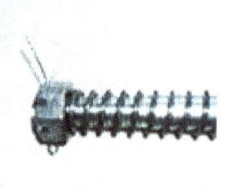

Cotter Pin through bolt in castellated, spring-loaded clutch bolt

Jay hung his feet straddling the shaft near the clutch. The protruding cotter pins on the clutch grabbed Jay's pants and shoes. Jay yelled as loud as he could for the driver to stop, but the combine was making too much noise. Fortunately, Jay's pants and old tennis shoes were rotted and lacked strength to pull Jay down into the shaft area. Jay was able to jerk himself loose with minor injuries. He never sat down on that platform again.

One day Jay was helping Ted, who was combining oats across the road from the house. Jay tried to bring the truck to the combine to empty the grain bin. He had done that before. The truck clutch was hard to push and the bare pedal was worn slick. Jay's foot slipped and the truck lurched breaking an axel. The rear axles were the weakest part of the truck. Joe had broken the axels several times and had some spares. Usually the axels broke at the wheel making changing easy. But this time the axel broke at the ring gear and ground the debris in the differential. The differential area had to be cleaned and any damage station where he bought the boys a nickel bottle of pop each. The boys were thinking that crime did pay.

Sometimes Joe liked to catch one of his work horses and ride it to the fields in the bottom grounds near the river to see if the hands needed anything. He had two that looked alike; one was broke to ride and the other was not. He picked the wrong one. It threw him off and stepped on his leg. J R was working nearby, brought Joe to the house and put him in Joe's 1939 Ford. He drove the Ford as fast as it would go to the hospital in town. Fortunately there were no broken bones, Joe healed quickly.

Joe brought home a yellow cat called Fluffy. It was an excellent mouser. Once, when corn was being shoveled from a crib, mice were running everywhere. The cat caught three mice at the same time. She had one held down under each front paw and one in her mouth. She had some planning to do to handle that situation. Sometimes when someone was milking cows, the cats would standby during the milking. They loved to eat milk squirted from the cows. They became very excited when milking was done for they knew it was their feeding time.

One evening when Joe was milking, his sons-in-law that were married to Joe's two oldest daughters of Joe's first family, came out for a visit. One reached under the cow Joe was milking and grabbed a teat. The cow jumped and kicked the bucket splashing milk on Joe. Joe grabbed a two-by-four board and beat a calf nearby for "causing" the cow to jump. He had several strong words about what the calf "had done." The sons-in-law quietly went back to the house unseen.

Mules

As was mentioned earlier, Jay drove a mule pulling a hay rake in the summers. Joe had several hay fields and they baled hay all summer beginning in late June or early July. Jay raked scraps left by the sweep rake as it brought hay to the baler. Another similar hay rake was used to rake the hay into windrows after it was cut and dried. An old man in his eighties raked the new mowed hay into the windrows for the sweep rake. He drove another mule that was a matched team with the one Jay drove. Its name was Young Mule. Both had been US Army mules with army numbers branded on their jaws. The mules were similar in appearance to the pair of mules shown in the photograph at right, above. Each rake had two shafts

Black Gelding[11]

Hay Rake[10]

to straddle the mules instead of one tongue for two horses to pull the rake; each rake was pulled by one mule.

The mule for Jay's rake was named Jude. Jude was a good mule, very serious in her attitude. She would follow the sweep rake faithfully. If Jay was asleep, which was the case many times in mid-afternoon, the mule would follow the sweep rake to the baler named Bird was retired. The day Bird was retired to the pasture her teammate, John, a brown, male mule, became sick with grief. He and Bird were the best of friends and

John look-alike and owner, Jake[12]

were always together when loose in the pasture. John would not eat or drink; he grieved so much he fell over and died in the middle of the afternoon the same day. Bird had to be brought back and put on the sweep rake again.

Sweep Rake

The hay was mowed by a tractor-mounted mower. A horse drawn IHC mower, converted to a tractor-drawn mower, was used for backup and helped when the primary mower got behind. The baler tractor pulled the horse mower.

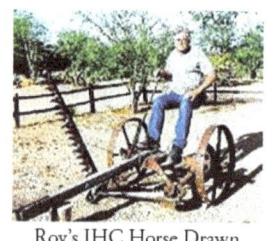

Roy's IHC Horse Drawn Mower[14]

When Wes, Jay's brother, was about thirteen, Joe bought a tractor-mounted sweep rake and mounted it on the VAC Case tractor. Wes was given the job of driving the sweep rake. After Wes was killed, Joe sold the VAC and bought a DC Case tractor. The DC became the sweep rake tractor.

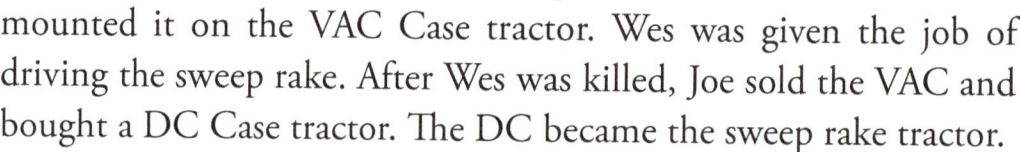

Tractor-Mounted
Sickle-Bar Mowers

Jay was given the job of sweep raking. He had to hold the hand clutch engaged with his foot so he could stop quickly if a tooth ran into the ground at a craw fish hole or a drill hole. Otherwise he would break the wooden teeth from the rake. It worked fine and never seemed to damage the clutch. Jay talked Joe into buying a tractor umbrella. That made things much nicer.

The supply wagon had baling supplies including baling wire, oil and gasoline for the tractors, feed and water for the horses and mules and a water barrel with drinking water for the nine men of the hay crew. The sweep rake tractor moved the wagon when the baler moved.

The drinking water was in a wooden forty-two-gallon vinegar barrel. A new one was purchased at the beginning of each hay season that lasted well into September. The truck used to haul the hay from the baler brought the supplies each morning. It

DC Case Farm Tractor[13]

would stop by the ice plant in town and get a 100 pounds block of ice for the water barrel. With the ice in the barrel, water at the ice plant was used to fill the barrel around the ice. The hay crew loved it. The barrel had a wooden bung in the bottom for filling the drinking cups. Sometimes Jay would tie Jude to the supply wagon. A few times she ate a crew member's lunch if it was in a paper bag; guess who was angry for the rest of the day and a few afterwards. It was a good thing that Jay was the boss's son. Jay was between nine and eleven during this time.

At the beginning of the haying season in late June or early July (right after grain harvest), the baler and peripheral equipment were moved six miles north to the first hay field. The hay fields were all with bluestem grass on land that had never been plowed.

Starting one season, several hands left their cars at Joe's house and rode the truck or equipment to the field. The first load of hay was loaded onto the truck six layers high. Each bale was approximately two feet by two feet by three feet, weighing approximately sixty pounds. All of the hands with their cars at Joe's house rode the loaded truck back to the house on the hay. As the loaded truck came to state highway 10, a paved road, Joe stopped to check traffic. He put the

Those further from the back end managed to hang on the hay that stayed on the truck. The explosives truck was loaded with dynamite and caps. The driver said that the caps would detonate with a ninety pound jar. No one was hurt seriously. Jay walked around to his dad and said, "Why do not you watch where you're going"? Joe mentioned that to others later.

Some of the hay fields were near the lead and zinc mines. As noted earlier, there were abandoned drill holes all over the hay meadows. The drivers of the horses and mules had to watch for them to keep the animals from breaking legs in the holes. The young boys that worked around the baler loved to ride pieces of corrugated roofing metal or scoop shovels down the chat (tailings) piles; warm bottoms were common. There were several abandoned shafts, approximately ten feet square at the openings, near the chat piles. The kids looked down into the four hundred feet deep shafts and could barely see water at the bottom. They threw rocks into then to hear then clunk on the sides before splashing in the water. There were no covers or guards around the shafts. Wood shoring kept the shafts from caving in. It was said that folks as far away as Chicago found permanent resting at the bottom of the shafts.

While Jay was raking hay he came upon a drill hole that had caved in and was the home of a family of skunks, a mother and several babies. Jay was highly tempted to try to separate the little ones from the mother and catch one. He had been told that baby skunks had no scent. However, better judgment prevailed, and Jay came home that night without smelling like a skunk.

Joe sometimes sold the hay on the meadow. Other times he sold and delivered the hay. Mostly he stored the hay in three of his barns. His brother bought some hay from him and shipped it to his customer by boxcar. When the boxcar arrived at its destination, it had heated and spoiled. It had been baled before it was completely dry. His brother wanted Joe to pay for the bad hay. He was very angry because he lost the price of the hay and his customer. He had tempted to try to separate the little ones from the mother and catch one. He had been told that baby skunks had no scent. However, better judgment prevailed, and Jay came home that night without smelling like a skunk.

Joe sometimes sold the hay on the meadow. Other times he sold and delivered the hay. Mostly he stored the hay in three of his barns. His brother bought some hay from him and shipped it to his customer by boxcar. When the boxcar arrived at its destination, it had heated and spoiled. It had been baled before it was completely dry. His brother wanted Joe to pay for the bad hay. He was very angry because he lost the price of the hay and his customer. He had come back for another load of hay, had it two-thirds loaded and was standing on top of the load yelling at Joe. He said that Joe had done him wrong and wanted Joe to pay for it. He threatened Joe and the hay crew saying he would whip them all, in effect, and that he did not have long to live. Joe did not answer.

Joe's brother had cancer in one of his eyes. The eye was removed by surgery and skin covered the eye socket. It was not a pretty sight. Joe did not want to disgrace him, but he did not feel he could pay for the bad hay. Joe's brother came to Joe's house and gave him another loud lecture demanding Joe pay him. Joe refused.

Joe, his Brother and Two of his Sisters

One day when the hay crew arrived at the field, the hay was damp from a shower the night before. A fellow from some distance away was there with his truck to buy some hay. While they were waiting, the hay crew got into a crap game with a pair of dice. The man with the truck joined the game. J R, cleaned out the man with the truck; he did not have enough money to buy hay. Joe

Chapter 5

Teenage

The four youngsters attended a school eleven miles away in a remote town whose main business was the school system. The return trip around the route was twenty-two miles with overhanging tree limbs swatting the students through open windows. The way there and back was on dirt roads all of the way. The total population of the town was approximately two

Steel Truss with Flimsy Floor Bridge

hundred. Besides the school, there was a dry goods store, a hardware store, a bank, a grocery store, a movie theater and a filing station. Highway 60 had been moved approximately one mile north when the lake nearby had been dammed in 1942. New bridges had been installed across the two rivers that came together nearby to form the lake. They were called the Twin Bridges. The old bridges were of the old steel truss-and-wooden-floor type. It scared young Jay to cross over them; the flooring rattled. The replacement bridges were of modern construction without trusses.

Most of the stores in the small school town did not survive, but the school system did. The four youngsters attended this school because the school bus came by their house. A much larger school was only six miles away with four miles of it paved road. The bus from that school came only within one and one-fourth miles of Joe's house.

At one particular time when Jay was around twelve years of age, he and his three siblings walked to the country Baptist church approximately two and a half miles away on dirt county roads. It was up hill both ways (of course it had down hills both ways, too). They walked the long way around hoping some neighborhood kids might go with

The Actual Old Country Church Recent photo recherché

them. The church had a revival. The revivals in those days (no TV or easy travel, etc.) lasted two weeks. They were held in the evenings during the week; people came. The little one-room church was always full. It was daylight when the kids arrived, but it was dark when they went home. One evening on the way to church Wes told Jay that when the invitation was given, the preacher was talking to Jay. Jay thought Wes was the one that should go forward; he was the ornery one. He was always getting them into trouble with his shenanigans.

Now Jay was a very shy kid, especially during his early years. It may have been agora phobia (fear of being seen by other people). He hid behind propped open doors in the summer when someone came, including relatives, and behind the high-back cook stove in winter. He tried to sit behind some big person when he could all through school, including graduate school, so the teacher would not call on him. The milk cow that hid in the underbrush and stood still so the bell would not sound (a shy cow) reminded Jay of himself.

At the church, all were well dressed except Jay and his siblings. Wes and Jay wore high top work shoes and overalls with worn, dirty coats. That is all they had. They seldom took a bath in winter. They were small for their ages. The other folks at the church were "tall as trees." What made Wes think that Jay would ever go forward under the circumstances; a most unlikely happening? But when the invitation was given Jay felt compelled to go forward with a sense of urgency. He hardly remembered the walk down the aisle; it was as if someone had him by the hand leading him (the Holy Spirit). When he sat down on the front pew he began to pray the sinner's prayer with the church pastor kneeling before him. All of a sudden someone pushed him over. He could not believe it. It took all of his courage to come forward. When he looked around his brother, Wes, was there. Both prayed for forgiveness and acceptance by the Lord. It was winter time, and the little church did not have a baptistery. They went to the nearby town with a large Baptist church that had a baptistery. After that experience Jay felt like he would like to do it all over again every time the invitation was given. Later, it became obvious why the Holy Spirit was urgent in His efforts to get the boys saved.

Recent Photo of Flood Gate There Now

The girls did not participate. Wes really wanted Jay to lead the way. Apparently, he was being urged by the Spirit to go forward and publicly profess his faith in The Lord; it was very fortunate that he did.

Wes was in the Boy Scouts at school and was doing well. He and a class friend by the same first name were both at the same level in the Scouts. They needed to camp overnight for their Eagle badge. Their scout master was the pastor of the local Friends Church. He was an invalid in a wheelchair and could not go with the boys. The boys took their camping gear after school and went into the hills south of the school. They went to the edge of the nearby big lake. It rained hard all night, and the boys found a cave to camp in. The next morning, they walked back toward the school. They had to cross a low-water bridge that was raging with the rain runoff from hills upstream. Unknown to them, one end of the bridge had washed out. They tried to wade across but the current was too swift, and they were both washed down the creek. Wes's friend was able to grab the cable holding a flood gate and get out. Wes was not as fortunate and was washed down the creek. He had his Scout backpack on. He obviously hit his head on the edge of the concrete of the low water bridge at the washed out end or rocks because there were injuries about his temple. He was found some time later down toward the lake. It was said that there was no water in his lungs.

Most farm flood gates were made of wood with spaced vertical slats suspended by a cable. The one there at the writing of this book is made of steel; the view in the photograph on the previous page is from upstream (from the low-water bridge).

Wes's scout master was very apologetic about the whole thing. He came to Wes's house and told Joe how sorry he was that he could not go with the boys. He gave Joe Wes's Eagle badge awarded posthumously.

Joe, J R and Jay went to Joplin, Missouri and bought Wes a new Boy Scout outfit. Joe and Ted took the death very hard. Ted had worked closely with Wes in the fields and had a boy the same age. For more than a year later Joe could be heard late into the night walking around with his light on. He dearly loved Wes.

Joe had Wes's body brought home for the wake. Many folks came by. Ted wailed loudly when he saw Wes in his casket.

The funeral was held at the little church where Wes was saved; it was approximately three months after Wes professed his faith in the Lord. Wes was fifteen. The church was completely full for the funeral; there were probably more folks outside than inside. Wes was buried next to his mother in the nearby town's cemetery. Neither Wes nor his mother had a head-stone. Vera and her husband made markers of concrete the best they could for both with the information of each on them. Bonnie, who inherited Joe's farm, and Vera, Joe's executor, together had nice markers placed on all of the family dead, including Joe's first family, after Joe died. Vera, Jay's half-sister, was married to a good Roman Catholic man. Vera became a Roman Catholic (catholic means universal, all inclusive) and tried very hard to live up to the church's strict discipline.

Vera and her husband, Claude, offered Jay the opportunity to consider joining their church. However, different churches with their various doctrines were confusing to Jay. Earlier he had tried to read through the Protestant bible and was distracted by its old English language. He had no animosity toward the Roman Catholic Church, but he just could not understand the difference between that and the Baptist church he was brought up and baptized in at the time. Jay was a slow reader and was thrown for a loop trying to read old English writings. He hated Shakespeare plays, written in old English. When he encountered Shakespeare's play Romeo and Juliet in school, he was not sure if Romeo was maybe an artist and had lost his paintings when he read, "Romeo, Romeo, wherefore art thou?" Old English was always distractive for Jay in the King James Version of the Bible. The Roman Catholic Bible has more books than the Protestant Bible.

Claude loaned Jay one of his bibles. Jay scanned through it. Jay was a slow reader and did not get far with it. The Roman Catholic faith just did not appeal to Jay.

In 1947 the weather was extremely wet. Joe had opened a wheat field on a Sunday afternoon to begin the wheat harvest that year in June. One truck load of wheat was combined. That was all Joe got from his approximately three hundred acres of wheat. It rained almost every day, and when it did not rain, the fields were so soggy that a combine could not go into the fields. When the ground froze in November, Joe tried to combine some of the wheat for feed, but it was black and moldy, not fit for feed.

The same Sunday in June when the first load of wheat was harvested, Jay and Ellen were in the truck load of wheat. Bonnie was there, too. Jay and Ellen were playing in the wheat, throwing it on each other, etc. A week or so later, Jay developed a terrible ear ache. Jay was taken to a doctor who found three grains of wheat lodged in Jay's ear. The wheat had swollen and caused the ear ache. It is a wonder that farm kids survive.

Twelve-year-old Jay was picking up where his brother left off, talking back to his dad. Joe had put up with a lot of back-talk from Wes when Wes was alive. Jay was helping Joe grease a combine several miles south west of town when Joe, who was holding the hose onto the grease zerks, yelled, "Pump!" Jay retorted a remark and pumped the twenty-five-pound capacity grease gun as hard as he could. Grease squirted and made a mess. Joe grabbed Jay and spanked his bottom with his hand. Jay could not remember his dad ever spanking him or Wes before. Jay walked the fifteen miles home through town where the bridge over the river was. He stayed out three days and did not go to work. When he decided to work again, he had lost his job as driver of the tractor pulling the combine. Alex, Ted's son, had been riding the combine controlling it. He was now the tractor driver, a much better job, and Jay rode the noisy, dirty combine. Jay knew he had it coming.

In the early 1950s the democrat-controlled Congress came up with parity on farmer's grain. Farmers were producing so much that they were not getting enough for their crops to make a living. Wheat was the big crop for farmers in the Midwest. The government put price supports on wheat of 2.05 dollars per bushel (parity) and limited the amount of their land they could plant in wheat. This was known as wheat allotments. Joe said at the time that it was socialism and would break the farmers in the long run; it did in the 1970s because the parity price had not increased in relation to other prices for products as they went up. The government also paid farmers to let land lay fallow (no crops planted on it). Joe was paid seventeen dollars per acre not to plant some of his land. Joe said he liked that good old democrat giveaway program called the Federal Land Bank. He said a democrat was someone who believed in something for nothing. Joe was a democrat, but he did not agree with their ideas.

Sometimes when Joe went by a local grocery store he would flip a coin with the owner for the price of a coca cola for himself and one for Jay. The agreement was double or nothing depending on who won. When Joe won he would say, "Boy, that's a good ole democrat coke."

Some virgin land (sod not disturbed) was obtained by Joe. It was several hundred acres. The ground was plowed for its first time and was planted to seed wheat. The first year the seed was called foundation wheat developed by Oklahoma State University (known then as Oklahoma A&M). Students came to the field and made sure there were no weeds to contribute their seed to the yield. The next year the yield was called registered, and the third and thereafter it was called certified. Certified seed was then sold as seed to other farmers. The wheat Joe raised was a strain of early triumph wheat. By selling his wheat as seed Joe could get six dollars per bushel instead of the 2.05 dollars. He had his own cleaner. He cleaned and sacked the seed and sold it to other farmers himself. One day in the late 1950s when he was cleaning seed the cleaner stopped. It was belt driven by an electric motor. Joe grabbed the belt and pulled on it to get the cleaner going again. His index finger went into the pulley and was severed. He took the finger to his house, and with some help he packed the finger in ice and hurried to the local hospital. The finger was reattached. It regained nearly full use.

The three surviving kids lived as if they were extremely poor. They had almost nothing to call their own. In the summer one year, Joe gave Jay a few dollars for helping in the hay fields. Jay bought some undershirts and undershorts. The two girls took some of the underclothes and used them for themselves. Jay was put out for a bit but soon realized they had nothing for underclothes. He got over it quickly.

One day when the three youngsters were in town they went into the Crown drug store. There was a small battery powered radio near the front of the store.

The three swiped the radio. They listened to radio stories on it in the evenings after school. Programs included Sergeant Preston of the Northwest Mounted Police, Inner Sanctum, The Lone Ranger, The Grave Digger, etc. The kids were not prone to steal and resigned themselves to doing without.

Reiterating, Jay was too small for sports. When he decided in the seventh grade that he was tired of being nobody and decided that he could make good grades, he observed how the other students that were making good grades were doing it. Math was taught by a civil engineer turned teacher. He graded on the curve. With a little studying he could do as good as, or better than, most other students because kids at that age were frisky and did not want to study. The same went for the other subjects; the key was study. In the back of his mind, Jay wanted to impress the pretty girl of his dreams, Nancy, a girl he fell in love with in the first grade.

There were two brothers, one in Ellen's class, who played string instruments, a guitar and a mandolin. They sang and played at the assemblies. The students loved them and clapped loudly their approval. The superintendent despised their music and scolded the students. He said they acted like hillbillies. Jay and most of the students were country folks, and they liked country music. Jay thought the superintendent was a bully.

Jay wanted to learn to play stringed instruments, but was too poor to endeavor the learning process. He did manage to talk his dad into taking his mother's guitar to town

Jay's Mom's Guitar

for repairs. It had a Hawaiian mural painted on it. The repair folks put new strings on it, and converted it to a steel guitar. Even though it was a standard guitar, it did come with finger picks and a thin bar. The repair folks removed the standard guitar's scratch guard and installed a black monstrosity. They removed the standard bridge and installed a tail piece because steel guitar strings are larger than those for the standard guitar which means it takes a stronger support to hold them. Actually, they "butchered" the guitar. Carol had bought it at a farm sale. As a steel, the guitar was not very good. The Choctaw seventh grade music teacher said that if any students wanted to bring their string instruments, he would teach them some on how to play them. Jay did that and learned some basics.

Now Jay managed to get in trouble by himself. Sometimes his nephew, Carl, who was three years younger, helped. When riding on the back of a truck the two boys and Carl's cousin got the dumb idea of throwing a cup of ice water on cars they met. The water barrel with ice water in it for the hay crew was aboard.

They threw it on a Henry J car that had the wing window open. The driver made a hurried stop and ran down the truck with Joe driving. The man and woman in the car were furious. They cursed and yelled that they should take the boys down to the river and drown them! Joe sat quietly and listened to their tirade. When they were through, Joe drove nonchalantly away. Joe had nothing to say about it. He knew boys were ornery.

The boys had seen many western movies with Gene Autry, Roy Rogers (Leonard Franklin Slye) and others noting that the cowboys shot guns from horses. They were riding Joe's old super-gentle mare named Bird. She was so easy to get along with that kids liked to ride her. One day the boys shot a gun while riding her; she left the two boys sitting on the ground. Hollywood horses surely must be trained not to flinch when they hear shots from their backs. In the photograph at right, Bird is in the foreground

Bird, the Gentle Mare

with two of Vera's girls and Jay on her back. In the background is Carl, the nephew, on another horse with two of Vera's sons.

Carl and Jay made a 410 shotgun out of parts they found on the farm. They wanted a one-fourth-inch steel water pipe, but there was not one available. However, there was a copper water pipe about the right size. It was not straight, but the boys straightened it the best they could. They put a cast iron corn planter sprocket on one end for the firing chamber.

The shell, then, was slid through the sprocket into the pipe. The sprocket fit nicely onto the pipe. A nut fit into the sprocket on its outer end, and the nut held a center punch

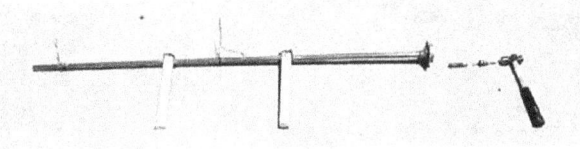

Replica of original Home-made 410 Shotgun

Yorkshire Boar Hog

iring pin. Two handles were attached to the pipe for holding wire sights were attached to the pipe. Of course it took two The boys bought a box of two- and-three-fourths-inch-long nsive at that time. The crude gun worked. The trigger-man id whacked the firing pin (center punch) with a hammer. ters when it breaks. The boys did not consider that, but they were fortunate the sprocket did not break. With the gun they shot huge wasp nests hanging in trees and such other targets. One day they were walking through the hog lot down toward the spring-fed creek. A big boar hog that probably weighed six hundred pounds was sunning himself with his head down toward the creek. The hog was a Yorkshire, a bacon hog. Joe said the Yorkshire pigs had long wheelbases. He made a tempting target. The boys were far enough away that they knew the hog would not be injured. They fired and the hog jumped as high as he could. The boys thought that was pretty funny. While they were reloading, they heard something. They looked around to see the hog bearing down on them in a big hurry with his mouth wide open; he looked like an alligator! They dropped everything and made tracks fast. The nephew, Carl, went one way and Jay went another. Jay cleared the four feet tall hog lot gate some fifty yards away with no trouble.

When he looked back to see where Carl was he saw him in the top of a small persimmon sapling. Persimmon trees are soft wood and not very strong. The sapling was swaying back and forth, and the hog was traipsing over the rocks around the base of the tree making chomping sounds. Jay's two dogs went with Jay; he sent his dogs to rescue Carl. The dogs were good at handling pigs and made quick work running the boar over the hill. Joe did not want the dogs working the pigs; they were too rough with them. One dog would get at one end and distract the pig while the other chewed on its behind. Sometimes the dogs injured the pigs.

When the boys used up all their box of two-and-three-fourths-inch shells they decided to try three-inch ones. The first one split the copper tube. But, the boys did not give up. They used the broken gun like a mortar by lighting large firecrackers and dropping them into the pipe. They put rocks in behind. Sometimes they would drop a second firecracker with a lit fuse in behind the first. Fortunately, no one was injured with the gun.

A football game one Friday night was on Jay's agenda. His close friend Mack Wolf, a full-blood Seneca Indian in Jay's freshman class, was going to the game from his uncle's house, which was less than a mile from Jay's home. Mack spent a lot of time with his uncle. Another friend of Jay came home with Jay from school. They all went to the ball game together with Mack's uncle. Joe had bought a gallon jug of sherry wine for some hired hands helping Joe pick corn. The weather was cold and the wine was to perk the pickers up. Jay did not drink. He did not like the taste of alcohol in any form. He never took to drink, including coffee; he just did not like the taste of coffee either. However, Jay filled a long neck, quart syrup bottle about half full with the wine. On the way to the game Mack drank some each time it was passed around. None of the others drank any. At the game, Mack was feeling good. He was yelling and making a fool of himself in the stands. Mack was a big guy and a good athlete. Even though he was a freshman, he was supposed to suit up for the game. He did not. He was too drunk. The school superintendent captured Mack in the stands and found out what happened. All of the boys involved were brought to the superintendent's office where the superintendent ranted and raved. He had the constable, the dad of the friend with Wes when Wes was killed, there too. The superintendent said that he was going to call Jay's dad. Also, he said, "Jay, I don't care if your dad comes here and bails you out of jail tomorrow or not." When the superintendent went back to the game the constable told the boys to get out of there and stay out of trouble. They took Mack home. Jay worried all weekend what his dad was going to say about the incident. If Joe knew, he never said anything. The following Monday morning the school's principal gathered the boys into his office and gave them three swats each with a big paddle. That was the end of that.

Joe had a large fish pond built at a corner of the forty-acre hog lot. Farm animals were fenced out of the pond. The Government Farm Conservation Agency had the pond built as a way to help farmers. It never filled completely. The soil was too rocky, and the pond dam leaked. However, there was enough water for swimming. The boys, Carl and Jay, built a diving board that worked after a fashion.

Homemade Diving Board in a Fish Pond

The imbedded photograph at right shows Jay entering the water with Carl right behind. A neighborhood boy is in the float. The deep part of the pond was no more than eight feet deep. Jay would go to the pond alone in the evenings and Sundays and swim.

Sherry, Dog Team, Jay and Carl

Carl and Jay built a cart and trained the two dogs to pull it like horses. At times they put a rooster in the cart. The actual photograph of the cart with a rooster in it is shown. The girl in the picture is Jay's younger sister, Sherry, who was born two weeks before their mother died of pneumonia. Jay is in the middle and Carl is on the reader's right.

The tractor-mounted sweep rake, mentioned earlier, can faintly be seen in the background on the right. Jay here is about sixteen (1951). Carl's mother and dad lived close by and came over often on Sundays. The road in the photograph is the dirt road on the north side and in front of the old farm house Joe and family lived in. Since the prevailing winds, except in the winter, are from the SW, dust from car traffic was blown away from the house.

Kids are innovative, even at a young age. They look around for items they can put together to accomplish their dreams. They are usually crude but they sometimes work. The gun they made did work until the barrel failed, and the diving board worked fairly well even though it was not so attractive to behold.

The dogs in the photograph were the squirrel dogs that became excellent hunters. When someone walked out on the porch with a gun the dogs headed for the forty acres hog lot and immediately treed a squirrel. They seemed to know where they all were. They learned from an older dog. When they had their first experience with a gun they ran, but when they saw how excited the older dog was when the squirrel he treed fell, the young dogs came back to the action. From then on they were squirrel dogs.

Jay did not eat squirrels, but he liked to run them through the trees with the dogs.

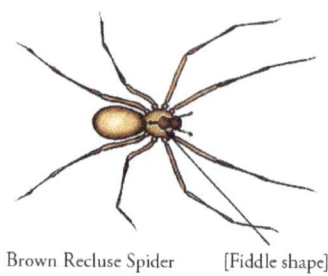

Brown Recluse Spider   [Fiddle shape]

It was about this time Jay was bitten by a brown recluse (fiddle back) spider, not once but twice. The spider must have been in the bed because one bite was on top of Jay's forearm and the other was on the bottom, both approximately two inches from Jay's wrist. Jay thought the sores from the bites would never heal. The scars are still there.

Red (Fox) Squirrel

Jay bought a couple of baby red squirrels for a quarter from a friend who had found them in a nest. They were old enough to feed on a doll bottle. The bottle fed the babies too fast and they would get milk coming out their noses, but they would sneeze and blow the milk away. The milk was whole milk, and the squirrels thrived on two feedings per day. They soon grew and ate nuts, bread and some tasty foods like bacon grease from the skillets and sugar from cloth sugar sacks. One day a neighbor girl who sometimes came home with Jay's two sisters was in the house. She liked bacon grease and, with her finger, ate some bacon grease from the skillet. One time a squirrel had peed in the skillet. When told of this, the girl was cured from eating from the skillets there again. By the way the kids liked to chew on corners of cloth sugar sacks. They called the corners "sugar tits." This usually happened on the way home from the store in town.

The squirrels were tame and could be handled like cats. None of the immediate family was bitten by the squirrels. Jay's sister, Bonnie, once knocked a squirrel off the table because it was hanging by its back feet from the rim of a large jelly jar eating jelly. The squirrel had no longer hit the floor than it was back on the table with the sister's finger in its mouth. It did not bite though. The squirrel liked to store its nuts people gave it in among the large tubes of a battery powered Wards Airline radio no longer in use.

Wards Battery
Powered Radio

In the summertime when the doors were propped open in the house, the squirrels lived outdoors in a large pen three or four feet off the ground on legs under a huge cottonwood tree in the yard. The pen was covered with hardware cloth to keep the squirrels from cutting their way out. There was a time when Jay forgot to keep water in the pen. One of the hired hands discovered this and watered them. Jay was ashamed and did not let that happen again.

When Jay was fourteen, Joe told Jay to grease the Massey-Harris combine one morning. It was hot and Jay slept on a pallet in the front room. He was sick during the night and vomited on the porch outside the screen door. He was still sick the next morning and could not handle the thirty-pound grease gun. His two sisters helped Jay into the back seat of the 1939 Ford car, put the grease gun in the trunk and drove to the combine about a half mile away. The girls greased the combine. The self-propelled Massey-Harris combine that Joe bought soon after WWII was equipped

MH Combine with Sacker Stand

Mass Harris Self-Propelled Combine

with a sacker stand like in the embedded photograph above, right. Joe's farm help built a wooden box for a grain bin on the sacker stand. Grain had to be shoveled out manually.

When bins were made available Joe bought the grain bin for the combine; the bin looked like the one in the right hand photograph.

After greasing the combine, the girls drove Jay, who was still hurting on his right side something awful, back to the house. Joe had just had a hand-cranked, eight-party line telephone installed in the house. The telephone was the only thing in the house that resembled anything modern.

Joe's family lived in poverty. Joe was born in 1890 and 1800s life style was what he was used to. With no woman in the house to want more modern conveniences, they were not a priority. Ellen called a doctor in

Crank Telephone

the nearby town. He came to the house in his convertible car and examined Jay who was lying on the girl's bed upstairs.

The doctor took Jay to the hospital in his car. By the time they reached town, Jay's right side below his belt was no longer hurting; however, The white corpuscle count was 1900 per square centimeter, a level, Jay was told, that was more than what most folks' appendix ruptured. Appendicitis seemed to be common in that area at that time. Other family members had it earlier.

When the telephone was first installed in the house, a friend of Jay came home with him on the bus from school to stay the night. The friend had never talked on a phone. Since there were eight parties on the party line, neighbors would listen in when someone used the phone. When the phone was cranked, all phones on the line rang. Jay told his friend that if someone on the line butted in, tell them to "shut up." So when the operator said, "Number please?" the friend said, "Aw, shut up!"

Talent, Big Black Gelding[11]

Jay was operated on with ether as ananesthesia. The last thing he remembered before going under was the surgery folks talking about windows. When he awoke he was very sick.

He drank some water and vomited it. His abdomen hurt something awful. It was much worse when he coughed. In those days the surgeons cut through everything to get to the appendix, including the muscles. It took several weeks to heal. Jay had to wear a girdle with the lower part removed. He had to eat soft foods for three or four weeks. The operation cost 425 dollars for the doctor's bill. The doctor had a farm, and Joe sold him enough hay to pay the bill. He had told Ellen that she would have to pay the bill since she called the doctor. Ellen fretted about that for a long time.

Bumble Bee

Horse Fly

Single Tree

Jay was off work for a few weeks after his appendectomy operation. At this time Joe was busy in the hay season. Jay, whose job was running the sweep rake, was now relegated to running the scrap hay rake again. Joe had bought the gelding (a stud horse that had been castrated) as mentioned before; he looked like the one in the photograph above right. The horse still acted as a stud, always looking around with his head high in the air. He did this so much that the bit in his mouth made his mouth sore. J his mouth and guided him with the bit under his chin. That work raking scraps on a hill in one corner of the eighty-acre field.

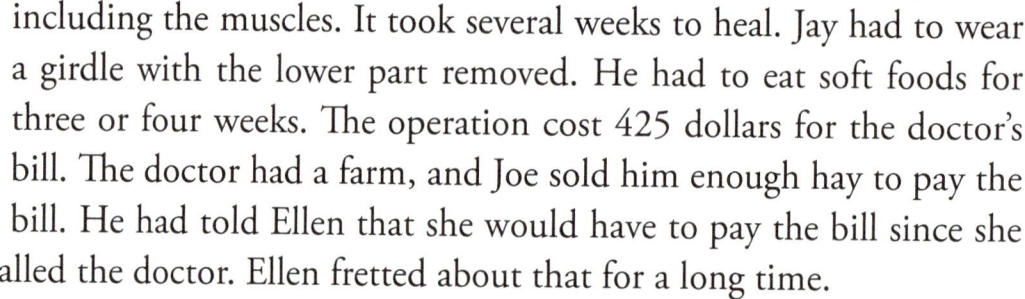

Hay Rake with Single - Horse Shafts

There was a bumble bee nest in the ground on the hill. The bumblebee is over twice the size of a horse fly and its sting is exceedingly painful. Bumblebees swarmed out of the nest and stung the horse. He ran full gallop down the hill toward the stationary baler set up at the bottom of the hill. Jay could not hold him without the bit in his mouth. Jay had accidently stepped on the trip that raised the teeth of the rake to dump it. The dump mechanism was activated by "dogs" in the hub of the wheels that rotated the teeth ninety degrees to allow the hay to exit. Apparently, Jay was standing on the trip while trying to halt the horse, but to no avail. The teeth were going up and down rapidly as the horse ran down the hill. Suddenly, one tug came loose from the single tree. This caused the horse to move out from the rake by about two feet jerking Jay off the rake while holding tightly to the reigns. He lost his grip for a split second, but he grabbed the ends of the reigns as he fell between the shafts of the rake. He was being dragged along in a prone position under the rake. Fortunately, one of the teeth hooked over the seat while the teeth were violently jacked up and down by the high speed of the rake and the trip was held down. Jay regained his senses as he looked up to see the hay rake teeth hanging over him. He let go of the reigns. The horse with the rake in tow rushed toward the hay baler as it was baling hay. The men operating the baler scattered. There were six men operating the baler. Two pitched hay brought to the baler by the sweep rake. One operated the elevator bringing hay up to the hopper from the pitchers and dropped blocks that determine the length of each bale after the hopper is clear. One is called the back-wire man. He pushes a length of wire with a loop on one end through the grooves of the blocks. Another fellow on the opposite side tied the wire around the bales. The sixth man bucked the bales, that is, he dragged the bales that exited the baler from the baler and stacked the hay. He also carried the blocks back to the elevator-control man.

When the baler crew saw the runaway rake coming straight at the baler, they ran for cover. The horse turned at the elevator and headed for the back of the baler. One wheel of the rake went upon the elevator and broke the rear sideboard off at its support stakes, and it hit the back of the baler bending the left wheel out of shape. The horse ran to the nearby fence. He stopped there and began to eat grass.

The rake was useless after that. It was the end of the hay season. Joe bought a wire tie pickup baler the next year, but the tie system was unreliable at that time. Joe hired someone with a string-tie pickup baler to bale his hay after that. From then on he had only enough baled for his livestock.

When Jay came home from the hospital he found that the girls had let his squirrels out to play with them. The male squirrel was killed by the dogs. Jay grieved about that for a while.

Joe had a hardware-cloth-covered metal cage built at the blacksmith shop for the other squirrel for the winter time in the house. The squirrel, named Nuts, did cut through the hardware cloth some but did not get out. Squirrels cannot take cold very well. They have to have a warm place to be in the winter such as a hollow tree.

Joe liked the squirrel. It was a lot of company to him in the winter. After Joe fed his livestock, he would build up a fire in the king heater, let the squirrel out to enjoy the rest of the day. The squirrel would sit on Joe's shoulder and eat nuts Joe would give her. If she was not hungry, she would hide the nuts in the old Airline radio. She hid the nuts around the tubes, which were quite large. She usually slept in the book pocket of Jay's mackinaw coat that Jay hung by the back door of the dining room. She lay with her tail over her as a cover. When someone came for a visit and the squirrel was in bed, she came out and put on a show. One evening after the squirrel had put on a show and had gone to bed, Jay's niece wanted the squirrel to get up and perform some more. She pulled on the squirrel's tail and the end came off. The squirrel jumped out of the book pocket and bit her, the only person she ever bit hard enough to cause injury. The niece was there during the next two weekends and the squirrel bit her both times. After that she left it alone.

One day in the winter Joe let the squirrel out to play after he had fed the cows and hogs. The squirrel got out of the house and went to the wooded hog lot. It was gone for several days. It came back and wanted to get into the house. Joe tried to get it out of the tree by the house with the two squirrel dogs with him. That was the wrong way to handle the problem. The squirrel jumped out of the tree and tried to get into the house but the dogs grabbed it and injured it internally. Joe rescued it and brought it in, but it died that night. It was suspected that the squirrel had gone to find a mate and had come home after the affair was over.

Grey Squirrel

Later, Jay found a small gray squirrel in a nest. He raised it and tried to make a pet out of it. Unlike red squirrels, which are more stable and less flighty, or nervous, gray squirrels are not so easy to tame, as Jay found out. The gray squirrel become mean and caused people to be afraid of him. Jay took it to a veterinarian and had it neutered. It was a male.

That did not help, so Joe took it to the barns around the silos. One day when Ted was getting hay from one of the barns the squirrel jumped on him. Ted batted it away with his hat. Sometime later, someone saw the squirrel in a tree near the road. It probably came to the stock tank to get a drink of water. The car came to a sliding stop, and the squirrel was shot. It was just as well, the squirrel was a nuisance.

3-D View Sketch of Red curved-block (tile)

One cold morning Joe wanted to light a fire in the only heater in the house. It was a coal stove Joe had bought used; Joe decided coal was easier to obtain and use than cutting and stacking wood. He bought and hauled the coal from Claremore. Joe went to the three-hundred-gallon gasoline tank he had for farm equipment, took a five-quart oil can, put some gasoline into it along with four or five corn cobs and brought it to the house. He lit a gasoline-soaked cob, threw it in on the coal and reached for another. The flame followed the vapor trail to the oil can and caught it on fire. Joe kicked the can toward the door and splashed burning gasoline onto his overall legs. He ran outside. Jay made a flying tackle and stopped Joe. Joe regained his composure and helped beat out the flames. The two ran back into the house to fight the fire, but the small amount of gasoline had burned itself out even though it was splashed onto the walls. The walls were covered with unpainted drywall and laths over the cracks. The floor was linoleum.

In 1949, Joe had a red curved-block silo made. It had two small steel rods lying in the grooves and a rebar in between on each block. Mortar was then poured in the grooves onto the rods and rebar enough to fill the grooves of both tile blocks (see sketch). The men putting up the silo, 74 feet tall, were well trained. They first dug and poured a strong foundation of high test concrete. The floor was left bare. They laid a few layers of blocks at a time. When the wall was too high to reach, the builders put together a circular platform and supported it with wooden beams. They raised the platform by hand onto wooden scaffolding braces. The material was raised by hand with ropes.

On the way down the silo walls were plastered with a special masonry coating to resist the acids from silage. It took them about a week or 10 days. Two of the workers stayed at the house. One was a middle-age man and the other was a young man. The young man slept with Jay; the older with Joe. At evening, the young man told Jay jokes. The two girls, Ellen and Bonnie, insisted on hearing them, too, and would not take "no" for an answer.

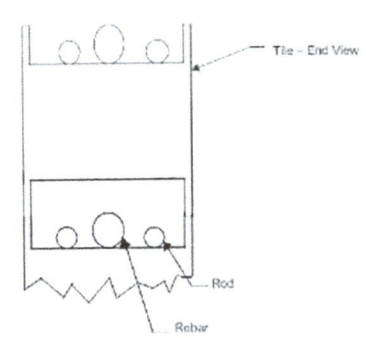

Wall Tile Reinforcement

Sargo, a cane about six feet tall, was normally used for silage. It was best. It was sweet and kept well in the silos. The cows loved it. It was cut and bound with a corn binder in the field. The bundles of sargo were then brought to the silo where they were chopped by a cutter-blower. The cutter-blower was hard pressed to blow the silage over the top. The biggest tractor, the DC Case, was used and at one time the Case agent came out and tied the governors back to get more power out. The tractor snapped a valve and rolled the end up the size of an egg. It knocked a hole in the piston of the failed valve. The engine was repaired by a special mechanic in town.

After the Case problem, the Farmall M was put on the cutter-blower. Joe wanted to tie the governors back on it, but the governors on the Farmall were enclosed and could not be tampered with. Later Joe bought a field cutter with its

own engine. It blew chopped silage into farm wagons, and it was hauled to the silo that way. Along with the cutter, Joe bought a blower without a cutter for the silos. However, if the hopper of the blower was over filled, the silage slug fell back in the pipe and plugged it. The six inch diameter pipe had to be taken down and cleaned out. Once, when Joe and his crew were filling a silo for a farmer NW of town, the pipe became choked. Someone had tied the rope around the pipe too far down the pipe. When the pipe was unbolted at just below the stoppage, the center of balance was above the rope. Instead of letting the pipe down vertically, the pipe toppled from the top, and as the top fell backwards, the goose-neck, the part that goes over the edge of the silo, struck Joe on the head. He was running as hard as he could away from the falling pipe. Fortunately, Joe had on a hard hat built like a hunter's pith helmet. It was given to him by an implement dealer.

While a binder was still being used to gather the sargo, J R, Joe's son from his first family, and Jay were binding sargo in a field. Jay was riding the binder, which gathered from a row-at-a-time and tied it in bundles after cutting it at the ground. J R was driving the tractor, and stopped near a ditch to take care of some personal business. J R was in the ditch a long time; Jay waited on the binder. He saw two girls off in the distance coming toward J R and Jay. Jay thought that surely J R would finish up soon; he had been there a long time. The girls were getting close, and J R was still in the ditch with his pants down. Jay's hope that J R would be out of the ditch failed. The girls were too close now to sound the alarm. They arrived with J R still with his pants down. J R had a few choice words to say to Jay for not sounding a warning. Jay realized that he should have yelled before the girls came too close. However, J R was a rounder and soon got over it.

Joe saw in a farm magazine the design of a false end gate for the farm trailers. He had his helpers build one for each trailer. The end gates sat at a slant at the front of the trailers. They had triangular wooden frames with the bottom braces acting as runners. A cable was fastened to each runner and stretched out the back. This would slide the silage to the back and make it easier to rake into the hopper. The hopper folded ninety degrees straight up out of the way so a trailer could pass. The false end gate could not be pulled directly with a tractor. However, a two-wheel tandem pulley cable system was rigged for the tractor pulling out the false end gate. That worked fine. As the silage was put into the silos, a series of aluminum buckets (without bottoms) were hooked onto the goose-neck attached to the pipe at the top. The aluminum buckets hung from the goose-neck inside the silo with a rope tied to them to direct the silage. Kids were used to tramp down the silage as it came in. Compacting was necessary.

Corn silage worked OK, but the pieces of cob would stick to the silage forks and make it difficult to get the silage out of the silo. Joe used corn a time or two when drought threatened corn production. Once soy beans were used when the beans looked like they would not make. Whoever shoveled the bean silage out during the winter smelled like hog manure for a while afterwards. Later Joe had a slab silo built. It was held together with galvanized rods around the outside banding the silo. It had a conical shaped top on it. In the photo above, the white silo is the slab silo being used as a depository for ground corn at this time. The tractor is belted to a hammer mill.

Oats were stored in the white silo once since the silo had a top on it. They were blown in with the silage blower; it was an easy job for the blower. The oats were on a government storage program. The government inspector found weevils in the oats and required Joe to treat the grain with a tear gas contained as a clear liquid in glass jars. The liquid was dumped from the jars quickly on top of the oats and a tarp was pulled over the dispersed tear gas. Joe, Ted and Jay climbed the silo, which was full almost to the top, with their jars and a tarp. They dumped the jars and pulled the

Actual Photo Showing Both Silos

tarp. Jay was immediately affected. He was very allergic to grain dust and such things. He could not breathe, but managed to get down the chute to the ground. After choking for several minutes, he realized that

Flat Bottom Boat

the other men were still in the silo. Jay started back in to rescue them somehow, he did not know how! As he started up the chute he heard the men climbing out of the silo and putting the door in place. They were a lot tougher than Jay when it came to breathing. The oats still smelled of the tear gas all the way to the bottom as they were removed later.

Vera's husband, Claude, gave Jay a flat bottom boat he had made. The boat was getting tired. Joe took it to the local blacksmith and had it rejuvenated for Jay. Joe and Ted made a large fish trap of hog wire and chicken wire. Someone ran over a chicken in front of the house. The chicken was roasted a bit, feathers and all, over an open fire and placed into the trap.

Cotton-mouth Water Moccasins

The two used the boat to put the trap in the river and tied it to a tree on the bank with a rope. The next night they could not raise it because it had too many fish; they dragged it to shore. Later Jay and a friend put the boat in a slough that had nearly dried up. The slough was cut off from the river. Several fish were trapped in the slough. The fish swam around in the slough with their backs out of the water. The two boys were shooting the fish with .22-caliber rifles. Jay's nephew, Carl, and Carl's mother were on their way to the slough when bullets were glancing off the water and whizzing all around them. A few hurried visitor shouts helped rescue the visitors. Carl had a limb in a sling, but he could not resist getting in the boat to shoot fish. When the boat struck a fish's back the fish took off making a great target.

Even the snakes were interested in the small fish. The fishermen shot at several huge water moccasins. Some were yellowish in appearances, as big around as a lady's arm and had designs that reminded the boys of bicycle tires, sort of diamond shaped. The snakes did not give the boys any problem. Though most of the fish got away, they did get some.

Yellow-colored Water Moccasin

Jay taught Bonny how to plow corn with a cultivator on the SC Case tractor. She helped out one day close to home. Another time Jay and Bonney were picking corn across the river and seven miles south of town near the old US Hyway 66, which was known as the "Sidewalk Highway" because it had only one lane paved. They picked corn with the two-row picker mounted on the M Farmall tractor. They put the corn in a trailer that had been made of a converted wooden-wheel wagon; it had truck axels with truck tires put on them. It was an awkward farm trailer. They put the corn in this trailer because it was the one in use being pulled behind the picker. Jay and Bonney drove the truck down mainstreet and picked up Ellen, at five o'clock at Main and Central in the 1936 International truck pulling the trailer. The main street was part of the US 66 and US 69 highways. Ellen was working at Woolsworth. The truck had poor brakes that were hard to push. A black Buick driven by a young girl pulled out from a side street and stopped. The truck with the loaded trailer could not stop in time and struck the car in the rear. Apparently, the driver of the car had no licence because the man in the car with her insisted they not call the police. The car had a dent in the trunk lid; the truck had no damage. Carl knew the girl. Jay and Carl went to see her to see if there was anything else that needed to be done. She just wanted to forget the whole thing.

One very wet fall, the two-row corn picker, mounted on the M Farmall tractor, became stuck in the middle of an eighty-acre field south of town. A wrecker was called from town. It became stuck in the gumbo mud of the field. Another wrecker was called to get the first out. They had difficulty getting the first one out, but the tractor remained. The picker stayed there until Ted brought over his team of mules from his home some 14 miles away and pulled it out after the ground dried some. In the meantime Joe borrowed a team of buckskin horses and a wagon. He hired several pickers, including some of Jay's school buddies, to pick by hand. They did not shuck the corn, which was ground for feed. When ground, the corn with the shucks on and cobs-in made a fine meal. Cows loved it. Actually, gathering the corn was called snapping it. The wagon had one high side. The pickers picked from the low side and threw the corn against the high side. As the wagon moved it knocked down two rows of corn.

Two men were assigned to pick up the two down rows. Each of the other pickers had one row off to the side to pick.

The pickers with the two down rows could not keep up. They were throwing the corn a long ways. Joe was next to the wagon and picked fast, moving the horses as he went. A down-row picker missed the wagon from a long way back and hit the team. It had a run-a-way down the corn rows. Joe ran the horses down on foot and ran them the rest of the way down the half mile rows and ran them all of the way back. They were not interested in running away again. Joe put Jay helping with the down rows.

Corn Picking Wagon

Ted and Jay were plowing corn down along the river west of town. The field was overflow land. Horse flies were terrible there. Seldom did horse flies bite humans, but these must have been desperate. They really hurt when they bit! Those things are somewhere around one-and-a-half-inch long critters and can deliver a strong bite. The men learned quickly to watch their backs. They looked over their shoulders as best

Horse Fly

they could, and if they caught a glimpse of a black spot on their backs they would swat it, or at least, rake it off.

There had been a house with a dug well on the highest part of the property. The well had a rope and bucket still there. Ted and Jay drew a bucket of water to drink; it was extremely bitter. When their eyes adjusted to the darkness of the well, they could see that the well was full of water moccasins! The river had overflowed the well recently.

Walking Plow

When J R was younger, he was plowing in the bottom land with a walking plow and a team of horses. He saw some girls walking along the end of the field. He hurried his team to get to the end while they were still there. His plow hit some roots where a stump had been and jerked J R up over the plow. People plowing with a walking plow usually tied the lines high around their waist so their hands would be free to hold the plow handles. Ted, who told about the incident, said J R was embarrassed, to say the least.

A carnival was in town and J R rode the Farris wheel. It stopped midway in its travel and a girl above J R peed on J R. He hollered, "Cut that out!" She said, "I can't." J R's plans were modified that evening.

J R and Ted were sacking oats in a grain bin. J R heard Joe coming from the house. He said to Ted, "It just will not work." Joe was close enough to hear J R. He stuck his head into the bin from the window in the driveway. He said, "Huh? What's that won't work?" J R said, "A windshield wiper on a goat's butt." Joe said, "Humph!" and walked off.

J R loved to tease farm animals. He turpentined a rooster once and said the rooster chased the hens in the barn yard as hard as he could go. He teased one of the ex-army mules (who had no doubt been teased by army personnel). The mule hated goats. J R would hide and nicker like a goat; the mule would try desperately to get out of the harness to find the goat. Sometimes, when J R rode the mule to water, he would kick the mule in the rib to see her buck. He would jerk up on the hame string that would slap the mule's belly. The mule would throw a fit. J R enjoyed putting a corn cob under a horse's tail. The horse would clamp down and perform a wild dance. A friend of Jay gave Jay a kid goat. The goat got into the pasture with the mule and the mule stomped it. The same friend gave Jay another. This one survived and became a nuance. It left goat pellets on the porch every night. Finally, Joe threw the goat in with a load of hogs that he took to Joplin for sale at the stock yards. He received twenty-five cents for the goat and gave that to Jay. It was thought that the goat became a "scapegoat" at the packing plant.

J R had an appendectomy operation shortly after Jay had his. J R's ruptured. J R had no health insurance and worked as a farm hand for approximately six dollars a day, which was normal for the farm area. J R had a family with three small children. They had no way to pay for the medical doctor or the hospital bill. J R's wife, Rose, came to Joe for help; she needed to pay the hospital bill for J R's release. Joe refused to help her; he said, "I ain't got it." Rose begged Joe for help over and over again in the barnyard, but Joe just walked away saying, "I ain't got it." Rose did not know where to get help. J R had been working for a neighboring farmer when he became sick. As a last resort, Rose went to him. The farmer loaned Rose what she needed. J R and his family were extremely grateful. They decided to move to California when he was well enough to seek work there. J R's oldest sister and her husband lived there with their family. They all lived in Bakersfield. J R came back at Christmas several times after moving to California and stayed with his next older sister, Lou, and her family. On one visit J R's oldest son, Jerry, with Jay, Carl and a neighborhood boy played "cowboys" using BB guns. All four had caps with the ear flaps down, goggles, gloves, coats and wraps around their faces. Jerry took off his goggles and was shot in the eye with a BB. It did not damage his eye, but Jerry complained that his eye hurt. J R and Rose took him to a doctor and found the BB was still in his eye. Jerry had no lasting problems with the eye. Jay was hit on top of his right hand index finger at the flesh end of the finger nail. The mark on the nail as it grows out is a weak line along the nail, and as the nail grows beyond the end of the finger, it splits there even as this book is written.

On the way back to CA over the old highway 66, Jerry came down with spinal meningitis and had to be put in a hospital a long way from home. Jay believes that was the last time the family came back to Oklahoma for a visit at Christmas. Several years after that J R, who was working on an oil rig off shore, went to sleep while driving home from the coast and hit a bridge abutment. The engine and transmission crashed into J R injuring him fatally. He died a few days later. He was in his early fifties. J R's two sisters in Oklahoma went to CA to see J R before he died. Joe did not go.

Jay made good grades in the tenth grade. However, his reason for trying so hard was gone. He gave up the idea of impressing the pretty girl, Nancy, of his dreams.

Joe had bought a new two-ton special truck and let Jay use the old 1936 International truck to go to ball games, etc., at school. One day after a B game that Jay played in, a friend suggested they go to a watermelon patch someone knew about. Several piled onto the truck which had the sides off at that time. They drove down the lane near the watermelon patch with the lights off. The owner's house was at the end of the lane, which was nearly one mile long and open at the far end. It was a moon lit night, and the boys broke open some melons. As they were eating, a car came slowly down the lane. Every one ran for cover. The car stopped for a while and then left. Jay and a friend crossed the road and, after a long wait, crept up to the truck. There was no one around. They jumped into the truck, but Jay had lost the keys. Jay hotwired the truck, an easy task, and they went home.

On Sundays, Jay's sisters dated in the afternoon. So did Joe. Jay found the keys to Joe's new truck, drove it out of the barn, and went back looking for his keys. He found them where he crossed a ditch. He then drove to the school to show off the truck to his friends. It had nine tons of ammonium nitrate fertilizer on it.

Joe was courting a lady he met at a restaurant. Joe ate in restaurants a lot because home cooking was not so too good with two girls that did not cook so well; they seldom had adequate food to cook with or the desire to do it. One Sunday afternoon, Joe and his lady friend, Fay, were playing cards (pitch) at Lou's house, which was about half way from Joe's house and town. Bonnie called Joe and told him that "Jay was killing Ellen." Joe came rushing home to find the kids all doing their thing but not fighting or quarrelling. Lou was a bit miffed and a bit amused at the false alarm. Ellen and Jay just had a disagreement over something and settled it themselves.

In his teenage years, Jay was very uncomfortable in the winter time. Many mornings he had to get up with snow on the floor of his upstairs bedroom and go down to start a fire before the school bus came. One bitterly cold night he could not sleep. He only had a couple of old ragged comforts his aunt made. He piled his coat and other clothes he had on top of the comforts, but he was still too cold to sleep. He tip-toed down stairs and brought in his two dogs one at a time. That was a big help, probably for all three, and it worked well until a neighbor's hounds bayed along the creek area in the hog lot behind the house. Both dogs ran to a window directly over Joe's bedroom and barked excitedly. Joe yelled, "What's going on up there?" He said, "Get those dogs out of there; what do you mean?" He grumbled a few other choice words. Jay carried them down and waited for Joe to go back to sleep. Then, he carried them back and was able to sleep the rest of the night. Jay promised himself that he would never jump out on a cold floor again when he was on his own; he never did.

Joe brought bones from the grocer's butcher department home for his dogs. The butcher saved the bones for Joe at no cost. A neighbor had two dogs that discovered the bone activity and decided to share in the feast. Joe saw them there and tried to run them off. Finally he ran them away one day and, from a distance, shot them with a shot gun. The neighbor told Joe shortly afterwards the wolves in the area were getting bad. They chewed up both of his dogs.

Joe did not believe in creature comforts. His vehicles did not have adequate heaters in them. When Wes and Jay went to town with Joe in the truck, they had to endure cold hands, ears and feet while waiting for Joe to come back. It was thought he went to the bank and to a restaurant while the boys froze. This went on for several years. On Saturday nights Joe would drop the kids off at a movie theater, give each a quarter apiece and come back for them later. Wes and Jay would buy a ticket to the movie for a dime, a sack of popcorn for a nickel and a funny (comic) book for a dime. Wes and Jay liked to follow the serials that went along with the cowboy movies. When the shows were over, the kids waited in the cold at a windy corner for Joe. They were afraid not to be there when Joe came back no matter how late he was (probably on a date at times). He would go off and leave them, and the kids knew it. This sort of thing continued long after Wes was killed. The girls would go to a country dance in a building just a block away and on the second floor. Jay would wait for their dad. Often he needed to go to a toilet, but there was none available. He was afraid to leave because of Joe's attitude; Joe did not like kids all that much. When their dad did arrive, Jay would talk him into waiting while he went for the girls. Those were miserable times. One time, Joe did leave Jay and Bonnie to walk home; not fun when you are tired, cold, and sleepy (it was long after their bed time). Joe had a stern, and perhaps, mean side. Sometimes when he was angry he would say to Jay: "You little bastard, you'll never amount to a damn." Jay never really knew what he meant, and he realized Joe was upset when he said that. Jay did not hold that against his dad.

Chapter 6

More Better

In the eleventh grade, he drove the old truck to school. Later, Joe helped Jay buy an old worn out 1941 blue Plymouth car, that had been a taxi, from a used car lot of old cars. He drove that for a while.

1941 Plymouth

Jay overhauled the car in the winter time in an open shed when it was so cold that his hands stuck to the tools. His dad pulled the car to town to have the valves, which were in the block, ground. He put in new rings and rod bearings. The bearings were very narrow. He did not replace the mains; a bad mistake. One worn-thin half of a main bearing slipped upon top of the other half and wedged the crankshaft breaking it. Jay, Ellen and Bonnie were in the car after visiting Lou and family. They were able to drive the car home in spite of the loud clunks. Joe let Alex, Ted's oldest son, help install a new crankshaft. They worked in the front yard. There was a barn with a concrete floor on the farm at that time, but it was full of farm things. The boys did not mind, though. They were used to doing things the hard way. They had few tools to work with, but they got the job done. It was good experience for both. Alex was good help. They did the job in good time.

Jay loaned his car to Bonnie to drive to the high school she was attending one day. There was a big hill near the Twin Bridges that led to the road to her school, Jay's former school. As she came down the hill to turn left onto the road over one of the two rivers that came together there, the steering wheel came off.

She ran across the gravel-road (Oklahoma State 60 highway) that crossed the two rivers just before they came together to form Grand Lake and was fortunate enough to get the car stopped before it went into the lake.

The class at the original school Jay attended had approximately twenty-five students, had five subjects to choose four from each year, and was twice as far to go over rough roads. The school that Jay changed to had several classes to choose four from. It was only seven miles away and five miles of it was paved.

Along about the time Jay was driving to school, he kept the car running with "baling wire." The tires were very poor and Jay had no money to buy tires for it. Nearly every week Jay had to boot the tires and patch the inner tubes. He broke the tires down with the bumper jack under the car to pop the beads loose.

1948 Dodge with Jay in High School Graduation Gown

When Jay traded the car for a 1948 Dodge, the Plymouth was completely worn out. Jay was so poor he had to use water for brake fluid. The car was immediately taken to the junk yard from the car lot where Jay, with Joe's help, bought the Dodge for 425 dollars (actually, Joe bought the car). The Plymouth was traded in.

Jay graduated in 1954. Nancy, of Jay's earlier fascination, attended her eleventh grade at the same school where she and Jay started. Her dad was president of that school's board. However, in her senior year she transferred to the nearby school as Jay had; he had a class with her. Jay had already ripped his pants with her by the crazy things he did, and he stayed away though she was still the girl of his dreams. Both were on the school's honor

Nancy

role for good grades. Along about that time Nancy became the state's dairy beauty queen and was the runner up in the national contest. She was the queen of sports there at the school, also, and was in a school play. Jay always thought she could have been a movie star; she was prettier than most movie stars.

Jay knew she could have had any young man for a beau she wanted, including a handsome, polite and well liked young man her age who lived in a very nice two-story sand stone house across a field from the girl's house. Jay often wondered why they never got together. Her dad made arrangements for her to ride with the young man to school as he took her dad's milk to town; the young man attended the same school in the town and was in the same grade. When asked once why he and Nancy never got together he said, "We just never clicked."

Nancy (seated); older daughter on her left - 2014

At the time, it was said she was sweet on a preacher's son who was porported to be handsome, a good athelete and in the same grade at the same school; she and her folks were said to be attending the preacher's church.

Nancy's cousin, a boy Jay's age, stopped Jay one night and asked him to follow a car. His girlfriend was in it with another boy. Jay did as he was asked. Jay never knew how that came out. Jay was driving the Dodge at that time. The cousins were related to each other through their mothers. The cousin's dad was a big farmer in Jay's neighborhood. Jay was hardly acquainted with the cousin. He hoped the girlfriend situation turned out OK. Jay never heard from the cousin again after that. He had the same first name.

SENIOR CLASS OF 1954

In the above class photograph, the fellow sitting on the right end (viewer's left) of the front row in the photo is the fellow who lived across the field from Nancy. The valedictorian is the attractive blonde in the center of the first row. The salutitorian is to her right.

Jay's senior class picture

There were approximately 132 students in the senior class. Jay is on the third row from the back and the fifth one from the viewer's left. Only the top half of his face is showing. After high school graduation, Jay only saw Nancy briefly. Once he saw her at the junior college in the nearby town where she had come back from attending Baylor for one year, he was told. He saw her one more time at the class reunion in 1979. She was very popular, and attracted lots of attention. Jay did not recognize her right off because she had changed in appearance somewhat from how he remembered her. He was terribly embarrassed. She was married at the age of twenty-one and moved away. Jay wanted to be inconspicuous and quietly left the activities when they began to dance. Nancy met him at the door and said goodby. She had no idea about how he would have liked to sit down and visit with her over old times. They were both married ; She had two daughters and he had a son. He just wanted to know if she ever even knew who

he was other than a remote class mate. She said at the door that she intended to attend the next reunion and would be there "come hell or high water." Jay never saw her again until 2014. He and Sandy went through the LA area where she lives and stopped for a short visit with her and her older daughter.

At the class's twenty-fifth year reunion in 1979 the number of Christian preachers from the class was impressive. It was amazing how the people in attendance looked young and vibrant. The fellows who brought their wives were proud of how attractive they were. All men are ugly, but those at the reunion were less ugly than most. Jay was privately proud of all of the people there.

Jay took a home economics course one semester in high school. He learned to make chili and used the recipe the rest of his life. He also made a shirt. It was not good, but Jay needed the shirt and wore it out. In the photograph at right the guys all made what they were wearing. Jay is the only one with the shirt. The collar was not good; the corners were

Home Economics Class of MHS 1954

round and fat. Too, the shirt was too short. It just did not look good. The class was an elective that gave the students some practical training for home life. Though, in later years, Jay's wife had a sewing machine and a serger, Jay was expected to do his own sewing. He had his own sewing machine that he used to repair boat covers, etc. Thanks to the home economics course, he did OK with that sort of thing.

Jay took Chemistry in his junior year. He was the lab assistant during his senior year. He became acquainted with several of the students that way. Jay used the few dollars the job paid to buy an old F-hole guitar. It had been cut to install a pickup designed for a round-hole guitar. It came with an amplifier. Jay learned some music on it. He was never as good as he would like to be.

When Jay's sisters married and left home, Joe married Fay, the lady he had met in a restaurant; Fay was a waitress. Fay was a sweet spirited lady who was in her fifties. She had been

Joe and Fay with the Big Barn in the background

divorced for some time and had a grown, married son. Things sure got better around the home. Electricity, running water, a modern electric stove, an eight-party line telephone and a refrigerator had been accumulated along the way before Fay arrived, but they were not properly used until Fay came to be the house mother. Other things were added such as a TV, propane heater, etc. She was an excellent cook. She kept the house clean and stocked with food. She had a washing machine with a wringer on it. She rounded up all of Jay and Joe's clothes and washed and ironed them. She was a big help all around.

Even though Joe had several head of cattle, he bought milk. His cattle were beef cattle (Herefords). There was never enough for drinking and cooking. Fay wanted a cow to milk.

Joe, Border-Collie dogs and Hereford Cattle

There was a roan cow in the herd that looked like a milk cow. She had lost her calf, and Joe decided to break her to milk. Joe ordered his hired help, including Jay, to run the cow into one of the barns. They put a rope on the cow and snubbed her to a beam. Joe milked her by standing next to her side right behind the right front leg. He leaned up against her and milked while she danced, kicked and snorted. Joe was sort of a wild man as was the cow a wild animal. They made a good match. This went on for a couple of weeks or more. One day Joe decided to take the cow to the house where there was a big barn.

The barn had a large hay loft and several horse stalls in it. The shed on the back side ran the full length of the barn and had some milking stalls with stanchions installed in it. However, the enclosed shed was full of hay. Joe decided to use one of the horse stalls, the one with an entrance door directly behind it.

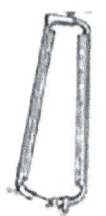

Stanchion

Cow Kickers

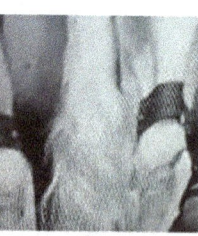

Kickers Installed

A stanchion was installed in the stall at the grain box in the big wooden manger. When the cow was brought to the house, she resisted all of the way. She was dragged stiff-legged behind a truck. At the barn she would not go into the stall. A flat clevis was fastened to the manger for the rope used to drag her in. The procedure was to rope the cow in the barn lot, drag her around to the entrance door with a tractor, stop and run the rope through the clevis and back to the tractor to drag her into the stanchion. When the cow was in the stall her

Clevis

head was fasten in the stanchion and kickers were put the on her back legs. The cow would allow the kickers and stanchion to be fastened on her.

The cow became resigned to the routine of being pulled in and milked by Joe sitting on a stool with the bucket on the ground. Eventually, Fay was able to milk her with Joe standing by for a while. Now there was plenty of milk. Jay pulled the cow in and Fay milked.

On an early Sunday morning when Jay was in his senior year, Joe had two semitrailer cattle-trucks arrive at the farm. They were loaded with steers and heifers bound for Kansas City stock yards approximately 180 miles due North. Joe had a two-ton special truck with stock racks on it. He loaded it with hogs for the

1951 Two -Ton Special Chevrolet Farm Truck

Kansas City stockyards. He and Fay left in the truck later that day. Joe liked to have his livestock in the stockyards early Monday mornings so the bidders, who were looking for their requirements for the week for packing houses, would be more willing to pay top prices.

Fay milked the cow before she and Joe headed for Kansas City. Joe told Jay to milk the cow the next morning. Jay saw no problem with that; Fay milked her OK. The next morning Jay arose early to do the cow routine. He roped the ornery roan cow and dragged her into the barn. The stanchion and kickers application went smoothly. Jay put feed in the trough and sat down on the milk stool with the bucket on the ground. The next thing he knew he was under the manger with a knot on his head. The cow was gyrating and snorting with her head still in the stanchion. Jay crawled out over the manger and went around to the next stall. The horse stalls had dividers about two-thirds the length of each horse. Jay could not find the kickers either in the barn or outside in the weeds. He had no idea of where they were or how the cow was able to get them off. Even if he could find them he was not sure he could get them back on or if they would stay.

Sometimes in the pasture when cattle needed to be patched up from a wire- cut, etc., a rope was tied around the flanks taking the fight out of them. Putting a rope on her legs was not an option. Jay threw a rope over the maverick's back from the protection of the divider. He raked the end under with a broken pitman arm made of wood. He tied a loop in the end of the rope and pulled the other end through the loop around the cow. Then, the loose end of the rope was thrown over a beam and tied to a post in the next stall. The rope was tightened enough to put pressure on the cow's flanks and to be very uncomfortable. Jay touched the cow on her back leg to see if she was ready to cooperate. The cow jumped and kicked as if she were trying to kick the side off the barn. Jay was already miffed and was getting angrier by the second. He pulled on the middle of the rope until the cow's back legs were off the ground. He tied it so the cow's back feet were dangling in midair. Again he touched the back legs to test the

cow's attitude, and the cow flailed frantically in every direction. Jay was plenty angry by now. He went to the house and readied himself for school. When he came out Ted was there to go to work. Ted asked Jay where he was going.

Jay said, "I'm going to school." Ted said, "What about that cow?"

Jay said, "I've had it with that cow!"

Ted said, "You can't leave that cow hung up like that. You'll kill her."

Jay let the cow down and unfastened the stanchion.

Cockleburs

Joe and Fay came back the following Tuesday late in the afternoon. Jay was studying in the dining room when Joe came in and said, "What's wrong with that cow?" Jay said, "That's the same old cow, two horns, four legs and a tail full of cockleburs." Joe said, "Aw, get that cow in the barn; what do you mean!" Joe had a few more unkind words to say while Jay did the rope and tractor trick. Jay told Joe that he could not find the kickers, and went on back to the house.

Fay came into the dining room and said, "You ought to go see about your dad. He's been down there a long time." Jay went to the barn, and the first thing he saw was the two dogs in the doorway. When he came closer he could see that the lower part of the cow's tail was gone. There was dirt and as milking and the cow was standing and shaking. There was no mystery about what had happened. When the cow pulled her wild dancing and kicking routine, Joe recovered, selected a club (perhaps the broken pitman) and gave the cow a thorough understanding about etiquette while being milked. The pitman arm was for pulling the sickle back and forth on a mower. The sickle had a ball on its end, and the pitman had a ball socked to attach to the sickle. The other end

Roan Cow (tamed)

was attached to an of-set post on the drive Fay came into the dining room and said, "You ought to go see about your dad. He's been down there a long time." Jay went to the barn, and the first thing he saw was the two dogs in the doorway. When he came closer he could see that the lower part of the cow's tail was gone. There was dirt and blood on the wall and on Joe. Joe was milking and the cow was standing and shaking. There was no mystery about what had happened. When the cow pulled her wild dancing and kicking routine, Joe recovered, selected a club (perhaps the broken pitman) and gave the cow a thorough understanding about etiquette while being milked. The pitman arm was for pulling the sickle back and forth on a mower. The sickle had a ball on its end, and the pitman had a ball socked to attach to the sickle. The other end was attached to an of-set post on the drive wheel.

Joe handed Jay the bloody, and damaged, milk bucket and let the cow out. Jay poured out the small amount of milk, mixed with dirt, on his way back to the house. Joe came in and said that he was through with trying to milk that cow and that she could hurt someone with her attitude. No doubt he was thinking of Fay. The cow staggered into an old orchard behind the house and lay down by an apple tree. Fay, Joe, and Jay had no sympathy for the cow, but Ted did. He carried water and feed to the cow for several days until she could get up. Joe told his help to take the cow back to the herd. The cow was tied behind a truck and pulled stiff-legged back to the barns and silos. She had reason to be stiff-legged now.

What happened next was difficult for Jay to believe. If he had not seen it himself, he probably would not have believed it. The cow became the gentlest cow in the herd. Herefords are naturally gentle, but this cow, not a Hereford, became a pet. Sometimes she would stand at the line of feed troughs in the way of the tractor pulling the feed wagon for the cattle. Jay would shout at her, but she just looked at him. Jay, then, would get off the tractor, put his arm around the cow's neck, take one horn in hand and lead her away from the troughs. She Disciples. He did what he was assigned to do; he established churches in the known world so that we can go to one and learn from capable teachers and preachers what God wants for us and from us. He did a good job.

There is more about that cow. When Jay was thirteen years old, he and his two sisters decided to milk that same cow. The three decided to catch the cow by driving her into one of the barns, get a rope on her and lead her down to the house. They never considered whether or not the cow was fresh (still giving milk since her last calf). She looked like a milk cow and they were intent on milking her. They ran her into a barn and threw their dad's silk lariat rope on her. When they let her out of the barn she took the three on tour of the rocky fifteen-acre barn yard, around the silos, around the all-metal Quonset barn, along the feed troughs, around the corals and working pens and around the herd before the three decided who was in charge; it was not them. They let go of the rope. Now there was another problem. Their dad's prized silk rope was still on the cow. They knew they were in a heap of trouble if they did not recover that rope right away, clean it and put it back where they found it. Fortunately, the rope was stiff. It relaxed on the cow, and she was able to get it off. They thought, "Whew!"

On one of Joe's trips to Kansas City with his cattle, Joe told Jay to "feed the cattle on the prairie" (called prairie because there were few trees in the area) while Joe was gone. They were in an open pasture ten miles to the north and had no shelter. A terrible blizzard came that following night. The next morning the snow had drifted four to five feet high in some places. The wind was blowing cold, around -10° F and nearly twenty knots (over twenty miles per hour) out of the north. Jay did not have good winter clothes. He knew it would be a cold ride to the pasture because he would need to use one of the tractors; none had cabs in those days. A truck would have no chance of getting through, especially on roads running east and west. Jay put on two pairs of socks, two

On one of Joe's trips to Kansas City with his cattle, Joe told Jay to "feed the cattle on the prairie" (called prairie because there were few trees in the area) while Joe was gone. They were in an open pasture ten miles to the north and had no shelter. A terrible blizzard came that following night. The next morning the snow had drifted four to five feet high in some places. The wind was blowing cold, around -10° F and nearly twenty knots (over twenty miles per hour) out of the north. Jay did not have good winter clothes. He knew it would be a cold ride to the pasture because he would need to use one of the tractors; none had cabs in those days. A truck would have no chance of getting through, especially on roads running east and west. Jay put on two pairs of socks, two pairs of pants, two shirts, the heaviest coat he had, overshoes and two pairs of gloves. His cap had ear flaps; they were nowhere near adequate.

Jay went to the barn and started the biggest tractor, the DC Case. He hitched it to one of three farm wagons; all had rubber tires. After pulling it to a silo and loading it with silage tossed down the chute, he pulled it to one of the barns and threw in several bales of hay and two one-hundred-pound sacks of cotton seed range pellets. He pulled out onto the road and headed north. Turning sideways to the wind he braved the snow drifts as the tractor plowed through them. Some of the heat from the exhaust and radiator would have been welcome, but the wind blew it all away. When Jay reached the pasture he was so cold and stiff he could not get off the tractor. He turned the tractor such that the exhaust helped a bit. After wriggling around for a few minutes, he was able to tumble off the tractor. Struggling to get to the gate, he was able to get it unfastened. Dragging himself back onto the tractor, Jay was able to drive to a Jay was in a hurry to feed them. Life was sure better going back with the wind. Upon arriving home and putting the tractor away, Jay was sure thankful for the warmth of the coal fire he built in the stove. His ears, fingers, and toes hurt for a while upon thawing. It was then Jay decided that when he could he would live in a warm part of the country; he now lives in southern Arizona as this record is written. Jay and his wife enjoy the year-around warm weather, and they do not have to shovel sunshine.

1956 mercury Hardtop Convertible

Fay talked Joe into paying Jay for working for him so he would have some spending money, some funds to buy clothes, pay for college, etc. The engine in the Dodge went bad. Jay had a rebuilt one installed, but it was not any good. Jay was now in local junior college. Joe talked Jay into buying a new car so he would not be working on it all of the time. They went to the Mercury dealer in town and Joe helped Jay pick out a new Mercury.

The car in the photograph is exactly like the one Jay bought except his was shiny black with white along the doors. The posts and trim inside were chrome, and the headliner was perforated white leather. It was a beautiful car. Jay kept it polished.

Jay had never had any work done on his teeth; he did not have the money. A lower jaw tooth on the left had a large cavity that gave Jay bad breath since he was twelve. At nineteen, he had enough money, thanks to Fay, to fix the tooth (it took a double filling), and to fix the crooked tooth in the front top on the left side. Jay had hid the crooked tooth with his hand when he talked. The tooth had grown in behind the baby tooth and behind the lower teeth. Without a mother to watch those things, and no dental appointments, bad teeth can happen in kids. The crooked tooth was pulled and a bridge of gold with a porcelain tooth attached was installed. The porcelain false tooth was attached to a pin on the bridge. It broke occasionally and had to be replaced. Later, nylon was used to replace the porcelain, but it wore out quickly. Some thirty years later, the bridge was replaced with a much better one that lasted without repair until the writing of this book.

At the time of the new bridge one of the front teeth that was longer than the other was cut down and capped. Then the front teeth looked presentable.

When Jay arrived on the campus of the local junior college, he had no idea of what he wanted to study. He ran into a friend from a nearby

Jay in Later Years

town. The friend had participated in driver's contests from his school. As they had driven in contests for their different schools, they became friends. Jay asked the friend what he planned to enroll in. He said he did not know, but he had heard aeronautical engineering was a good field. They both chose that as their major. The friend dropped out after a while. Jay continued; one semester he carried twenty hours while still working for his dad in the afternoons, evenings and weekends. It nearly killed him to get his studies done. He never did that again.

Engineering is a practical science. It takes the pure sciences such as physics, chemistry and mathematics and applies them to necessities and conveniences. In chemistry, if you mix two particular chemicals of the same consistency and One night, the college had a masquerade party. Mack, Jay's school chum through the tenth grade, dressed as an Indian, which he was, and Jay dressed as an Indian with a black pigtail wig and brown shoe polish on his face. The shoe polish burned for a while after being applied. The two won the prize for most unusual.

At the college Jay took a welding class. During an afternoon lab, Jay and a friend put a .22 bullet on the sidewalk and heated it with an acetylene torch. The bullet fired. A girl wearing a heavy coat was walking by approximately twenty feet away and was struck on the shoulder. She yelped with surprise, and the bullet went straight up a few feet. It fell harmlessly to the ground. No one was hurt.

Double-Neck Steel Guitar

Jay organized a square dance band for the student union. He had a guitar fellow from a nearby town, his neighbor fiddler and himself on a double neck Gibson steel guitar that he never mastered. The guitar had four removable round legs. The fiddler was an expert with a fiddle. He was full-blood Indian and had played at several barn dances, etc. He was in his late forties and had a stiff left arm bent at a right angle. He had been in an automobile accident. He was drunk and sideswiped a car while his arm was hanging out the window. However, he was the best fiddler around. They played every other Tuesday evening.

The draft board called up Jay for a military draft physical. He was sent to Oklahoma City on a bus. One of Jay's chums from the old school was called up at the same time. They were not too happy about being called for the draft physical. They did not answer the questions on paper very well. As an example, one question said, "Do you now or have you ever wet the bed?" The boys answered yes. A naval officer, a doctor, asked Jay about it. Knowing that the arrogant officer strutting around like a peacock had no authority over him, Jay said, "Can't you read? It says do you or have you ever wet the bed!" The doctor wrote anxiety on Jay's paperwork and walked away. Jay was sent to a psychiatrist who was there and who asked Jay one question. What do you feel about going to the Army? Jay said that he did not feel he was any better than anyone else to be drafted. The shrink wrote something and dismissed Jay. Jay felt smug that he had told off a haughty military officer. Jay's friend, a good athlete and physically well-developed, did not become acceptable for the draft while Jay, the runt, was.

Jay dated a girl that was on the high school driving team. She was a tall, good looking girl a year behind Jay in school. They thought of getting married and decided to do it secretly. They would keep it secret until the girl finished school and Jay finished junior college. They went to a town 30 miles away, in another county and got a marriage license. Someone the girl knew was willing to perform the wedding, but someone saw the notice in the paper in the town they had gone to and told local people. Word got back to the girl's parents and the marriage was annulled. The girl was 17. Jay was not old enough either. Later some friends who knew the girl much better than Jay told Jay that he was better off. The girl had been used by her older brother and had very loose morals. When she dated she would undress as soon as they left her neighborhood. Local boys did not want anything to do with her. That was the end of that.

Some of the friends that Jay knew had joined the Air National Guard (ANG) in Tulsa. The unit had F-80 fighter planes and a C-47 (DC-3 civilian version) cargo plane. Sometimes Jay rode around in the C-47 as a passenger when it was test flown to flightcheck the plane after it had some maintenance. Later the F-80s were exchanged for F-86D fighters.

F-80 Shooting Star

F-86D Saber jet Fighter

The ANG members drove to Tulsa one weekend each month. They drove US Highway 66. At the time, the Will Rogers turnpike was under construction. The folks in Oklahoma were told the turnpike would be paid off in twenty years; at the writing of this book it is still a turnpike. Politicians just are not honest. The turnpike in Texas from Dallas to Fort Worth became a freeway when promised.

Jay was not sure how to pay for college. He had no help; he worked his way through. His dad had promised to pay his way through college before he ran off with the girl at his old high school.

Book for Testing for Color Blindness; Special Glasses

Now he would not help. Jay tried to join the Air Force Cadets to learn to fly and serve there. He found that he had abnormal color vision (color-blind in red and greens). He could not take Air Force pilot training. Much later in life Jay was responsible for work in non-destructive testing for a company. The job required good color vision. A local eye doctor told Jay that he had helped policemen with color vision problems by making them special glasses. Jay asked him to make a pair for him. The glasses had a red lens on one side and no lens on the other. It worked; Jay could read all of the color dot pages in the color- blind test book. In the photograph on the previous page, normal folks see 8, 39, 6 and 42 reading left to right. Color-blind people see only 3 and 5 for the 8 and 6.

Jay kept up his monthly training in the Tulsa Air National Guard (ANG). On a two-week summer camp at an air base near Casper Wyoming, an F-80 fighter assigned to the Tulsa ANG did not get his gear down in time before landing. The plane skidded down the runway to a halt. The maintenance crew picked the plane up with a crane, and the gear came down and locked. The plane was towed into the hangar. The inspector general looked the plane over on the other. It worked; Jay could read all of the color dot pages in the color- blind test book. In the photograph on the previous page, normal folks see 8, 39, 6 and 42 reading left to right. Color-blind people see only 3 and 5 for the 8 and 6.

Jay kept up his monthly training in the Tulsa Air National Guard (ANG). On a two-week summer camp at an air base near Casper Wyoming, an F-80 fighter assigned to the Tulsa ANG did not get his gear down in time before landing. The plane skidded down the runway to a halt. The maintenance crew picked the plane up with a crane, and the gear came down and locked. The plane was towed into the hangar. The inspector general looked the plane over and said that it was not worth fixing; it had a wrinkled fuselage. The shops converged on the plane like buzzards. They removed the engine, the instruments, guns, etc. Spare parts were hard to come by. The bone yard at Tucson was called to come and get the plane. When the bone yard folks arrived they asked, "Where's our plane?" They were led to it, but they said, "We can't take that plane; it's not complete." All of the equipment was replaced on the plane. The plane was hauled to the bone yard and scrapped; that is government efficiency.

The food the cooks of the ANG prepared was horrible. They made "gob- balls" of ground beef the size of baseballs. When Jay passed by in the chow line, a cook slapped one on his steel tray. It slid off on the other side and bounced on the floor like a rubber ball; Jay kept walking without looking back. Mashed potatoes had the hard eyes still in. Most of the airmen ate in Casper, WY, at restaurants in the evening to avoid the chow at the base. One evening, Jay ordered trout for supper; it had a big worm in the meat. Jay never ate trout again for a while. The ANG group spent a couple of summers at Casper. One time in town, a friend who was in the ANG and in the jr. college with Jay, hailed a couple of girls in a car and tried his best to get Jay to go with him. Jay refused. handled the flowers roughly; Jay thought they deserved to be handled with more respect.

On one occasion, the girl and Jay took Ted, his wife and their youngest son to Oklahoma City to a special medical facility there. The son had muscular dystrophy, and the facility had experts in that field. There was not anything they could do to help the boy. The girl drove back. She drove at a high rate of speed which scared the passengers. It was two hundred miles to Oklahoma City. They drove it there and back the same day.

The girl took up with a local college graduate, while dating Jay, and married him. That was the end of that. Someone told Jay later that the girl had dated a college guy before Jay and became pregnant; the guy would not marry her. She jumped out of his car on a curve at a high rate of speed. She was taken to a local hospital where she lost her baby. Jay always thought of her as a good friend afterwards, anyhow. The college guy was later killed with two friends as they returned from Missouri, a wet state, with some booze. They ran under the trailer of a truck that had backed onto the highway to turn around.

After he finished junior college, Jay was sent to Lackland Air Force training base at San Antonio for basic training for three months with other ANG trainees from other states. At the beginning the stout Mexican women cooking and serving chow there were

1953 Plymouth 4-Door

hard to look at. At the end of the training they were beginning to look a whole lot better. During three months long Basic training, Jay could not pay the payments on his car; the pay to the trainees was somewhere around fifty- six dollars per month, and personal needs, including haircuts, had to be paid by the trainees. The lenders for Jay's car wanted to take the car, but Joe would not from other states. At the beginning the stout Mexican women cooking and serving chow there were hard to look at. At the end of the training they were beginning to look a whole lot better. During three months long Basic training, Jay could not pay the payments on his car; the pay to the trainees was somewhere around fifty-six dollars per month, and personal needs, including haircuts, had to be paid by the trainees. The lenders for Jay's car wanted to take the car, but Joe would not let them have it. Fortunately, military men were protected from such activities while on active duty. When Jay returned he resumed the payments. Jay knew he could not keep the beautiful Mercury and go on to college. He sold the car and bought a 1953 Plymouth four-door car cheap.

Whitehand Hall

The winter of 1959 found Jay in Norman Oklahoma living in the White Hand Hall dormitory just across the street north of the University of Oklahoma main campus. He had a room located just inside the door to the left of the entrance on the first floor.

Thanks to Fay, Joe paid Jay six dollars per day for working for him at first; later ten dollars per day. Chores did not count. After selling his car for what he owed on it, one thousand three hundred dollars, Jay had somewhere around five hundred dollars coming. Fay's mother died and Joe would

The University of Oklahoma

not give her the amount of her part for her mother's funeral. Fay's immediate family each paid part of the funeral costs. Jay, before going to the four-year college (actually five years for engineering) to finish his education, asked Joe for the money he had earned so he could go to school. Jay gave Fay what she needed and had enough earned ten each at the junior

college. Jay decided to enroll at the University of Oklahoma. He went to Norman, got a room in Whitehand hall and enrolled in school for the spring semester of 1959. The room was a double room, but Jay's roommate was gone visiting his girlfriend most of the time. He was an education major, which was an easy curriculum at that time. Most majors required 120 semester hours for graduation; engineering required 136 difficult hours.

Jay transferred to the 138th ANG Wing in Oklahoma City so he would not have to go so far for guard meetings. The 138th Wing was a sister wing to the Tulsa 137th wing and had the same planes. The forty dollars per month sure came in handy. The unit at this time had F-86D fighter planes.

Jay got a job for two meals each day helping an elderly lady and her middle-aged daughter with the kitchen, setting the table for the noon meal and serving the noon meal. That sure worked out well. Jay was able to borrow three hundred dollars from the National Defense Loan set up during the Eisenhower administration. Jay was the third one to get it at the University of Oklahoma. It had to be paid back at 3 percent over ten years after graduation. That was a life saver.

Joe and Ted did the farming. With Jay gone they could really use another hand for the fall wheat planting. The ground needed to be prepared and worked to the proper seed bed. A hobo was found sitting at the end of a wheat field near US 66 Highway. He was dirty and obviously lived the life of a hobo. He carried everything he owned on his back. He said he was hungry. Joe bought him some food, and Ted taught him to plow with a tractor. He did a poor job; sometimes he would go the full length of the field without tripping the plow into the ground. However, Joe kept him around and paid him regular wages by check. Fay called him Bo. Bo never went to town and could not cash his checks. Joe took care of that. In the following winter, Bo was allowed to stay in one of Joe's

Joe and Ted did the farming. With Jay gone they could really use another hand for the fall wheat planting. The ground needed to be prepared and worked to the proper seed bed. A hobo was found sitting at the end of a wheat field near US 66 Highway. He was dirty and obviously lived the life of a hobo. He carried everything he owned on his back. He said he was hungry. Joe bought him some food, and Ted taught him to plow with a tractor. He did a poor job; sometimes he would go the full length of the field without tripping the plow into the ground. However, Joe kept him around and paid him regular wages by check. Fay called him Bo. Bo never went to town and could not cash his checks. Joe took care of that. In the following winter, Bo was allowed to stay in one of Joe's barns. A coal stove was there for heat. Bo said, "If I get too cold, I'll go across the road into the woods and build me a fire." Bo was not quite right in his ability to think. He did stay through the winter, but moved on later. Jay saw him sitting beside the road in a small town north of Tulsa. That was the last time he was seen by anyone connected with Joe.

While in the Tulsa ANG, a friend of Jay's there had a date with a pretty girl from a town south of Tulsa. She had a niece her same age. The girl was in Tulsa visiting her sister and niece. The friend wanted Jay to double date with him. When Jay was in Tulsa once each month at the ANG, he dated the niece, Sadie, after that. During the 1959 semester at OU, Jay wrote Sadie often and she wrote him. The letters were delivered the next day. During the semester, the postal system initiated their zip code system. Now the letters took as much as three days; that is government efficiency.

Sadie

Sadie was naive and not worldly. She was not familiar with dating. That is the primary thing Jay liked about her. She was not beautiful, but she was attractive. She had a speech defect; her mother taught her "baby talk" when she was a small child. She never quite got over it. It was not really all that bad. Her mother had been in labor much too long when Sadie was born.

required in the library checking references in the text books. In group studies, each student had understood a part of the class material better than some or all of the others. By putting heads together, the puzzle was much more complete. Jay, unlike the majority of other students, was tight on time. He studied with an Air Force pilot that was being sent to college by the Air Force. They became good friends. The pilot flew the local ANG planes, the F86Ds, to get in his required flying time. One day he and another pilot flew to the firing range somewhere west of Oklahoma City. On the way back the planes ran into wind shear. They dropped several hundred feet all at once. Jay's friend panicked and pulled his ejection handle. The canopy failed to blow off, and the seat blasted the friend through the canopy breaking his neck. The parachute deployed and let the friend down normally, but he was found dead draped over a fence. The plane leafed down slowly and skidded to a stop in a pasture; it was in one piece. Jay was shocked; he had just studied with the friend a day or so before the tragedy.

A fraternity invited Jay to join their house. They gave a party for prospective candidates. Jay was impressed. They had lots of discipline, were required to maintain a certain grade point and had lots of entertainment. Jay did not have the money to join if he wanted to. One thing that Jay did not think was fair was the closet full of former tests in most of the classes. Some instructors were lazy and gave the same tests in their succeeding classes.

The University put out an all points notice to contact Jay one morning. An instructor told Jay of the alert when he came to his class. Jay was notified to come home at once; Fay was in the hospital and very ill. Jay headed home immediately. Fay had some kind of stomach ailment. After a couple of days she was feeling better and on the mend. Jay returned to school more than two hundred miles away. To Jay's surprise, Fay and Joe came to Jay's room in Whitehand Hall for a visit. Joe was president of the local county Farm Bureau as the money to join if he wanted to. One thing that Jay did not think was fair was the closet full of former tests in most of the classes. Some instructors were lazy and gave the same tests in their succeeding classes.

The University put out an all points notice to contact Jay one morning. An instructor told Jay of the alert when he came to his class. Jay was notified to come home at once; Fay was in the hospital and very ill. Jay headed home immediately. Fay had some kind of stomach ailment. After a couple of days she was feeling better and on the mend. Jay returned to school more than two hundred miles away. To Jay's surprise, Fay and Joe came to Jay's room in Whitehand Hall for a visit. Joe was president of the local county

Farm Bureau as well as a board member of the Federal Land Bank making loans to farmers at a reasonable rate. They had been in Oklahoma City on business.

Jay was sure glad when that semester was over. He went back home and continued working for his dad, Joe, during the following summer.

Chapter 7

Adult Responsibility

Now Jay was not good at making good decisions for his life. He fell back a lot and spun his wheels a lot. He should have kept his life simple and not tried to make some of his dumb decisions work. He would like to blame his faults on lack of parental guidance, but others in the same boat did not make the mistakes he did. If Jay had simply followed his Christian teaching and the leadership of the Holy Spirit, his life would have been so much more enjoyable without wrong decisions along the way.

Jay knew about persistence and could have made it work well for him if he had just been more level headed. Probably the biggest problem in Joe's life was that he felt alone most of the time. He just did not feel that he had anyone close; he did not like being a loner.

Worry about where the next meal was coming from was not a problem for Jay. He depended on the Lord who had always provided; Jay knew he would continue.

At the end of the summer, Jay told his dad that he was planning to get married, and go on back to school. The girl he was to marry was Sadie in Tulsa. Sadie was eighteen and had just graduated from high school. They planned to work to support themselves while Jay attended school. Sadie's mother, when Jay asked for Sadie's hand, told Jay to promise not to leave the Tulsa area. Apparently she knew that Sadie was not ready for the responsibility of domestic life; she was not prepared. Jay felt she could learn and told Sadie's mother he had to go where the work was for engineers.

Joe and Fay planned to attend the wedding which was to be held at Sadie's parent's house. On the way to the wedding Jay had a breakdown of the old Plymouth near Claremore, OK. He had just done a tune up with new plugs, points and condenser. The new condenser came apart and the car died. Fortunately (or unfortunately) Jay had kept the old one. He quickly found the problem and put the old condenser back in. As Jay suspected that all grooms had some doubts about getting married, he thought in the back of his mind that he was being told something. The breakdown really was not a show stopper anyhow; Joe and Fay were in their car right behind Jay following him to the wedding place. The wedding went off without a hitch with several of Sadie's kin there. The preacher was one selected by Sadie's mother. She played it smart; saved lots of money on a wedding. Some weddings cost several thousand dollars. After the wedding Joe and Fay stopped by the motel where Jay and Sadie were staying. It was on their way home.

Upon arrival in Norman, the newly-weds rented a small apartment close to the university campus. Jay got a job in a Book Store very near the campus. The store had a bar at one end and shuffleboard. Jay and another student ran the bar. The pay was sixty-seven cents per hour. Jay did the evening shift and the other student did the afternoon shift. The store owner told the boys that they could have anything over thirty-one dollars for each keg of beer. That did not work out so well because the other student and his wife both liked beer. Jay did not drink any alcoholic beverages; he did not like the taste. There never was any overage.

Sadie applied for a job at the university, but she could not type well enough. She was guided to a cotton picking job at a field nearby. She and Jay bought long cotton picking bags that drug behind the worker and worked at that for a day or two; they made enough to pay for the bags. This was before the school term began. Then Sadie got a job in a fast food place in a small community a few miles south of the university. That did not work out "so too good" either. Needless to say, the two were struggling financially

When Sadie's mother had taught Sadie to talk, she put "H" before words that were not supposed to have it and leaving off the "H" when it was needed, e.g., "Hellvis" for Elvis and "ouse" for house. The practice stayed with her and made it more difficult to get a job.

Meanwhile, Jay enrolled in a full load of studies in engineering. The bartending went OK for a while. One student, a bar fly, came in every evening to tell his troubles to Jay. That was OK, but it did distract Jay from his work and studying when the crowd was small.

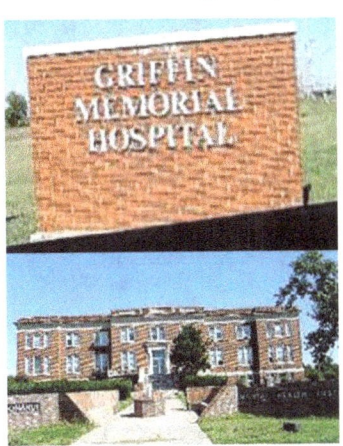

Griffith Memorial State Hospital
Administration Building

A couple was looking for a married student to live on their small farm and look after the place. They put an ad in the paper. Jay and Sadie took that opportunity. It was cost free, but it was nineteen miles east of town. The wife of the owners of the farm had been operated on for breast cancer. She was doing alright. She had worked at the state hospital in town. She told Jay he should apply there, and that there were several college students working there.

At the bar someone had left a magazine that had an article about how to handle the psychology test that companies were using to hire its employees. It was the rage at that time. People are like cows; they like to follow each other around. Companies are the same way. (Later, they all apparently realized that the idea of using psychology to hire people did not work well; it was phased out.) One thing that the magazine article said was that when asked for a drawing of the opposite sex, a man should draw a full page frontal view of a naked woman. Jay did that. He was hired and heard later that his bosses were told to not put him on women's wards.

Before Jay could tell the owner of the book store that he had another job, a strange thing happened. One night a fraternity brought in a sorority into the bar and gathered enough chairs around the long shuffle board table in the room for everyone. A "frat rat" came to the bar and bought every one beer, two or three at a time. The "bar fly" wanted to tell Jay his troubles, but Jay was too busy to listen to him. The" fly" stepped into the book store and called the police. The police stood at the door and checked the IDs of everyone. Some of the girls were under eighteen, the legal age for consuming liquor. The police were going to arrest Jay for selling the beer to minors, but the Fraternity guy who bought the beer told the police that he bought the beer, and Jay was not responsible what he did with it. The Police let Jay go, but the book store owner lost his liquor license. Fortunately for Jay, he had the job at the state hospital to go to. He started there a few days later.

The lady who let Jay and Sadie live in their farm house had some white pants that she took up for Jay. She and her husband were good to Jay and Sadie. They had another old house on their land. It was not near as nice, and they let an older couple live in it. The gasoline for the nineteen miles trip each way was a financial burden, and caring for the farm interfered with his studies.

Jay only made 180 dollars per month at the hospital for forty-eight hours per week job. There was an apartment close to the college and hospital. It was an upstairs unit within a few feet to a railroad track. The newly-weds quickly got used to the trains passing so near their apartment; the apartment was cheaper than the cost in time and fuel to live on the farm. However, at one time they were so poor that all they had to eat was a can of condensed milk and some corn starch. They made gravy with those items.

As things got better, Jay and Sadie moved into a house close to the hospital. The situation was so tight that Sadie and her parents talked Jay into letting her move back to Tulsa until things got better. Jay then shared the house with a

friend. As things improved, Jay rented a nice one-room second floor apartment close to the hospital. It had an air conditioner in one window where a pigeon nested. That was interesting and a source of entertainment.

This apartment had problems, though. The couple who lived next door was noisy. The lady was a nurse at the hospital; sometimes Jay's boss. When she came home around three PM she slammed the doors on her cupboards. The cupboards were on the common wall between the apartments. The problem was that Jay had a broken schedule. He come home at 7:00 a.m. slept for an hour and a half, and then went to class for three hours. Then he had labs for the engineering courses. After the labs Jay tried to sleep until he went on duty at 11:00 p.m. It was a rotten schedule. Sleep was sometimes interrupted by the kid next door working on his motor bike. Sadie stayed in Tulsa to a more orderly and quiet existence a lot.

The state hospital experience was a wild ride. Jay started out in geriatrics (older folks) on a men's ward. He thought several of the patients were normal. They carried on reasonable conversations with the nurses' aides like Jay. Some of the aids, including Jay, visited with an attractive younger woman in a full body cast on the woman's geriatrics ward. She was said to have tried to commit suicide. Jay worked the evening shift from 3:00 p.m. to 11:00 p.m. in the beginning. One evening he was helping a one legged ex-history teacher eat his supper when the man suddenly gasped, fell over in his wheelchair and quit moving. Jay called the nurse for help. The man was diagnosed as having died from a heart attack. Jay was told to help prepare the man for the morgue, including packing his large intestine with gauze. Later Jay requested to be on the night shift, 11:00 to 7:00 a.m. The request was granted. While Jay was still assigned to geriatrics, his job of the morning was to get the men up and into the day room by 7:00 a.m. A small man in an upper bunk did not get up on the first call. Jay went to each patient around 6:30 a.m., called him by name and told him it was time to get up. Jay went back to the fellow who was still in his bunk and said, "Mr. Doe, it is time to get up." "Mr. Doe" came out of the bed like a tightly compressed spring, socked Jay in the nose and sent him to the floor up against the wall. Jay bounced up, grabbed the little guy, stuffed him into a set of coveralls and dragged him out to the day room by the collar. It was good for Jay that no other staff members saw what happened.

Jay spent most of his time on the night shift. It was a hard way to go staying up all night and going to class on a broken schedule. After coming off a night shift Jay's mouth was dry with a bad taste. Once he was infected with staphylococcus between his left ear and the eye. It was large, but the hospital nurse and the university infirmary were able to clear it up without Jay missing work. One night Jay had the flu and the hospital nurse sent him home with some hystadill APC capsules. Jay took a couple and felt well enough to return to work an hour or so later.

Jay was not assigned a specific ward at nights. He worked on several different ones wherever he was needed. One night when he came to work he was assigned to work on the criminal ward. Before he arrived there had been a riot on this locked ward. There were four aids on the ward with the lead man a big guy around two hundred fifty pounds. All aides wore white uniforms washed by the hospital. The thirty-some odd criminal "patients," who were ordered there by a judge from somewhere for observation, were allowed to visit in the day room. The aides were in the office. The inmates rushed the office and tried to get the keys. The big guy was the only one who had keys. The inmates wrapped the telephone cord around the big guy's neck and ripped his white trousers trying to get the keys. The big aid managed to flush the keys down the toilet. The nurses, who ran the hospital for the doctors and administration people, did not have keys to the ward. They could not send in more aids to subdue the inmates. There were several university athletes working there. The superintendent, who had gone home, was called to bring keys. He let some aids into the ward. The fight was quickly over, and the inmates were each isolated in individual rooms. They were not allowed to congregate any more. That same night after all was quiet Jay decided not to study in the office. He sat at the long table in the day room. However he had not known about Wild Bill Hitchcock. Wild Bill always sat with his back to the wall. The one time he did not there in Deadwood, a crook sneaked in behind him and shot him. Bill held a hand of aces and eights ("the dead man's hand"). Jay sat with his back to one of the two doors into the dayroom, the one across from the office. He suddenly heard a deep voice, late in the night that said, "You got a match?" Jay must have jumped as high as the table. Fortunately, the guy only wanted a match for his cigarette. Someone had let the inmate out to go to the bath room and did not stay with him to put him back. Jay took him back and locked him in his room.

Jay worked all over the hospital. The best place to work was the veteran's complex located along the east side of the hospital grounds. This facility was modern and nice with air conditioning. It had four wards. The A ward was open for veterans that were responsible for their activities but were there for service related disabilities. They needed hospital mental treatment. B ward was locked at night, but the vets were free to roam during the day. C ward was locked at all times, but the patients were fairly easy to treat. D was for vets that needed serious mental treatment. Jay enjoyed working all of these wards when he got the chance.

The state side was not so nice. The buildings were old and not air conditioned except maybe for the infirmary. The wards on the state side were locked. Jay was assigned to a ward one night that should have had two aids. However the staff was shorthanded and jay was alone. A patient went into convulsions. Jay had been warned about patients with epilepsy. He grabbed a tongue spoon and ran to the patient who was lying on the floor writhing and snorting. A patient in the next bed hastily told jay, with a sense of urgency in his voice, to leave the patient alone. He said that if the epileptic person recovered and saw anyone watching, he would attack the onlooker. Jay went back to the office. The lights were off and Jay watched the epileptic person by the dim night lights until he got up, looked around and got back into bed. All of the patients pretended to be asleep. Jay waited several minutes and made his rounds with a flashlight. All pretended to be asleep including the person who had the attack of epilepsy. All was quiet the rest of the night.

The TB ward was one the aids were not eager to work on. Jay was assigned to the men's ward a few times. He was adorned in protective clothing from head to foot. There was a dressing room to change clothing before going in. A call come for Jay and another aide to come to the lady's ward and help subdue an attractive lady in her early thirties. She was completely naked and was uncooperative. The two men picked her up, put her on a bed and held her until she could be restrained. People were restrained by pulling a lady's cotton stocking over each arm, wrapping another stocking around the wrist and then pulling the first stocking back over the wrist and hand. The long length of the stockings became a lanyard to tie each arm to the bed railings effectively restraining the patients without cutting off the blood flow. Jay later worked on the TB pre-release ward a couple or three nights. Here no protective clothing was required; the patients were declared cured of TB. Jay was uneasy anyhow.

The children's wards occupied one building. The boys were on the ground floor and the girls were on the top ward. Their ages were from six to seventeen. Along about 1:00 a.m., Jay, who was substituting for a regular nurse's aide, and the lead aid were somewhat drowsy sitting in the office. They had checked the boy's ward they were serving, and all was quiet an hour or so before. A clunk from above in the girls ward was heard by Jay; it woke him up. He kicked the foot of the big football-player, regular aid and said, "I heard something." The lead aid said, "Let's quietly check the ward. They toured the boy's ward and all was quiet.

Now the children on the children's wards were not necessarily mentally ill; they were problem kids that no one could handle. Several times they had broken out of their wards by using bed parts, etc., for tools to pry open the windows and security screens. They were smart but difficult. They cooked up many ways to get out.

After satisfying himself that the boy's ward was under control, the lead aid quietly opened the door to the stairway leading to the girl's ward. When he opened the door to the hallway to the girl's ward office, the two aids found the hallway full of patients. The patients had rushed the lady aid on duty. She was alone that night and in the office when the girls demanded her keys. One patient had thrown a flower pot at the aid. That is what Jay heard. The aids from the lower ward sent the girls back to their ward. The nurse on duty was called and came right over. The girls were still milling around and making grumbling sounds. Their leaders were two seventeen-year-old girls. The nurse quieted most of the younger girls, but the two older ones persisted in their disturbances. They were heard to say, "Those sons-of-bitches won't come back here." The girls were stark naked. The nurse told the male aids to physically lay hold of the girls and put them in separate seclusion rooms. Jay thought that this could get to be a habit, physically handling naked women. He really did not enjoy it. That ended the problem for the rest of the night on the children's wards. Normally two aids were assigned to each ward. Another aid was sent to the girl's ward to help the other aid who was shaken.

There was a ward that had patients who did not respond well to treatment. They were seriously mentally impaired. Sometimes the floor felt sticky from the feces on the floor from the patients who had little or no control of themselves. Mopping was a constant task. The smell was hardly bearable. The locked ward's windows were closed in winter and the ward was sultry in summer and winter. In the ward was a hermaphrodite. The hermaphrodite would not leave the women alone when placed on their ward, and the men would not leave him/her alone when he/she was on their ward. The hermaphrodite was kept in a seclusion room for his/her protection. A middle-age, overweight woman with a protrusion from the vagina was how Jay described the unfortunate person. The patient's scream, which was its normal daily expression, could be heard into town. The seclusion room was kept warm for the patient because the staff could not keep clothes on him/her. Warm water spray was the method of bathing after which towel drying was applied.

Jay was on a locked ward alone one night. This was his first time on this ward. He was not familiar with the procedures. The patients were prone to break out, but Jay did not know that. He handled the ward in the same manner he handled other wards. However, this ward had door keys on a board in the office, and the aids locked the office door when they did their routine checks of the ward. While Jay was on his rounds, several patients sneaked into the office, liberated the keys and left the premises. Some were found sitting on a culvert end-buttress the next morning. Some were just walking around, etc. All were returned by mid-morning. No action was taken against Jay. Actually, there should have been two aids on at night because it was a difficult ward.

The runner job came open, and Jay became the runner. He went from ward to ward in the night collecting the day's report for each ward. One of his responsibilities was to report any aid he found asleep on the ward. He knew that previous runners always made considerable noise when they came around. Jay rattled the doors as he was unlocking them. He never caught anyone asleep. One of the wards he visited had a psychology professor in it as a patient. He had committed himself, Jay was told. If he was there as an observer, Jay was not aware of it. The hospital guard drove around the grounds at night. Sometimes, the guard let Jay ride from one complex to another, especially in inclement weather. They became good friends. The guard's wife was in medical school, which was located in Oklahoma City. The guard was glad to have company and someone to talk to. Because of that, Jay got to ride frequently.

There were living quarters and a cafeteria near the hospital grounds for the nurses' aids. They could live there at a very reasonable cost for room and board. Jay did eat in the cafeteria at times, but he never lived in the facilities. Much of the food was raised on the hospital farm, Jay was told.

Infirmary Building

The state hospital is gone now. Some of the buildings are still there, but most are for other uses.

A Baptist church in the local town became Jay's place of worship. He transferred his membership from the church in his home town. He appreciated all of the help the Lord gave him. He certainly needed it. Many times he asked himself

Griffith Hospital Chapel

if the strife was worth it. He considered throwing in the towel several times. Taking engineering courses and working forty-eight hours per week was an extremely hard way to go. He still wonders how he made it. Six work days per week was normal on the farm. The Lord's help and Jay's stubborn persistence was the backbone of his endurance.

On top of all of the work, studies and classes, Jay spent two days per month at the Air National Guard. This kept the draft folks off his back while he was in school. The 40 dollars per month helped him survive.

The engineering school's requirement for 136 semester hours of difficult class work was sixteen more hours than the other schools at the university. It took Jay five semesters and one summer term to finish his degree beyond the junior college work. He also took a course by correspondence. It was a very difficult course in math, differential equations. Believe it or not, he made a B in the course. It was rough to say the least.

Jay had to have a 2.5 grade point average to graduate. He had a D in strength of materials course, but he had A and B grades to offset it. The strength of materials instructor was a German. He was very strict. Some Arabs in the course made unusually good grades (part of why Jay made the lower grade). The instructor saw that the answers the Arabs gave on tests were like his book answers. He had a teacher's book to teach from and he took questions from the book. The teacher's answer sheet only gave shortcut answers; they were the same as the Arabs put on their tests. The teacher was sure the Arabs cheated and threw them out of the class. The consulate for the Arabs contacted the instructor and told him that his consulate had provided the answer sheet for the book. The instructor let them back into class, but he gave no more tests from the book. However, the damage was done.

During the 1960 fall semester, Jay and Sadie moved into a prefabricated house set up for veterans on the college campas. It was about twenty-by-twenty- feet unit with bolted sides and a pyramid top. They were painted silver. In the approximately four hundred square feet there was a kitchen, a living room, a bath room and a bedroom. It was tight, but it was livable, and it was furnished. For only thirty-five dollars per month with all bills paid, it was a good deal for the poor student who was not too proud to live there. Sadie went back to live with her parents during the last semester in the spring of 1961. Jay moved into a double unit for five dollars more a month and finished his studies there.

The double unit was at the south edge of the campus. It was nearly a mile to the engineering building. Jay managed to buy an old style Columbia bicycle. He ordered tires and a basket from Wards on credit. Jay had quit his hospital job, and borrowed enough from the National Defense loan to finish the second semester. He borrowed about three hundred dollars at 3 percent. He spent all of his time this semester studying. His grades improved dramatically.

One of Jay's classes was at the opposite corner of the campus from the engineering building. With the bicycle Jay could make the class at the far corner within the ten minutes allowed. One night, Jay parked his ugly bike in front of the library while he was studying. When he came out the bike was gone. He could not fathom anyone wanting to steal that thing; he had not bought a lock for it. He looked for the bike for days as he had time. He checked all of the bike racks on and off the campus nearby. He had no luck. He told the campus cops, but they never found it. One day when Jay was walking across the campus toward the library, he could hardly believe his eyes. There it was lying on the ground. He bought a cheap lock and kept it secured from there on. At night it stayed inside.

One day, about the middle of the semester, Jay was walking across the campus. A tall, good looking girl came swinging along. Her skirt was hardly more than a belt. This was the age of super short skirts. She suddenly stopped, turned to a guy close behind her and said, "Sweat it, little man." She then turned and walked on leaving the fellow who was following her and Jay, who was close by going the other way, dumbfounded.

Jay sometimes studied with three Arab students from Lebanon. One was red headed and was teased a lot by his friends. The Arab fellows made a coffee that was thick as mud. They served it in small child-like cups. Jay did not drink coffee; he did not like the bitter taste. The boys joked about dating Jewish girls. They said that there was a rumor about some of the married students having "key parties." It was said that they would put their door keys in a bowl and either the women or the men would each draw one out. The key they drew would open the door where they would spend the night. That sounded to be too stupid to be true. The Arabs thought that the rumored "key parties" going on among married students was hilarious but appalling. Jay became good friends with one of the Arab fellows and kept in contact for a while after they graduated. Jay enjoyed his better grades because of more and better quality study time.

He was on a team with his close Arab friend designing a turbine for a jet engine in a jet engine class. Another team designed the compressor for the engine. They were supposed to match in performance. They did not match well, but the instructor asked the students to suggest what they thought they should have for a grade based on effort and results. Jay and his Arab friend were given good grades.

One student was given a job in the school helping grade papers in a class that Jay took. Jay overheard the instructor say in the instructor's office, "They didn't think it was a joke." What was going on was that the student grading papers had approached some of the students with an offer that they would get a better score on tests for a price. He did remain in school and graduated.

Along toward the end of the semester, Jay was getting low on money. He could not pay for a gown for graduation. It was no matter. The graduation was held the weekend before the finals week. Jay could not go anyhow; he had to study for finals. He was not yet sure how the outcome would be. He graduated in "absentia," according to a friend who was there. His name was read at the graduation.

The "sheep skin", made of plastic, was mailed to Joe. Joe was so proud of it that he showed it to his banker and others. That was the first degree in Joe's family. It read, "Bachelor of Science in Aeronautical and Space Engineering." The aeronautical and space engineering school was a separate engineering school like the mechanical and electrical engineering schools. Aeronautics has to do with control of pressures on areas of aircraft wings and propellers. At sea level on a standard day (60° F, etc.), the static (not moving) pressure is 14.7 pounds per square inch (PSI). There is such a thing as total pressure, which is static pressure + dynamic (moving) pressure. Stick your hand out a moving automobile window and feel dynamic pressure.

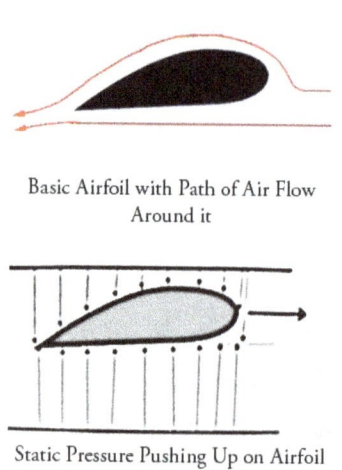

Basic Airfoil with Path of Air Flow Around it

Static Pressure Pushing Up on Airfoil

A basic airplane wing is flat on the bottom and curved across the top. Consider two particles of air at the front of an airfoil. One goes over the top and the other goes under the bottom. The two particles arrive at the trailing edge at the same time because the wing does not drag air along with it. We know that if it did, the wing would not fly. The particle of air on the top of the wing has further to go than that on the bottom; it has to speed up to arrive with the lower particle at the trailing edge at the same time. With the increase in speed, some of the static pressure pushing down is converted to dynamic pressure. At right is a static pressure diagram indicating the static pressure above and below the wing as it passes through the air. The difference is that along the top some of the static pressure has been converted to dynamic pressure.

Dynamic pressure is parallel to the wing and does not push up or down on the wing. Gravity is straight down; therefore, we are only interested in the vertical forces operating on the wing, namely static pressure pushing up on the bottom of the wing and the static pressure pushing down on the top of the wing. We know that pressure on an area is a force. The static pressure pushing down on the wing area is the downward force, and the force pushing up is the upward static pressure on the wing area. The static pressure downward sees the same plan-view area as the static pressure pushing up; downward pressure does not see the curve upward hump. It is the same as if you were standing over the wing looking straight down; you do not see the hump on the wing. So the static pressure up sees the same effective area as the static pressure down. The total pressure is the same all around the wing; it does not change from top to bottom. However, the increase in velocity over the top of the wing generates some dynamic pressure.

Another way to say it is that because the total pressure is constant (does not change), then the dynamic pressure has to come from the static pressure on top of the wing. It can be calculated by the equation $\Delta P = \frac{1}{2}\rho V^2$ (change in pressure = $\frac{1}{2}$ of the air density x airflow velocity x airflow velocity). So the static pressure pushing down on the plan-view area is less than that pushing up on the same effective area which means the force pushing up is greater than that pushing down and the wing rises provided the difference is great enough to overcome gravity. It can be proven by taking a sheet of paper and holding it by one end, two hands, parallel to the floor and blowing over the top; the loose end of the paper will rise. Jay wondered how much the Wright Brothers understood what caused wings to rise. He suspected that they looked at a bird's wing, copied the air foil shape and found it worked. Jay never saw what is told here in a text book nor heard it in a class room. He wondered if most aerodynamic professors fully under stood it.

Jay pieced the above info together like a puzzle over a period of time. Propellers are designed as airfoils and work on the same principal.

Sailing boats can sail into the wind by setting their sails such that they form an airfoil. As the wind passes over the airfoil-shaped sail it lowers the static pressure that gives a force in the forward direction at an angle to the line of travel. So the boat sails in one direction that has a forward component. Then the sail is swung to the other side of the boat and the direction of travel is shifted to that of the airfoil force, which is at an angle to the line of travel. Consequently, the boat has a zigzag course with a resultant in the forward direction.

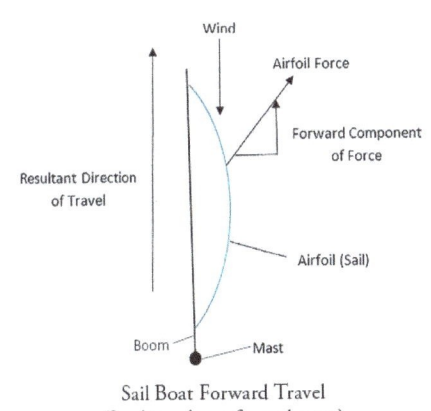

Sail Boat Forward Travel
(Looking down from the top)

Space travel depends on rocket engines. A balloon filled with air is a rocket engine. Jay as a young person thought that rockets propelled themselves by the exhaust pushing on the air around the rocket. That is not true; if it were, rockets would not work in space. With the wing, the area is held constant and the pressure on top of the wing is lowered. With rockets the pressure is kept constant (the same) throughout at any point in time inside the rocket motor, and the area on one end is reduced. Since the pressure is the same on each end, and the area is smaller at the opening end, the force on the end with the larger area is greater and drives the rocket in that direction. To demonstrate this, simply fill a toy balloon with air and simply open one end. The balloon travels opposite the open end.

All of the forces are inside the rocket. The nozzle, the hole at one end of the rocket, limits the amount of thrust of a rocket engine. It chokes at Mach one (speed of sound) of the exhaust gases. Jet engines and rocket engines are similar in performance; they both have a pressure chamber and a nozzle at one end. The basic difference is that rockets carry their oxidizers for their fuel while the jet engine gets its oxygen from the air. Fighter airplanes dump fuel in the exhaust pipe and burn it with the residual oxygen in the exhaust gases (after burner). This increases the pressure in the tail pipe. Another action, opening the nozzle area, is required. It has two effects. Opening the exhaust area larger decreases the area opposing the forward area resulting in a greater force forward, and the larger nozzle gives greater flow before choking. Choking at Mach one is caused by a standing shock wave at the nozzle.

The school posted on the bulletin boards the companies recruiting on the campus for seniors. Jay interviewed some and had three or four offers. He chose Chance Vought in Grand Prairie, Texas. Texas is a warmer place to live, and the offer was one of the better ones. The offer was for $731 per month. For Jay, that was a lot of money.

Jay and Sadie were ready to go to Dallas to begin their career in engineering, but they had no money. They thought that somehow the Lord would provide. He did.

1949 Chevrolet Coupe

They had borrowed Sadie's dad's old 1949 Chevy coupe. It was all they had to get around in. The transmission often locked up and the car had to be rocked to get it loose. They had lost their Plymouth trying to trade up to get a better car to go to Tulsa. The car they traded for was too much for them to afford and it was bought by Sadie's uncle in Oklahoma City. They tried to buy the Plymouth back but the dealer, contrary to his word, priced the car beyond Jay and Sadie's reach; another of Jay's bad decisions. Jay always depended on the Lord to take care of him; he sure did not do well by himself.

Jay and Sadie did not have the money for gasoline for the trip to Dallas to begin Jay's new job. Fortunately, Jay's aunt Alice sent eighty dollars for graduation. The two rented a very cheap motel until they could find a house to rent. Sadie found one and was able to rent it with a few dollars down. The two managed for three weeks on the eighty dollars. Jay was paid every two weeks; One week was held back. The first pay check was sure a blessing. The first thing they did was to buy some furniture on credit.

The first day on the job Jay was assigned to the propulsion engineering group at Chance Vought Aircraft Company in Grand Prairie, Texas. His boss was a fellow from England. The boss said that one time when he was on his way back to England his plane stopped on an island for servicing of the plane.

The service crewmen were natives who had long tubes on their genitals and were naked otherwise. A middle-aged English army officer stepped to the door of the plane and told the servicemen, "Get away from here, you bloody blokes; my wife will think I'm deformed." The boss was a good man to work for. Jay was told to go to the group's secretary to get supplies. When he asked for a hole-puncher the secretary giggled and told Jay, "No, you want a paper punch." Jay was embarrassed.

The plane in production was the Crusader, the American Navy's first supersonic fighter. Chuck Yeager flew it supersonic on its maiden flight.

One problem the plane had was that the pitot tube, the device in the airstream that was used for measuring airspeed, would ice up at high speed, and the ice could not be melted off with the pitot tube heater. There are several designs of the tube tips. The one shown in the photograph below is the slant back type. Another type is the slant forward toward of the outside (concave) type. The sketch below is of a velocity indicating system using a liquid in a U tube to indicate the difference between the dynamic (moving) pressure, Pd, and the static pressure, Ps. Velocity, V, is proportional to the pressure differences: $V \propto Pd - Ps$.

Chance Vought Crusader F-8 Fighter

All types were tried but ice attached itself to the tube regardless of the type and would not shed. The tube was heated for deicing, but the ice just would not come off causing the pilot to have no airspeed indication. Jay was asked to look into it as his first assignment. The research folks had a test rig set up near the supersonic wind tunnel. The supersonic wind tunnel consisted of several large steel tanks that looked like huge propane tanks. They were pumped up to very high pressure. Air flow from the high pressure tanks provided supersonic flow as the tanks were bled down. It took a day to pump up the tanks. A side port was used to provide flow to a system rigged for testing the icing of the F-8's Pitot tube. The air from the tanks was passed through a coiled tube immersed in glycol antifreeze with dry ice in it. Water was sprayed into the super-cooled airstream that was blown onto the Pitot tube inlet. It worked well. The internal heater of the Pitot tube was activated. Ice accumulated on the Pitot tube tip. It spun around the tip on a cushion of water melted by the heater, but it would not come off.

Jay looked into adding more heat with a heater made of carbon cloth, but that was impractical. Jay thought later that perhaps the answer was to blow the ice glob off with a puff of reversed air flow or simply turn the tube backwards so the blob would blow off in the slipstream. Trying to melt through the blob was not working.

 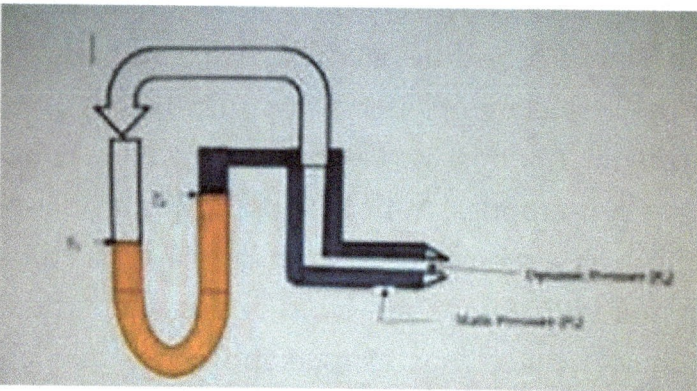

Pitot Tube   Pitot Tube Sketch

Jay and Sadie were doing fine getting set up housekeeping when Jay was called up for active duty in the Air Force through the Tulsa Air National Guard. Jay had moved his membership in the Air National Guard back to Tulsa. The reason was so that Sadie could see her parents once each month for the next seven months that Jay had left to finish his military obligation. There was a guard unit on the same airport where Jay worked, and he should have transferred there, or at least stayed with OKC. Neither the Dallas unit nor the OKC unit was called up. The Tulsa unit was called up right away after Jay moved back. Kennedy called up the Tulsa unit during the Berlin Wall construction. The Tulsa planes did not go to Europe; they went to Japan to carry cargo to Viet Nam.

KC-97

Both the Tulsa ANG and the OKC ANG had traded their F-86D aircraft for C-97 cargo planes. The C-97 was a Boeing B-29 with a cargo compartment built on it. It was pot-bellied and not great to look at. It had four R-4360 Pratt and Whitney engines which had four rows of seven cylinders each. It was not pressurized and was limited to 12,000 feet ceilings. It gave a smooth ride and some were used for airliners. Some were used for tankers (KC-97), but the birds that Tulsa and OKC had were cargo planes.

On active duty, Jay was assigned to the engine shop. Jay's duty was to help change engines if needed, do pressure checks on engines in for periodic maintenance, change plugs, etc. He had qualified by correspondence earlier as a jet engine mechanic. He had become proficient at auto mechanics by repairing farm machinery and his own cars. The change to reciprocating aircraft engines was not a stretch.

However, Jay thought that having a degree in aero/space might help him into Officer's Training School in the air force. He applied and was sent to Wichita Falls, Texas, for a medical examination and an interview. He was accepted. He was sent to Medina Air Force base near San Antonia, Texas for three months officers training. He had two years of AF ROTC in junior college. The ANG released Jay to go to training school at Medina near San Antonio. It had been a storage base for nuclear weapons (bombs) in bunkers scattered around.

Jay did alright though he was having trouble with social performance, which entailed going to the officer's lounge on a hill near the base and drinking with the boys. Jay did not drink. He was having trouble with a physiology course; Jay had never taken a course in physiology in college. He was not familiar with such terms as "identify with." And then at the six-week review, Jay learned that he was assigned to a weather station in Alaska, and that he was in the Air Force for four years. What if he did not pass the social rating and the physiology course? He could find himself four years doing menial work as an airman. When he applied for officer training, he did not understand it was for four years; he thought he would go back to his ANG unit. He asked for a release and return to his ANG unit. Fortunately, his request was granted.

He returned to Tulsa around Christmas and began his service there reassigned to the engine shop.

It was a hardship to move back to Tulsa and live on the few shekels he was paid by the ANG on active duty. Jay's unit stayed in Tulsa with their C-97 cargo planes. Jay did go on TDY (temporary duty) to McCord AFB in Washington, and he had a chance to go to the Far East as a crew member, but the big holes in the sides of the planes that came back were a bit discouraging.

Jay and Sadie rented an old "mother-in-law house" in the back of a house close to the airport where the ANG base was. He and Sadie lived on $185 per month. They had stored their furniture they bought in Grand Prairie, Texas, at Jay's dad's house. He checked out necessary tools with a tool box and set to work on the R-4360 Pratt and Whitney engines on the C-97. Later he had an opportunity to be assigned to a four-man engine test team led by a congenial master sergeant. He enjoyed that job. When the engine shop built up an engine that had been overhauled, it was turned over to the engine test group to be placed on the engine test stand mounted on a truck and proof tested. When needed the engine was then installed on a plane. Often, when the team showed up in the morning without an engine to test, they went to Grand Lake nearby and fished or rode around in one of the team's boat. Sometimes, Jay was given the fish; he really did not want them and put them in his bath tub until he could take them to a nearby stream the same evening.

One day at noon, Jay was walking across the hanger in front of a C-97 in which the number two engine was being removed. It was being supported by a chain hoist. It still had its four-blade propeller attached. As Jay was even with and nearly under the engine, the chain holding the engine broke and one end flew to the top of the hanger. The engine mounts were still attached but had been nearly removed. They held the engine, but the engine was looking down at Jay at approximately forty-five degrees. It all happened so quick that Jay did not have time to get scared. The R-4360 engines had four rows of seven big cylinders that could be changed individually. The engine weighed approximately a ton.

There was a master sergeant who was a real pain to the younger, inexperienced airmen. He harassed the young men by telling them to line up for overtime pay compensation which was a farce, yelling at airman to take their caps off in the hanger, which was ridicules, and such things that were not true. He was a detriment to the morale of the unit. Why he was kept around was a mystery to the men of the ANG unit. He was known as "Snakely", which was somewhat similar to his real name. He was tall and slender, too old to be soldering. No doubt he thought he was being funny. Jay was sure glad to be rid of him when the unit was released.

When Jay was sent on TDY (temporary duty) for a week at McCord AFB, it was a welcome break for Jay. The January weather there was warm compared to Tulsa's weather. The view was great with Mt. Rainer in the background. The duty was interesting, but Jay was glad to return to Tulsa after the temporary duty was up.

When the ANG unit was released after what seemed like a lifetime in service, Jay went to his dad's (Joe's), farm to pick up his and Sadie's belongings. Joe had given Jay the old 1936 International truck. The first thing required was to start the engine. The truck had been sitting in the driveway of the big barn at the house. There were ruts in the dirt floor and water had blown into the ruts and was trapped there under the truck. The starter would not turn the engine. Joe and Jay tried pulling the truck with a tractor to turn the engine. It would not budge. Jay pulled the pan off and found that the high moisture of the driveway had caused the pistons to rust to the sidewalls of the cylinders. He pulled the head and removed the rod caps. After soaking in oil all of the pistons were driven out. One of the rods was bent. The local International dealer in town was able to find a rod and rings. One of the pistons had a hole worn in its skirt. Jay checked everywhere he was told to look, including the mines parts suppliers, but to no avail. The worn piston had to be reinstalled after it received new rings. The cylinder walls were honed, and new rod bearings were installed. The overhauled engine ran very well. The cab and bed were smoothed and painted. The lights were replaced and a muffler was added. Tires were OK for Jay's use. Jay and Sadie loaded the truck with their belongings and drove it to Dallas without incident. Sadie drove the car. Jay had gone to LTV and re-established his job just after his release from ANG. Humorously, his new lead engineer, who had worked at Convair in Fort Worth, told him of an incident at Convair. It seems that an engineer had a bad habit of pinching women's bottoms. One complained to his boss who told the pincher to apologize to the woman he pinched. He didn't know which one complained, so he went around apologizing to all of the women he pinched.

A nice masonry house was rented. The truck was fitted into the garage. The couple settled into a routine life with a salary that was increased to $825 per month while they were away playing soldier.

Texas Book Depository

In the left part of the left photograph above, the faint buildings are buildings in Dallas. The Texas Book Depository with a sign on top can be seen just under the left-most light. This was taken before Kennedy was killed. The photograph on the right is of the Texas Book Depository. After a while, space was tight so a garage in Oak Cliff part of Dallas was rented to store the truck in. It was two blocks from where Oswald was captured in a theater.

The young couple was hard pressed to make ends meet so they decided to give the truck to Jay's aunt in SE Kansas.

Truck in Home in Grand Prairie

He thought the aunt and her husband would use the truck and keep it in a barn or covered; they did not. They did not even keep it covered. It deteriorated badly. Jay was disappointed. He could not afford to keep the truck in a shelter and did not want it abandoned to the weather. There was not anything else he could do to preserve the truck. Later, after it rotted to nothing in Joe's hog lot, someone asked for it to rebuild it. For Jay, it was the end of his knowledge of the truck's existence.

An old settler's day was to be held in the town near Joe's farm. Joe wanted to use the truck in the parade. Jay had given the truck to his aunt. He asked her if she would take seventy-five dollars for it back. She did and the truck was brought back to Joe's farm. Joe took it to a tire place that was sponsoring the parade and they put new tires on the truck all around for some reason; the old tires were not worn out. Then logs were loaded on the truck and Joe drove it down Main Street with a guy riding on the hood shooting a shotgun. In the photo below, Joe is in the center. The sponsor wanted to be paid for the new tires. What a waste. Joe pulled the truck into his forty-acre hog lot and let it rot to nothing along with the new tires. Joe never paid for the tires.

Joe has put several hundred thousand miles on it. He overhauled it over dirt; he had no concrete slabs to work on. The weakest part was the rear axles which he broke several times.

Joe with Shot Gun Rider on his Right, Sponsor on his Left

Chapter 8

Aircraft

After release from the Air Force Jay returned to Dallas to his old job, but now the company had changed its name to Ling-Temco-Vought. He was reassigned to the propulsion group.

The story told to Jay about the merger of the three companies is that Jimmy Ling caught a freight train out of Oklahoma and rode it to Dallas where he landed a job in a small salvage company. The company bought military surplus electrical cables for two cents on the dollar of the original cost after WWII and sold it back for two dollars on the original cost of the wires for the Korean War. Ling had acquired controlling interest in the salvage company. He took the windfall funds and bought controlling interest in Texas Manufacturing Company (Temco) located next to Chance Vought. Then he pyramided Ling- Temco to acquire controlling interest in Chance Vought. As the "owner" of Ling-Temco-Vought, he bragged that he had minimal education but had PhDs working for him, and said that "people were like grapes; they were always available and came in bunches." This angered lots of folks.

The increase in salary was a blessing. Jay felt fortunate to get back to engineering; he felt that being away too long might damage his career in engineering. He and Sadie started over. They rented a nice house in the south part of Grand Prairie. Jay was given a confidential clearance and assigned to the fuel systems of the propulsion group. Shortly afterwards he was given a secret clearance.

His lead engineer was a former engineer employee from Convair in Fort Worth. Their job was to calculate the fuel flow for the design team's plumbing on the XC-142 cargo plane. Chance Vought, now Ling-Temco-Vought (LTV), had won the competition to build the plane.

XC-142 Cargo Plane

It had four General Electric T64 turboprop engines. The wings tilted 90° and flew like a helicopter. It also had a horizontal prop on the tail for keeping the plane balanced. There was a cross shaft running to each propeller for the purpose of keeping all propellers turning at the same speed in case of engine failure. There were two fuel pumps; one was mechanically driven, and the other was electrically driven. Either could supply all of the fuel needs of all four engines. Jay, under the direction of his lead engineer, calculated the fuel sump duration time under negative gravity to within three places past the decimal using a slide rule. That impressed folks involved. The sump was required to supply fuel to the engines during negative gravity, including the plane being inverted for a given amount of time. The design engineers were impressed with the calculations, as were management. The sump was supplied by ejector pumps in the corners of the fuel tanks. Calculation of fuel flow from the ejector pumps was done with accuracy.

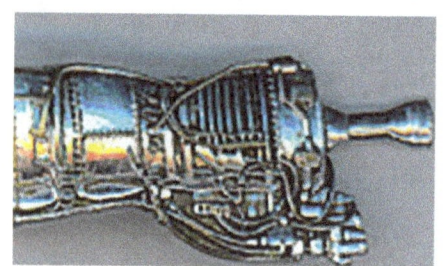

GE T64 Turboprop Engine

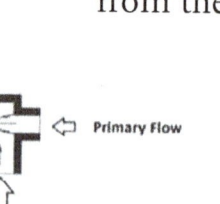

Ejector pump

The primary (motive) flow was supplied by the main pumps that pumped fuel to the engines.

To analyze the fuel system laid out by the design group on drafting boards, the lead engineer and Jay first had to determine the resistance, or pressure losses, in the fuel system. To do this they began at the engines and added up all of the loss factors back to the pumps. The loss factors, called K factors, were determined for bends, couplers, bulk head fittings, unions, straight lines according to length and size, reducers, etc. as they moved back toward the pumps. If the lines were parallel, the loss factors were added in parallel with the parallel formula which was the two parallel resistances multiplied by each other and then divided by the sum of the two resistances. If the lines were in series, the resistances were simply added for that line's resistances. In series, flow is constant and pressure losses are accumulative; in parallel, the pressure in each line is constant (equal) and flow for the parallel lines are additive. Resistance (K factors) for each item in the fuel lines was determined by empirical means and published in text books. The Darcy- Weisbach formula is used to determine pressure loss from the source to the engines. Essentially, it is ΔP= resistance factor (K) x 1/2 x fluid density (ρ) x velocity squared (V^2), or $\Delta P = \frac{1}{2} K \rho V^2$.

Once the total loss factors were determined and the maximum required fuel flow to the engines was known, pumps with the necessary capacity could be selected. The pump manufactures determined the characteristics of their pumps and published charts showing the flow the pumps could pump under different pressures loads. The required pressure to deliver the required flow for the engines plotted against the pump's capability showed which of pumps available was capable of delivering the maximum fuel that could be required by the engines.

When the fuel system was tested on the first plane, the plane was placed on a set of scales in one of the hangars. The operators of the scales were below the platform in a basement-like room. The plane was fueled from the ground level at a pressure port. There were float valves in each of the two tanks. The floats operated the valves by controlling the bleed ports on each valve. When the bleed port was closed, the spring-loaded valve closed itself because the area of the valve became larger with the bleed port closed, and the pressure times a larger area was enough to overcome the spring. One of the shutoff valves failed and fuel poured from the vent ports of the tank. The vent lines were sized for just such an event. That part worked OK. Fuel ran into the scales' pit setting off the fire alarm. The scale operators came out of the pit like jacks-in-a-box. A maintenance man mopped up the fuel with a rag mop. He set the mop down beside his mop bucket when he had cleaned up the fuel. The mop caught fire by itself (auto ignition). The fuel was JP4, a mixture of mostly kerosene with some gasoline in it for starting purposes. The fire was stomped out and the mop was set outside the hanger; it caught fire again in the early rising sun. Jay had spent the night assigned to be at the plane if engineering was needed.

Military people were wondering if the XC-142 would stir up debris that would get into the engines when the wings were vertical and the engines were running full power. The plane was designed to land in the jungles of South Vietnam. Jay was told to measure the air velocities at different locations around the wings with the plane tied down and wings vertical. He borrowed a portable secretary recording-machine (dictaphone), one with a blue plastic belt to be recorded on, and looked for a microphone for it. The belt recorders were large in size at that time.

 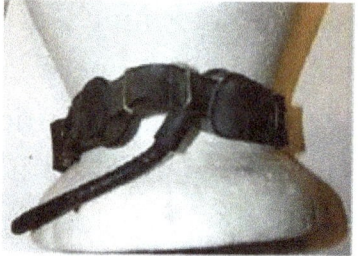 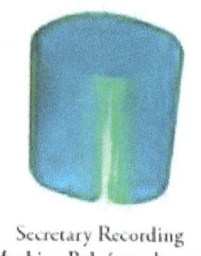

Throat Microphone

Secretary Recording
Machine Belt (translucent)

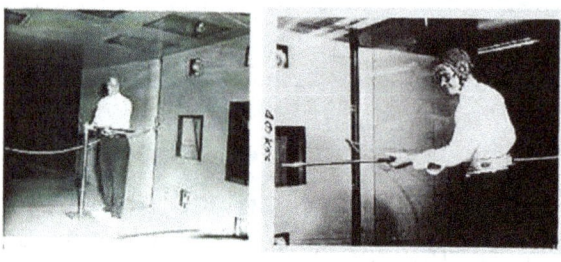

Jay in the LTV Wind Tunnel Calibrating Pitot tube setup

He went to an army surplus store for a noise-canceling throat mike used by B-17 pilots. He farmer-rigged the mike to the recorder. Then he calibrated a pitot tube in the low speed wind tunnel to see if a man standing in proximity would affect the readings. An aircraft airspeed indicator was installed on the setup in order to read air velocities. After a grid was marked on the pavement beneath the plane, the airplane's engines were run up to full power with the wing in the vertical position. With one try, the data was good and a velocity map was drawn. Later, a coworker asked Jay why they didn't use a dummy in the wind tunnel; Jay said, "They did." Jay was strapped to a post. At high speed Jay was leaning almost horizontal.

Slide Rule

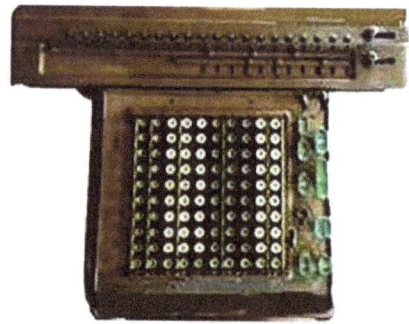

Freidan calculating Machine

Calculations were done on slide rules for multiplying and dividing. Adding machines were used for adding and subtracting.

In the propulsion engineering department was a contract engineer (not a regular employee of LTV). He was a single fellow that claimed to be an atheist, but in his foul language he mentioned God often. Jay doubted that he was truly an atheist from his language use.

He was a likable guy and became a friend to Jay. He owned a small plane, and Jay went flying with him from time to time. One day when the friend was chiding Jay about his faith in the Lord, Jay said, "If you are right and there is no god, what have I lost; I have been a better person trying to follow the Bible. But on the other hand look at what you have lost if I'm right." The friend said nothing but shrugged it off. The man had been on Tarawa during WWII. He said he was in one of the first waves, and the Japanese soldiers shot at his feet under the personnel carrier he took cover behind.

Now Sadie became pregnant while Jay was still on active duty. Sadie wanted to be a mother, and did not want to wait. Ling-Temco-Vought insurance covered Sadie's pregnancy. Jay and Sadie bought Sadie's mother a first-class American Airlines ticket so Sadie's mother could come down as soon as the baby was born. Her mother came down on the plane approximately two weeks before the baby was born. That defeated the purpose of the airline ticket that Jay and Sadie sacrificed to buy; they were still very poor. Sadie's mother wanted Sadie to nurse the new born child, but Jay was against it. He knew Sadie was slow thinking, and that she probably would embarrass herself and Jay by nursing in public, especially in their church they belonged to. He insisted that the child be raised on bottles.

Sadie's mother was a bit ornery. She would wave at truck drivers along the highway while sitting beside her husband, who was driving; he tried to smile and said nothing. She bragged about turning her charm on cops to avoid tickets. She was attractive. She pointed out to Jay a man's name in the Tulsa telephone book. It was Richard Large listed with the last name first and his nick name last. When the baby came, Jay took Sadie to the Methodist Hospital in Dallas.

Sadie had a hard time just as her mother had with her. In the waiting room were several expectant fathers and Sadie's mother with Jay. She nearly went berserk waiting for the baby to arrive. Instead of pacing like the others, Jay spent his waiting time consoling Sadie's mother. When the nurse brought the new born baby in, Jay and mother-in-law were relieved. They wondered why the baby had a big blister on the top of her head. Later they understood that it was caused by a suction cup used to help with the difficult birth. The baby was named Carla. Jay and mother-in-law went back home and spent most of the night talking; they unwound that way. It was here that Jay told Sadie's mother that Sadie did not like domestic life being in charge of housekeeping. Jay knew that Sadie's mother was a very good homemaker, and he wished that some of it had rubbed off on Sadie.

Sadie and Jay attended the local Baptist church in Grand Prairie where they gave 10 percent of their meager salary faithfully to the church. Even though Sadie's brother eventually became a preacher, Sadie's family was not churched people. Sadie's grandfather on Sadie's mother's side was a preacher in a charismatic church. The IRS required Jay show proof that he tithed every year. He would bundle up his canceled checks and send them to the IRS. The churches he attended did not send him annual statements.

Sadie and Jay had made friends with a young Spanish couple who lived across the street from them in their first house in Grand Prairie. The woman and her husband fought a lot. They were violent in their scuffles with each other; she threw things and he popped her on the head with the soft part of his fist. She called the police several times without arrests. Sadie began to throw things when angry. Once she called the police who came out and gave Jay a lecture. Jay and Sadie had only had angry words. That severely damaged the marriage. Jay became so angry he wanted her parents to take her to their home for a while; her parents were coming down that weekend. They took Sadie and the baby, Carla, back with them. After a while, Jay and Sadie cooled off, and they got back together.

In another incident, Carla went into convulsions during the night. Jay grabbed her and held her near a window fan until she recovered and cooled down. Jay and Sadie rushed her to an emergency room at a local hospital. Upon examination, the doctor told Sadie the child was anemic. Sadie admitted she was feeding the baby ice cream because "that is what she wanted to eat." That situation was corrected.

1957 Oldsmobile

Both Sadie and Jay were no longer happy being married to each other. They tolerated the marriage and did work together the best they could.

One Saturday morning Jay had Sadie take the Oldsmobile, the car they had for trips to Tulsa, to an Oldsmobile place in nearby Arlington for repair of a power steering leak. The car was nearly worn out and had some rusted out spots. It had several mechanical problems. Sadie had left the sink full of dishes; the water had been there so long that it had become putrid. There were diapers in the stool; Sadie used the tub for urination. Jay wanted her folks to see how she was keeping house when they came that morning, and perhaps, to help her do better. As soon as Jay had talked to the mechanics about sealing the power steering unit and was out of sight, Sadie beat it back home to clean up the house without the car repair.

Taylorcraft

Jay was in their other car, a worn out Renault, and went to Arlington for a flight lesson.

He could not afford to take lessons often. However, he did manage to solo with about nine hours of lessons. He soloed in a Taylorcraft, a plane with huge wings that caused the plane to float "forever" on landing. It was short coupled and had a bad tendency to ground loop on landing; its pilots had to pick a point a long way off and keep the plane's nose stuck to it. Jay was tense when up there alone. When he first soloed, he looked to the east and saw a dot coming toward him at his level; it was a Crusader. Jay turned his plane on the left wing and headed down. When he leveled off he saw that the Crusader pilot had seen him and turned to the north. When he landed he felt as if he had been run over; his mouth was so dry he could not spit. Even though Jay could not fly often because he could not afford it, he continued to build up hours when he could.

Solo Certificate

Aerocoupe

He took one hour in an Aerocoupe. It was like putting on a pair of pants. It had no rudder petals; the control surfaces were all coordinated to the yoke. It seemed weird to fly, but it was fun. It has a tri-cycle landing gear; Jay was used to tail draggers.

Jay did most of his early training in a J-3 Piper Cub. It had tandem seating.

J-3 Piper Cub

The drive way of Jay and Sadie's home was Jay's work shop. The house had a single car garage. A noise like that of a small plane engine coming toward the neighborhood caught Jay's attention. He looked up to see an F-86D flying parallel to a street a block or so west. It became quiet and two puffs of smoke came out of the plane. Then a parachute lying alongside of the plane was visible. The chute slowly became vertical as the plane slid out of sight. The plane had an engine failure, and the pilot ejected by first blowing the canopy and then the seat with the pilot in it. It was a Texas Air National Guard plane stationed on the same airfield as was Ling-Temco-Vought. Several officers from the guard unit came to Jay's house to interview jay about what he saw.

Vice president Johnson came to Dallas and visited LTV. He climbed upon one of the airplane assembly stands with his wife, Lady Bird and gave a speech to the workers gathered around. After the speech, Johnson asked if there were any questions. Someone standing close to Jay said, "Yea, how do you hide a ballot box?" He was referring to the incident in San Antonio when Johnson was running in the primary for a democrat party nomination; the ballot boxes disappeared for some time as the story was told to Jay. When they reappeared Johnson won by forty eight votes. Some of the names were in alphabetical order and some were from tombstones. There is a book written about Johnson. It is called A Texan Looks at Lyndon. The book tells of several crooked deals Johnson was implicated in. One was a case where a man was shot nineteen times in the back with a rifle; it was ruled "the worst case of suicide in Texas history." When Johnson ran for president, the democrats were telling voters that if they voted for Goldwater, our country would get heavily involved in Vietnam. Jay voted for Goldwater, and sure enough the country did get heavily involved in Vietnam.

Jay was not happy with Johnson or the Kennedys. He thought that the Kennedys traumatized America by their bungling of the Bay of Pigs and taking the United States to the brink of nuclear war with the USSR. He liked Ike, but he was not fond of Truman though Jay felt sure that Truman made the right decision to use the atom bomb. He felt the bomb saved far more lives (American and Japanese) than it destroyed of the enemy. However, Truman fired Jay's hero, MacArthur. That did not set well with Jay.

Sadie and Carla

Sadie and Jay settled in Grand Prairie, TX, with their new baby, Carla, during the early sixties. The November 1963 day when Kennedy was shot, Sadie called Jay and told him of the shooting. Jay said, "Aw, don't kid me that way." She said, "He really was shot." The telephone served four desks of engineers. Jay told the three around him of the incident, and everyone ran to the phone. Nobody could call out because all of the phone lines were tied up. That was Thursday. Work was suspended the next day. The independent TV stations suddenly went on with their regular programming while the alphabet, secular news media (MBC, ABC and CBS) stations broadcast only what was going on in Washington with the assassination until Kennedy was buried. Although it was a national tragedy, Jay felt it was time to move on after four days of mourning.

A tragedy on another occasion was traumatic for Jay. He and Sadie were at a televised country music show in Dallas on a Saturday night. Jim Ed Brown and his sisters were performing when it was announced that the plane carrying Patsy Cline and Jim Reeves had crashed in Tennessee. Jay thinks that it may have been the same program that Johnny Cash and June Carter were on. June called Johnny "Old Golden Throat." They were not married to each other then. On these Saturday night programs, several other country music stars appeared including Carl Smith. In Fort Worth in a similar type show, Jay and Sadie saw Hank Williams Jr. He was young and very much under the thumb of his mother at that time. Jay and Sadie had taken their baby along; she danced to the music.

One day Jay came home from work to find his house empty of wife and child. They had taken their belongings. He knew that the in-laws had come to Dallas and taken his family away. Jay knew this meant divorce and that Sadie and her family were planning to file in Tulsa. Jay's counselor told Jay to go around the neighborhood and get notarized signatures from the neighbors that had seen Sadie at the home in Texas recently to show that she was a resident of Texas. One of Jay's friend was a notary public and went with Jay to gather the signatures. After that was done, Jay's counselor advised Jay to take the terms offered by the Tulsa lawyer because it was about as good as he would get. They offered to not ask for alimony, seventy five dollars per month child support and a weekend per month visitation. Jay was reluctant because he wanted custody of the child who was somewhere around one and a half years old. He felt Sadie was not capable of giving the child a proper home with her attitude toward domestic life. Too, he thought the visitation was not practical. Jay felt that Sadie's mother set it up that way to keep Jay away as much as she could. Jay finally gave in at the persistence of his Counselor. He did try to visit when he could. After the divorce was agreed on, Sadie's dad had the gall to call Jay and demand he pay for all of the time Sadie spent visiting at his home. Jay, in effect, told him that what he wanted was not going to happen.

Shortly after the divorce, Ling-Temco-Vought had a cutback in personnel because the military services decided not to go into production with the XC-142. It had a serious flaw; the cross shaft that kept all of the propellers turning at the same speed was too weak and caused some failures. It was a thin-wall stainless steel tube that could not take the stress put on it.

Jay was offered an opportunity to go to Detroit to work on what was called the Missile B project, but the military dubbed it the Lance Missile. It was a forty-mile range, self-contained rocket capable of carrying an atomic warhead. The military planned to use it for tactical field operation in Western Europe for keeping the Russians out.

Jay sent all of the furniture he and Sadie had accumulated in the two years since Jay was released from the Air Force to Sadie at her parent's house. Jay's company paid for the moving of the furniture. Jay had bought a new Ford F-100 pickup, put a camper on it and put in as much of his personal belongings as he could get on it. He arrived in Detroit in January of 1965 and never saw the ground until mid-April.

He rented a house in Utica, a short distance from the Redstone Missile Plant on 15½ Mile Road on Van Dyke where he worked. A friend Jay had worked with in Dallas was there.

Jay and His 1965 Ford Pickup   Jay at his Rented House in Utica, MI

One evening there was a huge snow storm. Jay's friend who lived in up-state Michigan stayed overnight at Jay's house because he did not think he could get home. The storm continued throughout the night. The next morning Jay and friend were the only ones that showed up for work. They spent that day, all day, trying to get home because they had to drive almost into downtown Detroit to turn around. Snow was piled higher than car tops along the side and in the crossovers.

There were abandoned vehicles along the outside lane of the streets.

Lance Missile

The friend that stayed overnight with Jay had also worked at the LTV plant near Dallas. The two were assigned to the Lance missile project. The missile had a tank filled with liquid fuel and another tank filled with a liquid oxidizer. A small solid fuel rocket was used to pressurize the tanks. A spring-loaded relief valve on the rocket device was not holding a steady pressure in the tanks. The friend, who had a master's degree in mechanical engineering, suspected that flow around the lip of the relief valve was being affected by the gas flow past it causing the valve to chatter. The two did some calculations and found that the gas flow was causing unsteady lift on the valve lip. The recommended fix was to change the shape of the lip and dampen the spring.

Soon after Jay arrived in the Detroit area he had his new truck serviced. He noticed the underside was all red from rust. He had seen cars piled high in the many junk yards there; some looked to be around five years old and were rusted out. Jay asked the service man if he could undercoat the truck. He did with soft grease that looked like lithium grease. He said it was soft so it would heal if scratched. He even undercoated the hood. Detroit is said to have a salt mine under the city and the roads are salted daily. They said that if it did not snow or sleet, it was going to. Cars there sure took a beating.

At a movie house in Grosse Pointe Jay watched a movie and was at his truck that had some three thousand miles on it. Another man leaving the theater asked Jay if he had any trouble with the engine. It was a newly designed six cylinder engine with seven main bearings. The seven main bearings made the crankshaft very stiff. The fellow told Jay that his had knocked out the wrist pin areas of his pistons and the pistons had to be replaced. Jay told the man that he had not had any trouble yet. Jay kept an "ear on the engine" for any signs of problems. Sure enough, at about five thousand miles the engine began to rattle. Ford replaced the pistons and wrist pins. The engine was warranted for twenty-four thousand miles. It was overhauled three more times before the warranty was up and needed it again. Jay traded it off before the warranty ran out.

There was an attractive, dark haired Polish girl who worked at the Detroit factory. A friend of Jay offered to introduce Jay to her. Jay was not really ready to date, and besides, the girl would not go out with anyone without the date met her parents first.

Fort Knox

When the middle of April came around, Jay took his two weeks of vacation and went back to Oklahoma. On the way he went through Kentucky to see Fort Knox. The photo at right was taken on a very cheap camera while Jay's truck was in motion.

Ryman Auditorium
(Opry House)

Ryman Auditorium Stage

Jay stopped in Nashville and went to the Ryman Auditorium Opera House. It was on a Friday night and Jay went there to buy a ticket to the Saturday night Grand Old Opera show. However, the performers were there practicing. Jay went in and sat down. He saw Wanda Jackson doing her part for the Saturday night show. Roy Acuff and his band were there with others. Jay was close to the stage; there was hardly anyone there. His cheap camera made subjects look much farther away than they were. The photographs were taken by Jay on the Friday night he was there.

Since Jay had seen the show, he decided to go on to Oklahoma. Four years later when Jay wanted to see a show, the tickets were sold out for Saturday evening and only poor seats were available for the Friday night show.

Jay went to Oklahoma City employment office looking for an engineering job. North American's Aero Commander executive aircraft company at Bethany in the Northwest part of greater Oklahoma City was looking for Aeronautical engineers. They hired Jay, but it took a while to get the hiring process completed. It was June before Jay reported to work.

Jay, Jay's Friend and German wife at New York World's Fair 1965

On the way back to Detroit from Oklahoma City, Jay went by way of Washington, D.C. He visited a college friend who had been called up when Jay was and sent to Germany. While there he married a German lady. They all went to the World's Fair in Jay's new pickup. When they entered the Holland Tunnel on the way back to D.C. they were asked if they had any extra fuel in the camper shell. Jay said, "No", but he remembered later that he had put his five gallon Gerry can in its holder and it had

New York City with Empire State Building in Background

gasoline in it. No harm was done.

While the friend was at work his wife had toured Jay around D.C. the day before. They lived within walking distance of their apartment to the D.C. sights. She pointed out places to go and returned home. Joe went into the interesting places. The one he enjoyed the most was the Smithsonian Institution.

On his way back to Detroit Joe parked at the Union Station in New York City and took a picture with the Empire State Building in the background.

Jay at 1965 Indianapolis 500

Indianapolis 500 1965 First lap with Pace Car

While Jay was preparing to move to Oklahoma City, he and a young friend, who was not married, decided to go to Indianapolis to the Indianapolis 500 race. They put a camper stove, some groceries and sleeping bags in the camper of Jay's pickup. They arrived the night before the race and found a parking place a few blocks from the gate to the race. As they walked up to the gate to buy tickets, they saw many folks sleeping on people's lawns, under bushed, etc. The two went to the gate and found that the only tickets left were on the infield. They took them. After sleeping in the camper overnight, they walked to the track early to find that all tickets were sold out; people were being turned away.

They went to the infield placing themselves on the first turn near the fence. It was a warm sunny day. People were stacked several deep standing on the infield. Cars zipped by at a high rate of speed with a roar. The roar of the first lap with all cars bunched together was deafening.

Then they thinned out and the cars came around one or two at a time. The boys could not tell who was in the lead, how many laps were run or hardly which car was zipping past them. When the race was over Jay and friend walked to the pits. On the way, they walked past the convertible pace car with the most beautiful legs in it that Jay had seen; it had Connie Stevens with James Stewart sitting in the back seat. The boys walked next to the car so close they could have reached out and slapped the actors. When they reached the pit area they found newspapers that had pictures and the winner of the race already printed and being distributed. They wondered how that was done so fast.

The boys went back to their pickup and noticed the streets were clogged. They waited until the crowds thinned and started back to Detroit. They were jammed up with a slow moving line of traffic leaving town miles long. The boys pulled off to the side and fired up their camper stove to cook supper. After they ate, the line had disappeared. They pulled onto the two-lane highway again heading to Detroit. They caught up to the crowd and followed it slowly for a long ways. They arrived back in Detroit late. Stores were still open. Some stayed open twenty-four hours per day. Some factories there worked three shifts. Jay did his grocery shopping at night.

Chapter 9

Roller Coaster

Jay rented a large U-haul trailer for his move back to Oklahoma in June. North American Aero Commander paid for the trailer rental. A rental house on the corner of the street to Aero Commander and US 66 highway was available. It was a two-bedroom house.

A fellow from Canada that Jay had gone to school with moved in with Jay. He was in the evening law school at Oklahoma City University. He encouraged Jay to enroll there also, since there was no graduate evening-school in engineering at the University of Oklahoma some forty miles away. Jay knew he needed a higher degree in order to gain some stability in his life. Jay had learned by now that the aircraft industry was like a roller coaster. When the government put out a request for bids for a new aircraft, it required the companies bidding to show engineering staff capable of handling the new aircraft. All bidding companies went out and hired a full staff of engineers. Only one company won the contract; all others had to dump their engineering buildup. That was not good for engineers. Contract engineering companies were set up to help the aircraft companies alleviate the roller-coaster fiasco somewhat. Jay enrolled in law school.

Jay's roommate had to go home to Canada every year because he was a guest in the United States. While living with Jay, the friend brought back a girl he knew in Canada. She lived with the friend for a while. One day, Jay broiled some steaks he had bought. He put barbeque sauce on them with some onions. The sauce was burned somewhat. When the girl friend saw that the sauce was burned by the grill she threw a fit and yelled at Jay; they had not cost her anything. Jay had cooked them that way before and knew the steaks were not hurt. He scraped the sauce off and the stakes were fine. The girl cooled down.

John Wayne in Oklahoma City Parade

John Wayne came to Oklahoma City and rode his horse in a parade. Jay was there and called John's name as he rode by.

The camera used was a very inexpensive thing and made the shot look five times further away than it actually was. John looked at Jay and waved as Jay shot his picture.

At Aero Commander Jay worked in the fuel system engineering. His first job was to design a fuel level sensor for the 680 aircraft main fuel tank in the fuselage. The Tank was segmented and the top portion was not measured. The sensor itself came from vendors, but Jay had to design and draft the positioning of the unit. With the vendor's help the new unit was integrated into the gauging system.

Aero Commander was building a new version of the 680. It was a 680T, a turboprop driven airplane using AirResearch engines. Word came down that the turboprop engines were very difficult to start in cold weather. Aero Commander assigned three 680T

Aero Commander 680T

airplanes, each with an Aero Commander engineer along with the pilot and an Air Research engineer aboard. The one Jay was on was a research plane, the first plane used to prove in the new design. The pilot was the test pilot for Aero Commander. They were all to take the three planes to Duluth, MN, in early January 1966. The temperature was -24°F with wind that produced a wind chill of -55°F. On the way, one of the planes was diverted to headquarters back east. However, all of the engineers went to Duluth on the other planes. The research plane was not finished out; therefore, the engineers that were on the plane that went east boarded the other plane that went to Duluth. Jay and the test pilot were assigned seventeen thousand feet altitude on instruments. Somewhere over Northern Iowa and southern Minnesota, the left engine flamed out. The test pilot looked nervous when he said, "I'm going to start that bugger!" He dropped the plane to thirteen thousand feet and activated the start switches. The engine caught and came up to speed. He called the area control and told them that an engine flamed out, and he was at thirteen thousand feet with the engine restarted. The controller told him to stay at that altitude. The pilot said that he thought the cause of the flameout was ice that had formed at the engine inlet and had probably flaked off passing through the engine. Visibility was hardly more than the end of the nose of the plane. As they approached the Duluth airport they encountered heavy snow; the pilot and engineer could not see ahead, but they could see cars on the road strait down. Jay saw that as a phenomenon. The test pilot was an excellent instrument pilot. He brought the plane into the Duluth airport perfectly and landed it in deep snow with the low belly of the fuselage settling down with ease in the snow. The snow was so deep the runway lights were just faintly diffused lights beneath the snow. The pilot taxied to the general aviation parking area and left it to soak in the -24°F temperature at the airport. The other plane came in a short time later. All went to a motel for the night.

The next morning the pilot of the production plane tried to start its engines. The left engine was the first to be attempted at starting. It would come up to 60 percent speed by the starter, but when the fuel was added it would light and flameout. Several attempts were made. Finally, the engine caught and began to gain rpm, but suddenly there was a grinding noise and the engine quit. The oil had not lubricated the bearings properly and they failed. Now the six men on site were dependent on the test airplane to get home. The other plane would have to wait until a new engine could be brought in to replace the failed engine.

Heater muffs were applied to the engines of the test plane. They were kept on until the nacelles were so hot they were painful to the tough. Then Jay held the yellow muff, which was a flexible tube about a foot in diameter blowing hot air, in front of the inlet of the engine while the pilot cranked it. The ground was covered with slick ice. Someone held Jay's coat tail while the engine spun up. It fired up OK, and the other engine was started through the same procedure. All piled aboard and the plane took off heading back to Oklahoma. About one hundred miles south of Duluth the Duluth tower called to say that one of the Air Research engineers had left his billfold on the counter at the airport. The passengers said, "Keep going; they can mail it to him." The test pilot turned 180° and headed back to Duluth. The passengers wanted to lynch the test pilot. He landed and taxied to the terminal. There he shut off the left engine so the man from the terminal could hand the pilot the billfold. Now the passengers were really upset with the pilot. All wondered if the engine would restart. It did and all went well as the plane returned to Aero Commander manufacturing plant at the south end of the Wiley Post airport. Air Research had their work cut out for them.

The second semester of Law school ended in the spring, and Jay paid his fees for the third semester. He had taken two semesters of each of four subjects: Contracts, Torts, Property and Court Procedures. Contracts were taught by one of two deans. He came in inebriated to many evening classes. One time he said, "I want you all to understand that there is no such thing as justice; there is just good lawyers and bad lawyers" in a slurred voice. That did not set well with Jay.

Leonard and Wife

During the summer recess in 1966, Jay had gone to Wichita to visit his friend, Leonard. Leonard's wife was a nurse. She had a beautiful nurse friend a few years younger than Jay. Jay asked her to ride back to Oklahoma City with him in his new car. Then he would bring her right back in the Aero Commander Flying Club airplane of which Jay was a member. On the way back, they ran into a rain storm and landed at a small airport near Perth, Kansas. While they waited for the storm to break the pretty lady played the organ in the airport waiting area. She won Jay's heart. The storm did not break. Leonard and his wife came to Perth and took the stranded couple to Wichita. The next morning, Leonard took Jay back to Perth where he boarded the little plane and flew back to Bethany, the suburban town where he lived and worked. It was during this time that Sadie, Jay's former wife, wrote Jay a letter proposing that she and Jay get back together. It did not happen.

When Jay Joined the Aero Commander flying club, it had a Luscombe 8F all metal, two-seat aircraft. He arranged for flying lessons at the Westheimer Field in Norman where the plane was kept. The field was originally a naval flight training field, but was now the north campus of the University of Oklahoma. Joe had already soloed in Texas. He checked out in the Luscombe quickly and began accumulating enough hours to go for his license. One time when Jay was flying from Miami, Oklahoma, back to Oklahoma City, he came across a lone cloud not bigger than a section of land. It was extremely active floating around by itself with lightening and movement. What a strange phenomenon. Jay reported the weird cloud and its activity to the flight service station at Wiley Post Airfield in Oklahoma City. The station passed on the information to other flyers.

On a weekend before Jay had obtained his license to take passengers Jay dropped by the Flight Service Station at Wiley Post field. He asked for a weather report between Miami and Oklahoma City. The station told him that there was a front near Chandler, but he could get under it. As Jay approached Chandler between OKC and Tulsa, he could see that the front kept getting lower. Finally he could see it was on the ground, and he turned around to go back to OKC. He was in the soup. He was glad that he had had three hours of instrument training. By watching the artificial horizon instrument, he kept the wings level while increasing the power to climb out. Airspeed was closely watched, too. When he broke out on top he angrily called the flight service station and told them of his plight. They nonchalantly told Jay to look out for the 707 coming from Tulsa on its way to Will Rogers International Airport. Jay never saw the jetliner.

Jay had accumulated enough flying time to go for his license. He made arrangements with an examiner that did license testing for FAA. When the examiner came to the Westheimer Field in Norman, Oklahoma, to test Jay for his license, he asked Jay a question about aerial maps. He asked Jay to point out a restricted area. Jay was excited and pointed to a wrong area. The examiner folded his notes and started to leave. Jay quickly realized what the examiner had asked and pointed to the right area. The examiner was satisfied with the other answers Jay gave, including planning a course to a town to the SW. For the check ride Jay did things right including the walk around, checking the engine for oil level, looking for bird nests, checking the fuel level, etc. On the ride the examiner asked Jay to set up the Omni navigation system for a given course. Jay did that OK. Then the examiner pulled the throttle, after a few maneuvers, and told Jay he just lost power. Jay looked down and saw the octagon shaped practice field used by the Navy. He circled down for a perfect landing. The examiner said, "Let me have the controls; I really like flying these things. They are fully acrobatic, I understand." He did not do any acrobatics, though. He did fly it around for a while and landed it. He gave Jay his signed paperwork. Jay paid him and gave him a fifth of whisky, which was standard practice Jay was emphatically told. With his license to carry passengers, Jay flew to Tulsa to pick up his daughter, Carla. He landed at the Tulsa International Airport, parked in

the general aviation area and rented a car. His former in-laws did not know he had flown in to pick up 3-year-old Carla, or they may have been a problem. It seemed that they saw themselves as in complete control of everything. As Jay and Carla were landing at Westheimer Field back in Norman, a plane that did not fly the proper pattern for landing flew over the top of them just missing them by a few feet and touched down just ahead of them. They were gone before Jay and Carla reached the tie-down area. Had not Jay had Carla with him, who needed his full attention, he would have done everything he could to report and discipline the offender for his dangerous tactic; a plane on final has the right-of- way.

Jay and Luscombe 8F

Lou and Luscombe 8F

Another time Lou, Jay's sister, went with Jay as he flew to Tulsa to pick up Carla. They rented a car in Tulsa and drove out to pick up Carla. They visited with the child there. Then they flew back at night following the Will Rogers Turnpike. The landing at Miami was a bit hectic without runway lights.

The flying club appointed Jay the maintenance officer for the plane. A new prospect wanted to go up to see how the plane flew. Jay was asked to take him up. The prospect was a young fellow who had joined the Aero Commander Company. Jay invited the young man out one evening to go for a ride. Someone had left the switch on and the battery was down. Jay thought that was no problem, that the generator would charge the battery while they flew. He set the brakes and propped the plane. They flew around OKC and Norman. When they returned to Wiley Post it was dark. The tower was closed. They entered the pattern and cut power to lose altitude. All electrical equipment went off. Jay tried to raise the flight service station service station by adding power, but the "coffee grinder" radio could not find them. He wanted them to turn on the runway lights. He then landed by watching the width of the dashed lines in the middle of the runway. He could see them by the reflection of the lights on the Aero Commander buildings at the far end of the runway. When the lines looked wide enough, he rotated and set the plane down in a good landing. The prospective club Passenger said nothing. When they taxied to the tie-down area, the young man got out, walked away and was never seen again by Jay. Needless to say, he did not join the club. The problem with the battery was that the relay connecting the generator to the battery was activated by the battery. Jay quickly fixed that by having the relay activated by the generator.

Jay and Carla's cousin flew to Tulsa on a Sunday afternoon to take Carla back to Tulsa. They landed at a small airport north of Tulsa. Sadie and her parents were there to pick up Carla. Sadie's dad accosted Jay; that irritated Jay for some time afterwards. It also sealed the prospects of Jay and Sadie ever getting back together. Jay always thought Sadie's parents wanted Carla for themselves. They knew Sadie was handicapped and needed help as a mother, but mostly Jay figured they were just selfish. It may have been that they thought in the back of their minds that they had failed Sadie. Probably, Sadie wanted to be like other women and be a good house wife, but she was not up to it. Sadie and her parents are all dead at the writing of this book.

In the summer of 1966 after Jay had enrolled in law classes for his third semester of law school, Jay saw a large advertisement for engineers at Boeing in Wichita. Jay decided

Carla and Cousin in Tulsa

to see what they had and sent in a feeler reply to the Boeing advertisement. They were interested and sent Jay application forms. When he sent in the forms the manager of the propulsion division of Boeing came to OKC to Jay's house to interview him. Boeing promised Jay a substantial raise and financing for graduate school in engineering. Not only would they pay out-of-state tuition, they would pay Jay fifteen dollars per semester hour besides. Jay was highly tempted. The pretty girl was there that he wanted to get better acquainted with, and he preferred an engineering degree to a law degree. After all, Jay was shy and was not suited to be a bull slinging lawyer. There is a sign hanging in a public place in Kansas City that says, "If it had not been for the first lawyer, there would not have been a need for any more."

Jay accepted Boeing's offer and moved to Wichita. There he began work on the SST (Super Sonic Transport). Boeing had won the contract to build a swing wing SST to compete with the British-French Concord. He was assigned to the fuel system. The fuel for the engines was used to cool the leading edge of the wing. This could create two-phase flow, which is liquid fuel and vapor flowing together in the lines. The lines had to be large enough to accommodate the two- phase condition.

Jay began by looking at work others had done in this area. He found some work that had considered a formula that could be applied. It was called Henry's law. Jay and his lead man in the propulsion division went to Phillips Petroleum refinery in Bartlesville, Oklahoma, to see some work their R&D department had done on the subject. They found little useful information for the SST application. Suddenly, the program was stopped. Boeing aerodynamics engineers discovered that a delta wing was a better design than the swing wing Boeing had proposed to win the contract. But Martin Marietta had presented a delta design in their proposal.

This blew the politician's minds. The Federal government was funding the SST project. They were so frustrated that they simply shut the program down for good. The program had lasted for about two years.

B-52

Jay then worked problems of the B-52 fuel systems. A computer program was being written to calculate the amount of fuel in the curved-shaped B-52 fuel tanks no matter what the attitude of the airplane was. Jay and another engineer calculated sample situations and attitudes of the tanks by hand to verify the accuracy of the computer program written in fortran IV (formula translation) language. There was a flaw in the program, but an engineer in the group was able to help the programmer find it. The program was a success. The fuel tanks in the B-52 were nearly big enough for a man to stand up in.

Jay wrote a computer program for an air scoop located in the big bird's tail. He was amazed at the size of the B-52, but it was smaller than the Boeing 747 airliner that came through one day.

Boeing had an engineer's union. Jay resisted joining because he felt it was too much like socialism. However, managers told all of the engineers that the union represents you whether you participate or not. The union, called WEA (Wichita Engineers Association) negotiated merit raises each manager received for his group and the cost of living raises. Most of the managers were former WEA members. One good thing that the union did was to create a totem pole. According to seniority, engineers could tell when they might get laid off in the roller coaster aircraft business. This would give the engineers a heads-up on their possibility of layoffs and an early chance to look for another job. The aircraft industry was plagued by the military system of asking for bids from several aircraft companies for one contract as mentioned earlier.

At Wichita, Jay's first residence was a one bedroom duplex on Oliver Street not far from Wichita State University. The owner lived in the other side. It was crowded with the tiny rooms. After a year there a house in Rose hill became Jay's new home. It was much better, but it was a long distance from Boeing and the university. Next, a one bedroom house was rented on South Hydraulic in Wichita. This house was close to Boeing and in a more rural area. A nursery field was across the road. It was a good place for Jay to jog in the evenings. There was a garden spot at the house. The owner lived in a farm house less than a quarter of a mile away. The owner and his wife had horses and a daughter about Jay's age.

The owner's daughter sometimes rode near the rent house. The fence ran close to the house. The girl gave the horse fairly loud verbal instructions as if she wanted to attract attention. Jay had a steady girlfriend and was not interested.

One big problem with living in the small house was that the city sewer treatment system which was approximately a half mile away. At times the aroma drifted in from the treatment area. It was like living in an outhouse.

The garden spot was nice. Jay and his uncle, who lived nearby, put in a garden. When the potatoes were ready to dig, Jay dug his share and put the tops back in the ground since they were still green. The uncle came over and began digging his share. He pulled the tops that Jay had stuck back into the ground and told Jay that a gofer got their potatoes. Jay did not intend to play a joke on his uncle and told him what he had done.

Jay filled an old Survelle gas refrigerator with his share; they were too many for him to ever use. The uncle wound up with most of them. Fortunately, none went to waste.

When Jay arrived in Wichita in the summer of 1966, he enrolled in mechanical engineering graduate school at the local state university. No make-up courses were required though Jay's bachelor's degree was in aero-space engineering.

Approximately thirty semester hours were required. Jay spent most of his evenings and weekends studying to maintain a B or better average. He did play touch football on an occasional Friday afternoon and a mild poker game a time or two on Friday nights. Jay did not do a lot of game playing. He dated some, also. His Uncle nearby obtained a black pup from his neighbor and gave it to Jay. The uncle's wife called the pup Jiggs. He was an active, comical dog. At night he could be heard playing "football" with a plastic milk jug, his favorite toy. He liked cats. Someone had put a female cat out at Jay's rented house. She had kittens that Jiggs adapted. One day the mother cat decided to move the cats from the house to the garage. She was thrashed by Jiggs when she picked up a kitten by the neck.

Jig and "Football"   Jig and Cats

The pretty lady that Jay wanted to get better acquainted with in Wichita would not date Jay. He did not know why. Leonard introduced Jay to another of his wife's nurse friends. She just was not the one Jay wanted; he wanted the pretty one. Later, Jay was told that the pretty girl was pregnant and was getting an abortion in Denver. Jay was still interested in her, and met her for coffee at a restaurant one day. They visited casually, but she was aloof because Jay was dating her other friend.

On a Thanksgiving Day, Jay rented a Cessna 140-tail dragger. He and the current nurse friend flew to Oklahoma to visit with Jay's parents. The sky was overcast in Oklahoma and Jay was not sure they could get down through it. Fortunately they found a hole in the overcast

Cessna 140

and dropped down. Jay recognized the town, Vinita, below and flew the Will Rogers Turnpike to their destination. Before landing, Jay switched fuel tanks from the right side to the left. When they landed, Jay had the right tank filled with aviation fuel.

He left the switch on the left tank on the way back; it took a full right tank to fly from Wichita. When the two arrived back at Rose Hill, near Wichita, where he had rented the plane, the right tank was empty even though the switch was still on the left tank. Jay did not rent that plane again.

That nurse friend moved to Kansas City to study for her master's degree in nursing. She came to Wichita on weekends. She and Jay eventually went their separate ways, but Jay never tried to date the pretty one again.

Leonard had dropped out of college. He had been attending Wichita State University. Jay offered to pay his enrollment fees if he would get back into college. Leonard took him up on it, but he enrolled at a church sponsored university with high tuition costs. However, he finished college with an industrial engineering degree, and later got a master's degree at Oklahoma State University in industrial engineering. Good for him!

At Boeing there was a pretty girl that Jay became interested in. She would have dated Jay, but she was a former girlfriend of another friend who was attending graduate school with Jay. Jay went to her apartment one Saturday morning for a little while. The weather was snowing, and Jay had to do his chores and study. That is the only time Jay came close to dating her. Too, she was Roman Catholic; Jay felt there was not too much promise of a future there.

Leonard took Jay to a church sponsored social organization for single people. There Jay met Sandy, a small, cute woman twenty-six years old.

Along about that time Jay had a hemorrhoid operation and was in St. Francis hospital. Jay's aunt and uncle who lived in Wichita came by for a visit. While they were there, the two girls, Sandy and then the pretty Catholic girl, came by.

Sandy

What an awkward situation. None of the visitors were invited. That was the last of the pretty girl relationship. The other, Sandy, was attractive in many ways. She worked at Boeing at this time. How they all found out about Jay being in the hospital is a mystery to Jay.

At about this same time, too, Jay was introduced to another very attractive girl who lived with another young woman in an apartment. She was a high school teacher at a large campus in the far Northeast part of Wichita. She had a master's degree. The date she and Jay had was to watch a KU basketball game on her TV in the basement. Jay went out and bought some popcorn. They simply watched the game. She must have been disappointed that Jay was not more aggressive. When they kissed goodnight, she became somewhat seductive. This lady was a divorcee too, and Jay wondered if two divorcees could make a go of it. He was busy and liked Sandy, whom he had just met. Jay wanted a wife who was a nonsmoker, not a drinker and a Christian. Sandy was a nonsmoker and a non-drinker, as far as Jay could tell, and claimed to be a Christian though she was a follower of an organization that Jay found later to not be Christian. Jay learned why it is important not to be unequally yoked. If both are of the same faith, life is so much easier. Sandy played the piano and had an accordion along with a beautiful singing voice, a plus.

In a class at the graduate school was a student that was a pilot who sometimes ferried planes for Cessna. He had a partner who was a test pilot at Beech Aircraft. The student

Cessna 152

asked Jay if he would like to ferry planes with them. Of course Jay was interested. On the first day of the year, the three had three Cessna planes to deliver to Ogden. Utah. Two were 152s and one was an executive Citation.

They met at the Cessna airfield near the Cessna plant January 1, 1966. Jay had never flown a 152 before. He was pointed to his plane. The test pilot flew the other. Jay was a bit uneasy about flying a plane he was not checked out in. It was easy to fly and was no problem to get into the air. Jay had flown Cessna 172s. The 152 was easier to fly, a lot like driving a car. They left Wichita early in the morning and headed west toward Dodge City. As they passed Dodge City Jay was appalled by the stench of the feed lots below. A storm was raging just west of Dodge City. The test pilot's plane was faster, and he was out ahead of Jay. They ran into the storm and lost sight of each other. They were in radio contact but could not find each other in the overcast. The test pilot was leading the way, and it was imperative they keep each other in sight. The test pilot radioed that it was foolish for the two to be flying around blind in the storm. He decided that they should land at the Dodge City Airport and stay there until the storm passed. When they landed, the wind was so strong that people at the airport had to come out and walk the planes in to the parking area. The two pilots stayed several hours. The clouds cleared up but the winds remained. The test pilot was a bit miffed about it all because he wanted to fly the Citation. The two took off around two o'clock in the afternoon and headed for Goodland. The plane that Jay was flying had a starter failure. The test pilot propped it. After they had flown for half to three-fourths of an hour, Jay looked down and asked the test pilot what town was below them and slightly to the rear. The test pilot checked his navigation and said it was Dodge City. They dropped down to get out of the strong north wind as much as possible. They arrived in Goodland close to 5:00 p.m. After refueling they headed west to Denver. Along the way they ran into two more fronts. They flew so low that they had to rise over fences and farmers feeding their cattle; it scared and scattered the cattle.

Cessna Citation

As they approached Stapleton International Airport (closed in 1995) the tower asked the test pilot that had contacted them if the second plane had a radio. Jay cut in and confirmed communication. The tower sent the two west toward the mountains and landed them to the east. The north and south runways were very busy with commercial aircraft (the wind was out of the north).

Jay feared the plane would flip over due to the strong north wind, but he was able to taxi the plane to general aviation parking. The test pilot decided to leave the planes there and went to the terminal where he bought a ticket back to Wichita. Jay waited at the general aviation terminal for the pickup plane and fell asleep on the carpeted floor. The pickup plane was a six-place Cessna that belonged to the Cessna flying club. It was a new plane flown by a young pilot with his wife. Jay was awakened by the young club pilot. He looked up to see the most beautiful face on a woman he had seen for a long time. She was very fair with golden hair that hung down to her shoulders. When Jay gathered his senses he was introduced to the club pilot's wife. The pickup crew allowed Jay to fly the new plane for a while. He was tired and the pretty wife exchanged seats with him and

helped with the flying. There was snow on the ground at the Cessna field, but they landed without incident. Jay did not fly with the ferry folks again.

The test pilot did check out Jay in the Beech club's bonanza. Sandy was with them in the back. When the pilot asked for a power off stall, the plane headed straight down with Sandy screaming in the back. Jay

Beech Bonanza

was careful not to stall that plane on approach. The plane had a habit of fish-tailing sometimes in a cross wind. Jay understood that the Debonair was a Bonanza with a standard tail for that reason.

Boeing rounded up several people who had pilot's licenses for testing a project of using low-light level TV cameras for flying B-52s at four hundred feet above the land surface to get under the Russian radars. The rout that was recorded and shown on a TV screen in a dark room was over San Francisco and to the northeast. The idea was to see if the pilots for the test could identify the land marks. Jay missed the first which was a highline on a hill near the ocean. He spotted the next, which was some ships in storage. He identified all of the rest. There was a problem with the camera lens; bugs smeared the cover just like they do on a car windshield. Chemicals were tried to remove the bugs without satisfactory results. Since car washes did a reasonable job, a cover was taken to a car wash where it was found that hot water with pressure cleaned the cover. The process was applied to the B-52s. The planes were to fly in low, rise up, let go of the bomb(s) and turn away (toss bombing). It was tried with the B-47, but the wings were not strong enough and some planes were lost, one near Tulsa. The B-52 wings were strengthened.

Jay did a check ride with a lady instructor pilot in Wichita. Sandy was aboard. The instructor pilot had Jay do an emergency landing. Normally, when the instructor saw that the emergency field was made, he/she would say, "Add power and climb out" without landing. This instructor had Jay put the Piper 180 down in a small pasture with cattle in it. The ground was frozen with deep cow tracks. It was a bumpy ride. Then she had Jay taxi down wind and take off into the wind, hoping the cows would stay put. Jay always wondered about her.

Punch Card

One of Jay's graduate classes required the problems be solved by computer programs written by the students. The university had one old IBM 1620 computer. It filled a large room with its vacuum tubes and relays. It was slow, was very limited on memory and could not pinpoint mistakes. It used punch cards to enter the programs and data. Programs were hand-written in fortran IV (formula translation) on eleven-inch-by-seventeen-inch sheets of paper with eighty columns of spaces on a grid to accommodate the punch cards. A program consisted of several cards called a deck. Jay numbered his cards in a deck to be able to place them in their proper place in case the cards were shuffled. The cards were originally punched on a 026 punch machine. Then the machines were upgraded to 029. That was confusing because the symbols on the two different machines did not match. Cards punched on the 026 machines had to be converted by punching new cards in the 029 format. Boeing had two IBM 360 computers

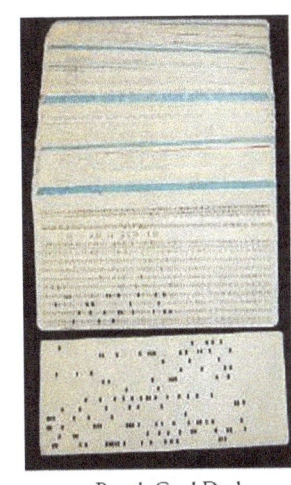

Punch Card Deck

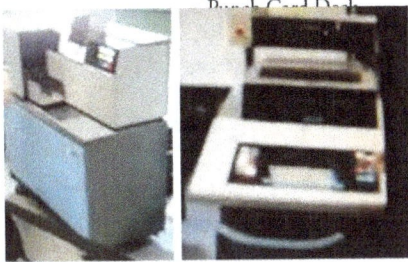

The IBM 1130 Computing System

using 029 keypunch cards. Some of the student engineers converted their decks and asked the Boeing operators to run their programs when they had time. The 360s could tell the programmer where the mistakes were to a reasonable extent.

Later, Boeing purchased an IBM 1130 for hands-on by the engineers. It was placed in a glassed room in the engineering department and was a huge help for the engineers and graduate engineering students. It could be used by the students after hours for their graduate studies. Boeing was friendly to the local university and encouraged it where they could. Many of their engineers were students there. The 1130 could automatically convert 026 cards to 029. It was a boon to the engineering department.

Jay became fairly proficient on the 1130 and at programming in fortran IV language. He was irritated with his professor who required him to learn computer programming while taking his course, thermodynamics, which was very difficult without the added burden of learning and applying computer programming. This course took a mammoth amount of time. What was worse the university operators had only enough time to run his program once every 24 hours? A tiny mistake, such as a period out of place, would fail the run. Jay had to search every character to find the mistake. He often stood at the computer window begging the operators to run his program on Saturdays before the

1130 became available. Later, though, Jay was glad he had learned to program. He did some computer analysis for the scoop at the base of the B-52 vertical stabilizer.

Chasing girls took too much time. Jay concentrated on his studies. He worked hard in all of his spare time studying. He made the grades necessary to gain a master of science in mechanical engineering. It was fortunate he did not have to go back and pick up any undergraduate mechanical engineering courses.

Oscilloscope

Pressure Chamber and Vibrator

In early 1969, he was finished with class work and began working on his thesis. The thesis was a study to determine the effects of a long tube on pressure measurements. Would the long tube dampen pressure vibrations giving erroneous readings? Long tubes may be required to get the transducer measuring pressures away from a hostile environment. To do the study, Jay built a pressure chamber, with the help of some university machine shop employees, and attached it to a vibrator that could reach a very high range of vibrations. He then attached a piezoelectric transducer to the chamber and a Statham strain-gage transducer to the end of a pipe filled with the same liquid (water) that was put into the pressure chamber.

The transducers were attached to an oscilloscope with a Polaroid camera for recording the responses of the vibrations induced by the vibrator.

Jay always thought that grants were given to college professors to study their projects they had graduate students doing.

The oscilloscope was not fast enough to capture the full trace of the vibrations the transducers were sending. Jay and his advisor felt that a faster recorder was needed; they felt the rounded traces on the oscilloscope were not good enough. A Honeywell light-sensitive recorder was applied with good results.

The Statham strain-gage transducer failed; the strain wire fatigued. This cost Jay several weeks on his project. It was unfortunate the university did not have the funds for two piezoelectric transducers. The project would have been easier. Jay hired Sandy's two nieces to help extract data from the traces to be loaded into a computer program Jay wrote for the project. It was found that there was a peculiar quirk in the system that gave data off the normal damping trace. Jay's advisor told Jay to remove it, but Jay realized that the several points there indicated that they were real. He left it on the plot, and they were later challenged on his oral defense of the thesis.

When the experimentation was complete and the thesis written, Jay prepared to defend his thesis. A grade point average of B was required for graduation of graduate students. Jay met that requirement. All that was left was to defend the thesis to a board of professors that Jay picked. Jay was told that he could be questioned on anything he had been taught throughout all of his college course work. Jay reviewed diligently as much of his former studies, such as physics, as he practically could. He selected his former graduate school instructors as much as he was allowed thinking that the questions they would ask would reflect on them if Jay could not answer. However the math professor asked Jay some questions Jay could not answer; they had to do with "modern math" (set theory, etc.). Jay's advisor told him to say "I do not know" if he was not positive of the answer. The math class Jay took in graduate school was completely new to Jay; he had never encountered "modern math" before. Curls, sets and unions had entirely new meanings to Jay. Jay froze up when questioned by the math professor, and gave "I don't know" to each of his questions. The automatic controls professor jumped in and asked jay questions that he had drilled his classes on. The answers came easily and saved Jay's bacon. When Jay presented his thesis, the experimentation data of his project showed the outlier group of points when the data was plotted on a graph. When asked during his exam what they were Jay said he did not know. It was obviously a characteristic of the equipment and perhaps a good follow-on thesis project to discover the source of the outliers. Jay's advisor, who was in charge of the thesis project, gave Jay a B for his thesis because Jay did not remove the outliers. His advisor disagreed that the outliers were real and, consequently, marked Jay down some on the Thesis. Jay passed his orals anyhow and received his master of science in mechanical engineering.

A Dale Carnegie course on effective speaking, influencing people, etc., was recommended by one of Jay's graduate teachers. Jay did well in the course after a rough start and won several prizes. He never applied much of it, though.

Jay had dated Sandy for a long time. She told Jay that she was a Christian and had taught in children's Sunday school in the West Side Christian Church. He felt good about that. Sandy and Jay met in 1966 and were married in 1969.

Jay, by now, knew that Sandy had a stubborn streak and was hard-headed about some things. It took Jay a while to convince himself that marriage was the right thing again and that Sandy would stay through thick and thin. They were married in Oklahoma at a Baptist church, her lifetime girlfriend's church in Ponca City. Her friend had lived a short distance away while the two girls were growing up.

Joan was the maid of honor, and Royce was the best man. These two were current friends of Jay and Sandy in Wichita.

Jay and Sandy's Wedding Pictures

Jay, Sandy and Wichita Friends

Jay, Minister and Sandy

Sandy's Friends, Sandy, Jay and Minister

Sandy and Jay

Sandy had lost her job at Boeing and had gone to work at Beech Aircraft. Jay and Sandy lived in the small house Jay had on South Hydraulic in Wichita. They moved to a house in Andover. Boeing had a cutback in engineers and Jay was laid off. The Boeing engineering union had told the engineers where they were on the "totem pole" for layoff. Layoffs were a common practice in aircraft factories. Jay knew when his time was coming and looked around for another job. His advisor in graduate school had come to work for Being and was cut back, too. The two went looking for another job together. Jay took a job at Beech Aircraft Company. Sandy was working in the mail room at Beech at the time; she was bumped from her job by someone with higher seniority. However, as a wife she did not need to work.

When Jay had dropped by the Grand Ole Opry house in 1965 on a Friday night, it was open, and performers were practicing for the Saturday night show. In 1969 Sandy and Jay took Sandy's mother and dad to a show at the grand Ole Opry. The only tickets they could get were for the Friday night show. It was nearly sold out, and the tickets were for the upper balcony to one side of the stage.

Jay enjoyed working at Beech. An engineer there with the last name Beach sometimes needed to call vendors. When he told them who he was the vendor would say, "Yes, sir, Mr. Beach! What can I do for you?"

Jay and his lead engineer at Beech became good friends. The lead engineer was second generation German. Jay asked him if he thought in English or German. English was his preference.

Beech Musketeer

Jay had become a member of the Beech Flying Club. One day at noon, Jay, his lead engineer and a fellow engineer friend flew in a Beech club Musketeer to a small lake east of Wichita to view the friend's cabin on the lake. On the way back the plane began to vibrate. Jay cut the throttle to minimum flying speed to lessen the vibration. Later, another pilot lost the tip of the propeller of that plane. Another time, Jay took his lead engineer, his wife and child and Sandy on a ride in a Musketeer one Sunday afternoon. As they approached the Beech field, they were landing from the north. They were approximately one hundred feet above the end of the runway when the right wing dropped nearly ninety degrees. Jay immediately applied power and cranked the ailerons far left; the plane leveled out. There was a strong cross wind from the west. The passengers did not seem to be concerned, but Jay felt his hair was on end. Beech buildings were on the north end of the field; the wind from the west rolled over the buildings causing the right wing to drop. Jay landed downwind where there were no buildings on the south end, and advised other traffic of the problem by radio. One pilot radioed that he was going to land on the east/west grass strip.

The club had a Bonanza K model. It was a big plane and fast. Jay, his uncle, Sandy and his uncle's son flew to northeast Oklahoma. Jay had made the trip several times, but on this trip with the Bonanza for the first time, the destination came a little faster than Jay expected. The group arrived while they were still at cruise altitude. They let down in Missouri and came

Bonanza at NE Oklahoma Destination

back to the airport in NE Oklahoma where they landed. At the destination in the photograph at right is Joe, Sandy, Fay and Lou. They flew over Grand Lake. When they returned to land, there was a squall coming in from the north. Jay followed a plane in the pattern that had landed. The other plane suddenly turned back onto the runway to taxi to tie down. Jay added full power and pulled up the gear. He had full flaps and knew he did not dare pull up the flaps until they had good flying speed. He circled around and landed; he had the right-of-way because a plane on final has that right. The other plane's occupants scurried away before Jay arrived.

At Beech Jay worked fuel systems. He wrote a computer program for determining the performance of fuel systems. To analyze a proposed fuel system, Jay used the Darcy Wiesbach formula. The first step is to determine all of the resistance items in the fuel lines. As stated before, resistance values for each component, called K values, have been determined empirically (experimentally) and published in hand books. The loss factors were then multiplied by flow to determine the loss of pressure from the pump to make certain the proper pressure and flow at the engines were adequate. To begin, the analysis starts at the engines. For lines in parallel, K factors are determined for each parallel line and then added by adding the total for each line, multiplying them together and then dividing by the sum of the resistance of the two lines. Those in series are added directly. When all of the resistance factors for the lines, bulkhead fittings, elbows, etc. were added properly, the total loss was plotted against the performance capability of the pump supplied by the pump manufacturer. The performance of the fuel system was determined by where the plot of the pressure loss vs. flow crossed the performance of the pump plot.

Jay in De Havilland Aircraft

Jay was assigned to design the HVAC ducting for the De Havilland executive aircraft Beech bought from England without interiors. Jay drew up the duct work for the heating, venting and air conditioning system (HVAC) for the new plane. He then drew it isometric (in 3-D) to help manufacturing build the parts. The 3-D drawing was for the opposite side, but the actual part drawings were OK. Jay worked for Beech for one year.

Olive Beech owned and ran the company. It was said she paid less income tax than an engineer making twelve hundred dollars per month. She eventually sold the company to Raytheon.

While working for Beech Jay bought an Allis Chalmers WD tractor with a two-wheel trailer and disc harrow on the trailer for a small price. He had a walking plow he pulled behind the tractor to plow up a large garden. He used the disc to smooth

De Havilland Aircraft

the garden. He bought an enclosed truck bed to keep the tractor in. The rent house in Andover where they lived had a 1-car garage, but the 1966 Chevy was kept in it. When Sandy and Jay moved from Andover, they took the equipment with them.

WD Allis Chalmers Tractor

The aircraft business was stressful for Jay because of the roller coaster employment in that line of work. He wanted a more stable life. An advertisement appeared in a Wichita paper for a mechanical engineer in an oil company. Jay answered, and two people from that oil company's research and development lab came to Jay's house to interview Jay. They made an offer, and Jay accepted. The company had a moving company move the new hire. The couple found a rent house right away and moved into it. They rented a garage and put the tractor and equipment into it. Jay was amazed that he could still buy parts for the tractor, including lenses for the lights.

A fellow worker had five acres that Jay and another friend used to raise a large garden. They raised a large patch of potatoes and sweet corn along with onions, etc. All three participants enjoyed plenty from the garden.

Chapter 10

Oil

When Jay saw the advertisement for an engineer at an oil company in Oklahoma, he thought that this might be an opportunity to get out of the aircraft business, since now he had a master's degree in mechanical engineering. The offer from the oil company was more than the $1200 per month he was being paid by Beech. Jay was hired to oversee the industrial lubricants lab work for the three chemists formulating oils and greases of the research facility. There were four technicians doing the work. Jay was responsible for the technicians' work and the lab supplies, etc. There were two PhD chemists who worked outside the lab but were in the same overall group. They both told Jay to look out for a particular chemist in the industrial lab; he was a back-stabber looking for a way to climb the corporate ladder. They were right. The research lab's villain looked for all ways to make himself look good at the expense of others. In an empty room next to the supervisor's office, he listened with his ear to the wall when someone was being evaluated or disciplined or when the superintendent's boss was in the superintendent's office. He was a menace to the moral and satisfaction of the others in the lab.

The research lab had an industrial lubrication section and an automotive oils section. It was financed by the marketing department.

The automotive section had three chemists, four technicians and one engineer to evaluate the engine oil formulations after testing. The chemists formulated the engine oils with the many additives (around eight) such as Zinc diaryidithiophosphate wear inhibiter, silicon antifoam, antioxidant, detergent to keep sludge suspended, viscosity index improvers (VI), etc. The light base oil was lighter than the lowest viscosity range of the multi-grade oil being formulated. It was mixed with the higher weight oil to get the exact lower viscosity of the oil being formulated. Then the VI, a polymer (liquid plastic) with a flat viscosity vs heat response, was added to make the multi-grade. For Example, if 10W-40 oil was to be formulated, the lower viscosity of the blend of the base oils would be Society of Automotive Engineers' (SAE) rating of ten viscosity for winter. The VI improver, then, would be blended to hold the viscosity within the rating of forty when the oil was hot. Sample oil formulations are shown at right.

The oil formulations were tested according to SAE standard tests. For long wear a 302 Ford engine on a dynamometer stand was used. It was called SAE VC Aunt Minnie driving test. First, the engine, even new engines, were disassembled, cleaned thoroughly, measured to be within tight specifications (rings were ground to proper gap, etc.) and carefully rebuilt such that each engine was as near to each other as possible eliminating variation among them. The tests lasted for three hundred ninety-two hours with start, drive at moderate speed, drive at higher speed, each for a specified time and then stops in each cycle. At the end of the test the engine was broken down and the engineer rated the parts for varnish in the valve cover, wear of valve lifters, sludge and varnish in the pan, etc.

SAMPLE OF AN OIL FORMULATION

ADDITIVE		SERVICE STATIONS		INDUSTRIAL	
	AMT~%	BRAND NAME		AMT~%	BRAND NAME
Oxidation Inhibitor	1.5	Hitec-686		0.8	ECA-448
Or	1.1	ECA-4493		1.1	OLA-229
Rust Inhibitor	1.2	Amoco-9717		1.3	Amoco-9217
Dispersant	2.5	Amoco-9250		5.1	Lubrisol-990
Detergent	1.3	Amoco-9217		1.3	Amoco-9217
Anti-Wear	1.5	Hitec-Z-682		1.1	Hitec-E-682
VI improver	8.5	Acryloid-955		7.6	Acryloid-955
Anti-Foam	0.1	DC-280		0.1	DC-280
Base Oil-Light		5710			5710
Base Oil-Heavy		5717			5717

A Sample of Oil Formulations

The rust test on a formulation was done on 455 CID 1977 Oldsmobile engines. It was called the SAE IIC test and lasted for thirty-two hours. Each eight hours a sample of the oil was drawn and analyzed in the chemistry lab. Chilled water was run through a special valve rocker cover; water was condensed all during the test and wound up in the oil. The engine was run at a nominal load and rpm on a dynamometer stand. The amount of water condensed was measured on the dip stick. Then at the end of thirty hours of testing, the engine was run at one hundred horsepower and 3600 revolutions per minutes for two hours to drive the water out. The engine was broken down and rated for rust, etc.

The third test was primarily an oxidation test with other performance characteristics measured along with it. It was called the SAE IIIC test. It ran at one hundred horsepower and 3600 revolutions per minute for sixty-four hours on a 455 CID 1977 Oldsmobile engine. Every eight hours a sample of the oil was taken and an equal amount of the same oil was added back. The viscosity was plotted to see when and if the oil is oxidizing (getting thicker). If the oil does oxidize, it usually happens all at once in an eight-hour period. When that occurs, the oil gets so thick it will not drain out of the pan and the test is stopped. The engine parts were rated by the engineer.

The industrial lubricants were tested for film strength and wear. One of the tests was with a cup with three steel balls (steel bearings approximately three- eights inch in diameter) held stationary. The cup then was filled with a lubricant to be tested, and a fourth ball bearing was mounted to a vertical rod. The rod then was spun with a load on it. After a period of time, the unit was disassembled and the wear marks on the three balls in the cup, were measured. From that the performance of the oil can be determined. Varying amount of load on the rod with the single ball was another parameter used to determine the oil performance. If the four balls weld together during the test, the film strength has failed and the oil was considered a failure if that load is below that required for the film strength. The used ball bearings were discarded after the tests.

Some of the lab personnel took the discarded balls home. One of the PhD chemists, Eric, who worked with the lab but worked in another area, had a "beanie flipper", a Y shaped wooden device with rubber bands attached to each side and a leather pouch at the end of the bands. He had a tom cat in his neighborhood that woke him up every night as he came down the street yowling loudly. Eric shot at the cat with a steel ball. The ball missed the cat and rattled around in a neighbor's garage two houses down and across the street. Lights came on in the affected house while Eric, in his underwear tip-toed back into his house. Shortly afterwards, Eric's wife joined a local play-house. Jay thought the plays were lousy. Eric's wife took up with a younger man in the playhouse group and divorced Eric; she took both of their young children with her, as Jay recalls. The wife was pretty and Eric was such a nice guy. Jay sure hated to see the break-up. During an oil company strike, Jay and Eric worked on the same work gangs. Jay could tell that Eric was hurting terribly.

When Sandy and Jay first moved to the oil company job, they rented a house. It was a fairly nice house with a back yard. A back street coming into the neighborhood was half paved while the other half was dirt bordering an open field. One day when Sandy and Jay were coming home along that street, their dog, Jig, was in the back seat. He liked to go places with the couple. They passed a boy on a bicycle going the same direction on the dirt section. As they were beside the boy on the bicycle, Jig stuck his nose close to the boy and said, "Woof!" The boy threw his gallon of milk he was carrying into the air and lost control of his bicycle. Sandy asked, "Do you think we should go back and help the boy?" Jay said, "No! I don't want to get beat up by a kid."

Jay had helped a local farmer with farming, driving his large John Deere tractor working his fields. A cat had been dumped in the parking lot at the oil company. Jay was the last one out of the lot and brought the cat home. Jig and the cat did not get along well; the cat was afraid of Jig. One day as Jig was going through the doggie door the cat caught him from behind, clawing and biting. Jig said, "Woo, woo!" as he tried to get loose. The farmer had several cats, and Jay took the cat to the farmer and let him out without the farmer knowing about it. Later, Jay was helping the farmer load an outbuilding onto Jay's trailer for delivery to a buyer, the cat came to Jay, his old friend. He went under the trailer and Jay threw him out of the way by the tail. The farmer was indignant at the rough handling of his newly acquired cat.

Sandy and Jay went to Tulsa to see Carla from time to time. They brought her to their home in the oil company city. She told Jay and Sandy that she went to the refrigerator one time for some ice cream, but it was gone. She said her mother, Sadie, told her that a mouse got it. She later found the container behind the couch. Since then the expression that a mouse got it was used by Sandy or Jay when one was looking for something to eat in the refrigerator, and it was gone.

Carla and Sandy

One time, Carla, who was six years old, told her dad and Sandy that Sadie and her new husband wanted to adopt Carla. The couple thought about it and decided that they could not control the situation there in any way. They felt it would be best for Carla if the new husband was made totally responsible for her. Adoption would end the mischief the grandparents caused, especially when visits were made with Carla. Sandy and Carla got along great. Sandy and Jay agreed and told Carla that they could remain friends. She would be welcome at their home anytime. They thought the grandmother was engineering the situation and would be glad to have full control there in Tulsa. Later, they sent Carla a 3D projector with pictures they had made for her. The child's grandmother sent them back with a threatening letter. The couple thought the grandmother was extremely cruel.

Ethylene glycol antifreeze formulation testing was done by testing the new formulations with chemicals and metals found in engines along with their radiator materials. Antifreeze of ethylene glycol formulation is most common.

After soaking over a period of time at high temperature and comparing the results with known high quality antifreezes of other brands, the integrity of the new antifreeze formulation was verified. The formulations were tested to be sure they were compatible with other brands (so they could be mixed without adverse

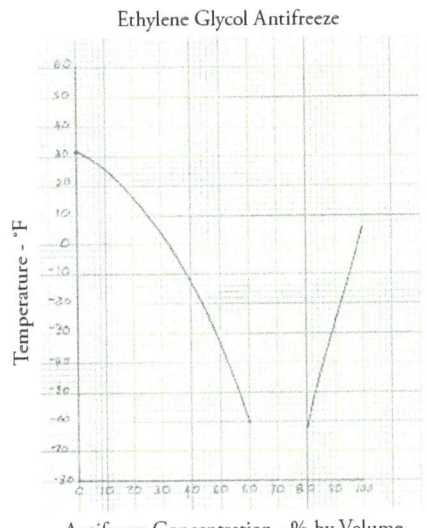

Antifreeze Concentration - % by Volume

effects). The chemists were responsible to evaluate the results. The basic material in the antifreezes is ethylene glycol, which has its coldest freezing mixture with water at about 70 percent antifreeze. This antifreeze without any water mixture freezes above 0°F. In moderate climate antifreeze mixtures are around 50 percent each. It freezes around -30°F. Water has a higher heat capacity than antifreeze and can carry away more heat. However, higher concentration of ethylene glycol antifreeze gives greater protection of the engine and radiator metals. Engines with proper size and condition of their radiators will operate satisfactorily in most areas of the Unites States on a 70 percent ethylene glycol antifreeze mixture. At that mixture there is no concern about freezing at any temperature the engine might see.

Formulation of grease was an interesting industrial oils product. The chemists blended oil with clay and additives in a hot vat and whipped the mixture like whipped cream. Grease releases the oil onto a bearing when a bearing gets warm from friction. That is how it works, holding the oil in suspension until needed and releasing only the amount needed to keep the bearing lubricated.

Sandy's girlhood friend's husband worked in the computer building of the oil company. The friend's church was where Jay and Sandy were married. Jay attended the large Baptist church in the town. A friend at the lab was in the know of the church. The pastor of that church was dictatorial. He had everyone holding hands while singing hymns. Sandy agreed to join the church with Jay if the church would accept her baptism in the Christian Church; she had been immersed. The dictator preacher refused; he said if she wanted to join his church, she would have to be baptized again. She refused and, that was the last time she came close to joining a Christian church again.

The engineer that covered the automotive testing of engine oil formulations resigned and moved back to Pennsylvania, his home state. Jay was moved into that position. Not only did he oversee the technicians in that area and rate the engine parts after an oil formulation was tested, he was assigned to test alcohol as a motor fuel. This was around 1974 area. The first "oil shortage" was declared. Gasoline was around thirty-nine cents per gallon. Jay thought that the oil companies wanted more and banded together to create the hoax that there was an oil shortage to get the price up; it worked. The price went to seventy-nine cents per gallon.

The Fuels and Lubricants manager wanted the alcohol study because the oil company owned the second largest coal company in the United States. Methanol, wood alcohol, can be easily made from coal. Methanol is CH_3OH, or CH_4O; that is one atom of carbon, four atoms of hydrogen and one of oxygen. Coal burning in the absence of sufficient oxygen produces CO (carbon monoxide). CO in the presence of a catalyst and H_2O (water), produces methanol (wood alcohol). It has an energy content of approximately nine thousand BTUs per pound while gasoline has approximately twenty thousand BTUs per pound; it is apparent that gasoline has approximately twice as much energy as alcohol. That means that the fuel systems must supply twice as much alcohol to the engines for the same performance on alcohol as with the performance on gasoline.

A Ford Pinto was purchased for alcohol testing. Jay and a technician opened the power jets in the Pinto carburetor to twice flow area. The engine ran fine.

Then by mixing fuels in one gallon cans, they mixed isooctane hydrocarbon fuel with N pentane by volume starting at 80 percent isooctane, which is 100 octane, and 20 percent N pentane, which is 0 octane. This gave an 80 octane fuel mixture. Then the isooctane percent was increased in succeeding cans in two octane numbers through 100 octane numbers of mixtures. The timing of the engine was adjusted for each of the mixtures establishing an octane setting for each timing setting through car acceleration tests. With that information the octane value of the alcohol could be determined.

To adjust the timing setting for each fuel octane, the Pinto was run on the fuel and accelerated on an abandoned airport. On each mixture, the timing was adjusted until the engine no longer knocked on acceleration of that mixture as the timing was reduced. A chart was established showing timing settings vs. fuel mixtures. Then the car was accelerated on alcohol until the timing was just at the point where the engine no longer knocked. The timing setting for the alcohol compared to the same timing for the hydrocarbon mixtures (isooctane and pentane) at that setting determined the octane rating of the alcohol. It was around 106 octane number for the methanol.

A fuel-injected Volkswagen engine was purchased and run on the alcohol.

Twice size injectors by Bosh were used for fuel delivery. They worked fine.

A 302 Ford engine was set on a dynamometer and run on the methanol. The methanol was purchased by Jay in fifty-five-gallon drums at 99.9 percent pure methanol. The Ford's carburetor power jets were bored to twice their standard flow area sizes. Over a short period of time the carburetors were dissolved by the alcohol to the point that they would not work, and could not be repaired. They were replaced with new ones. After a week of run time and sitting idle for a weekend the cylinder walls of the 302 Ford were rusted considerably. Elastomers such as gaskets, diaphragms, etc. were damaged by the alcohol, which is a solvent.

Emissions were very good with the alcohol. Most of the byproduct of burning the alcohol was water. However, an automobile dynamometer was set up in a separate building. There the volume of exhaust gas was measured with a Roots blower. Oxides of nitrogen and carbon monoxide were measured by infrared. Oxygen was measured by an oxygen meter, and unburned hydrocarbons (unburned fuel) were measured by a flame ionizer device.

Jay was invited to Bartlesville, OK, to the ERDA (Environmental Research and Development Agency – forerunner to EPA) lab to witness a test of automobile emissions by Dr. Franklin. Jay had thought that smog was just a hoax to fleece the auto owners for expensive emission controls on their cars. It was not. Dr. Franklin had a large Plexiglas tube that he introduced carbon monoxide (CO), oxides of nitrogen (NO, NO_2) and hydrocarbons (unburned fuel such as butane, propane, hexane, pentane, etc.) into together. He then turned on a fluorescent light (producing ultraviolent light) mounted just above the tube. Immediately, a brown cloud was formed – smog! Jay was convinced that automobiles could produce smog in sunlight. When Jay flew around cities, including Wichita with its relatively flat area around it, he could see smog once he was above three thousand feet.

Jay was sent to the University of Michigan at Ann Arbor to study automobile emissions for a week. There he learned about the three bad guys that produced smog: CO, HC and NOx. Catalytic converters were added to car exhaust systems to convert (oxidize) the CO to CO_2 and HC to water and CO_2. Ford added an exhaust gas reactor to their engines to further burn the CO and HC as they came out of the combustion chambers. The reactor consisted of an air pump that pumped fresh air into the exhaust at each exhaust valve where the gases were hot and would burn. It worked fairly well, but catalysts assured lower emissions by oxidizing the burnable carbon compounds.

Now the NOx gases were a different story. They were already oxidized. To reduce them with a reducing catalyst would also reduce the CO_2 back to CO and perhaps the HC back to unburned fuel. So, what to do? It was found that the NOx was formed when the combustion temperatures reach 3,000° F. Therefore, by recycling some of the exhaust gases back to the combustion chamber, the combustion temperature did not reach the 3,000° F mark. Automobiles then were fitted with exhaust gas recycle (EGR) devices that recycled approximately 6 percent or less exhaust gases. Jay did some testing with exhaust gases. An engine on a dynamometer was tested by using 100 percent exhaust gases into the air intake and adding approximately 21 percent oxygen to it. It ran fine; however, the exhaust gases were cooled in a fifty-five-gallon drum before recycling.

The trip to Ann Arbor was interesting. Jay decided to drive and take Sandy along. Jay had his 1966 Chevrolet serviced, including aligning the front end; a bad mistake. They left town on Friday afternoon and planned to drive to Jay's dad's home that day. They would spend the night there and go to Indianapolis Saturday. From there they would make Ann Arbor Sunday. As they left town, they noticed the front tires were squealing on turns.

Jay's 1966 Chevy

They knew the front end was not aligned properly. The front tires were nearly new and squealed on every turn. The Chevrolet place that did the alignment was closed. The couple decided to drive on to Jay's dad's farm and get the front end aligned the next morning in the town nearby. The spare bedroom there had not been used for a while and Fay had sprayed around it to drive away the bugs.

In the night, Sandy said, "Something bit me!" Jay said, "Aw, go back to sleep, it was probably a mosquito." Sandy said, "No, something bit me and it hurts."

Jay got up and turned on the light. Sandy looked down and saw a scorpion on the neck of her night gown. She did an active war dance complete with hollering and screaming. The scorpion fell to the floor and Jay killed it with a shoe. Scorpions are not poisonous in that area, but have a sting like a wasp. Now, they were wide awake in the middle of the night. They knew they would probably get no more sleep that night, so they decided to go on toward St. Louis and get the front end aligned there early Saturday morning. By the time they arrived in St. Louis, one of the front tires was worn down. They looked for a Chevrolet dealership for an alignment, but when they found one it was closed, a standard practice for other Chevrolet dealers. They drove on. They had a reservation at a Holiday Inn in Indianapolis. They arrived at around noon. Their room was not ready. They waited in the hot car for two to three hours for the room to be cleaned. They were dog tired. When they were let into their room it was a mess. The bed was not made and had something spilled over it. A tray with food and drink containers was sitting outside the door. The travelers had to wait longer for the room to be serviced. The raunchy bed spread was put back on to the bed. The couple was not happy with Holiday Inn!

By now, one of the front tires was bald. Jay knew he had to get another tire before going on. The only one he could find the right size that Sunday morning was a scalloped tire that was taken off a police car. Jay thought it would soon be worn round and bought it. The station mounted it and the two moved on toward Ann Arbor. A hundred miles or so down the road, the tire replacement started to go flat. A filling station nearby fixed it. They arrived in a town called Ypsilanti near Ann Arbor. They had a room reserved in the Howard Johnson Motel there. In the trunk was a spare can of gasoline. It spilled on their suitcase and doused their underclothes. They had to send them all out to be laundered the next morning. They went nearby and purchased some supplies for school. On the way back to their room they decided to check the temperature of the large swimming pool water. As Jay stooped down to feel the water, his foot slipped on the wet sloping, edge and he fell in. Sandy laughed. He went back to their room in sloshing shoes. Jay laid out all of the wet papers in his bill fold, put on his bathing suit, as did Sandy, and they went back to the pool. People were in the hot pool at the time of the accident. They were still there. Jay and Sandy stepped into the hot pool with them.

Later, they decided to get something to eat. They drove from the parking lot to the street, and the oil light came on. Jay checked the oil level; it was OK. They drove back to parking and the lifters begin to rattle for lack of oil pressure. The next morning Jay called the Chevrolet dealer in Ypsilanti. They came and towed the car. At noon Jay called the dealer and learned that the oil pump had broken, probably because the scalloped tire vibrated it to failure. The dealer wanted to put a new 283 CID engine in it for around the price Jay had paid for the car. Jay told them to put a new pump in it, change the oil, align it, put the spare on in place of the bad tire and bring it back. The engine had not been driven far enough after the pump broke to damage it. It ran fine and never used oil or even leaked. At 81,000 miles the engine was still running very well without any problems. Upon return home Jay took the worn out tire to the dealer that did the wrong alignment; they replaced the worn out tire with a new one.

The manager in charge of the alcohol study (the lab supervisor's boss) wrote a paper, 750118, for SAE and presented it at an SAE convention in Detroit in 1975. It presents alcohol as an automobile fuel. Jay's name is on the cover of the report. He was at the convention, too.

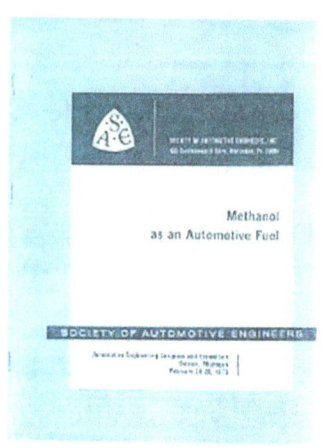

Alcohol as an Alternate Fuel Report

The report tells of the many problems of using alcohol as a motor fuel including its difficulty in starting the engine on the alcohol under 53° F. The starting problem can be overcome by mixing 4 percent butane with the alcohol. It also tells that the known reserves of coal in the United States would last the country for five hundred years at the usage at that time.

Jay did not believe that there was a fuel shortage. The alcohol project was stopped by upper management. Knowing that the project had great potential, the lab's supervisor went to headquarters in Houston to plead for continuation of the project. Auto manufacturing engineering could fix the problems discovered. The management said, "We can sell all we can make of gasoline and we can produce all we can sell." The lab supervisor's boss was severely disciplined for going around his local boss.

Jay could not go out on the street and buy gasoline from the major oil company service stations during the "fuel shortage" (1973 to 1974 time frame). He could get all he needed from the independents because they had contracts for their supply. One day during the "shortage," word came down that the refinery would shut down in three days because there was no place to put the gasoline. All of the 250,000 gallon capacity white tanks on the forty acres tank farm were full, all of the service stations were full, all of the trucks were full and even the abandoned service station tanks were full; there was no place to put more gasoline. The oil company's management said that the government would not let them sell the gasoline. Say what? Before the three days were up, there was plenty of gasoline everywhere, but the thirty-nine cents per gallon gasoline was now seventy-nine cents. That is surely what the oil companies were after. They pulled the same trick again in 1979 to get the price above one dollar per gallon.

Jay came up with an idea to eliminate oil spots on driveways, parking lots and garages. It would catch oil leaks at the source, put it into a container by manifold vacuum and then filter it back into its source. Jay offered it to the oil company, but they turned it down, releasing it back to Jay. Jay teamed up with the shop mechanic that built unusual apparatuses for the oil company research lab. He then did research to see if anyone else had applied for a patent in that area at the library at Oklahoma State University. With the help of a lawyer who sometimes worked for the company, Jay received a patent. It cost Jay about one thousand dollars for patent drawings and the attorney. The patent was granted; however, Jay and his partner never built one.

Jay had bought a bicycle shop in town for nine thousand dollars on a loan, and Sandy helped run it. They never made a profit from it even though it brought in approximately ninety thousand dollars per year gross for each of the three years they had it.

This was the era of the twenty-seven-inch wheels with skinny tires. Their best bike they sold was a Takara made in Japan. They also sold Vista, which Jay understood, was formerly Columbia. It had fat tires for paper boys, etc. The

Front View of Bike Shop

light weight bikes with skinny tires sacrificed strength to save weight. They were really made for adults for long distance riding. When parents bought the light weight bikes for their kids, they invariably came back with bent forks and/or frames. The young riders were jumping square curbs; the light weights could not take it. The bike shop sold several new forks, if they could not be straightened, and a myriad of rims because the rims were usually ruined by the curbs. Jay and a friend were able to lace both three-across spoked rims and four-across, as well, in approximately fifteen minutes. The

Show Room of Bike Shop

charge for a new rim laced on was fifteen dollars with the rim costing $3.50 from the supplier and selling for seven dollars to the customer. Later they were able to purchase rims and hubs together with spokes laced on for seven dollars each; they sold them for $15 and did not have to put labor into them other than truing them.

Jay painted the sign pointing to the entrance on the side of the building by first drawing the sign on a grid paper. See the photograph at right. Then he scaled the drawing up for the wall and drew the scaled up grid on the wall using correct measurements with chalk lines. It turned out good. The signs on the window were painted by a young man who worked in advertising for the local newspaper. He wanted to do the wall, too.

Sandy with Josh inside with 1972 Oldsmobile Tornado in the Background

Sandy became pregnant with son Josh. She could no longer run the shop during the daytime. Jay and Sandy tried to sell the business, but could find no takers during the time they had before Sandy could no longer be at the store. They decided to auction the contents. The lab's trouble maker came into the store, his first time ever, nosing around asking questions; no doubt he was spying for the new lab superintendent, who replaced the recently retired superintendent. The new superintendent was a PhD chemist. The trouble maker had always been at odds with Jay; he wanted the job Jay had when Jay was hired. He worked at building confidence with the new lab superintendent. The new lab superintendent was an athletic type. He bicycled to work at times. He had a tiny farm east of town. The trouble maker spent time on weekends and evenings "helping" the superintendent with his farm work. The young superintendent was arrogant, filled with himself and gullible; bad news for Jay.

The bike shop was closed and the contents auctioned off. The auction generated enough money to pay the loan at the oil company's credit union.

Sandy was around seven months pregnant. She and Jay rented a plane with the plan to fly to Fort Scott, Kansas, to see Sandy's aunt and Uncle. Coming from the north was a storm front. They tried to go around it by veering off to the south.

Jay lost track of the ground check points while skirting the front. He knew that he had to fly due west to pick up Interstate 35 in order to return home. He tried to pick up the flight service station at his home airport and ask for a fix and heading to that airport, but they could not locate him. The plane had no transponder. As he was talking with the flight service station, he saw the campus and football stadium at Oklahoma State University. He was due south of his home airport and simply flew the thirty or forty miles back to his airport. Later, the FAA called to chew on Jay for getting off course and momentarily not knowing exactly where he was. They were convinced that Jay knew generally where he was and that he could find his way home, which he did. Jay and Sandy landed and drove to Fort Scott in their Tornado. Jay and Sandy bought the 1972 Oldsmobile Tornado car from a wealthy lead chemist at the lab. It was a front wheel drive vehicle with a 455 CID engine in it and front torsion bars hooked behind the back of the front seats underneath. The car rode with a rocking motion.

Later, in the same plane, Jay was going for his bi-annual check ride with an instructor. On takeoff the instructor pulled the power off at about one hundred feet above the ground and said, "You just lost power!" Jay nosed over to not loose airspeed and stall. The instructor shoved the throttle forward yelling, "No! No! Keep the nose up!" The plane bumped the ground hard on the main landing gear, but no harm was done. They went on with the check ride. Jay had never been told or witnessed anything like that before.

Jay's dad, who was eighty-four years old, became sick and was in the hospital. He had an enlarged prostate gland and did not empty his bladder each time he urinated. One day he found blood in his urine and his doctor put him in the hospital where he was operated on. Jay came to the farm to take care of it for the

few days Joe was expected to be in the hospital. He had several head of cattle, but they were in poor physical condition. Jay told Vera about the cattle, and she talked to Joe about it. Joe told Jay to go to a feed supply company in Kansas and buy some cotton seed meal. Before Jay could get started the next morning, Joe had Fay call to tell Jay to not get the feed. Jay realized he could not do anything for the cows or any other help around the farm. He contacted his sister, Bonnie, who lived a few miles away, to look after the farm and then went back to work. A short time after Joe came home he hemorrhaged and was taken back to the hospital. Jay came to see him but Joe said, "I don't know you" because he was very sick in intensive care. He died several days later. At the day of the funeral Fay told Jay that Joe left everything to Bonnie in a will he had written when Jay ran off with the girl at age sixteen. Joe must have felt really hurt. Fay tried to get Joe to change the will. He was working with his attorney, but did not get the change done. Bonnie told Ellen and Jay she would share with them but not the family of Joe's first wife. She did not, and Jay was informed that Bonnie's husband told her that if she did share, he would leave her. Jay drove himself and Sandy to the church at the funeral. Bonnie's husband tried to man-handle Jay at the church by pushing him around. Jay drove to the cemetery and left from there after visiting his mother's and brother's graves in the same cemetery.

Joe's farm equipment was auctioned. Jay understood that Fay got what she and Joe accumulated while they were married. Fay asked Jay to come to the auction, but Jay had to go to a weeklong school in Houston. It was a "take you apart and put you back together" school called Managerial Grid written by a couple of PhD "head shrinkers." Jay went through several of those where he worked throughout the rest of his career. He did not go to the auction. He really wanted to forget some of the hardships of the farm life anyhow.

E. W. Marland found oil on the 101 Ranch near Ponca City, Oklahoma. He built a refinery and processed the oil. He had a mansion just east of the refinery.

It was quite nice with an outside social area for dancing, etc. It was still there in the 1970s. E. W. had built a new mansion on a large tract of land approximately a mile east and a few miles north of the refinery. It was a very attractive mansion with a swimming pool and many other niceties. It had a wall around the mansion area with an artist studio along part of the wall. E. W. and his wife had adapted a couple of children; they were the children of E. W.'s wife's family. When E. W.'s wife died, the adapted girl was an adult. E. W. married the girl, as the story goes. The town's folks could not accept that and called it incest, Jay was told.

E. W. lost his newer mansion but kept the artist studio where the Marlands lived during the 1929 depression. It was then said that E. W. was a broken man seen north of town drilling for oil on leased land. Jay was told that E. W. had made a fortune in Pensylvania and lost it. He came to Oklahoma where oil was found in a creek on Indian land near a place called the 101 Ranch (where the black cowboy, William Picket, developed bull dogging for rodeos it was said). It was a good find from which E. W.

built his oil company. When E. W. died his wife moved away; some thought she moved to get away from the sharp wagging tongues. A housing development was built on the east side of the mansion property. Jay and Sandy owned one, and sometimes when Jay came by the artist studio at night, he saw lights on in it. The rumor was that E. W.'s wife had returned and was living in the quarters.

Conoco Tank Farm, formerly E. W. Marland Oil Company

As the story goes around Ponca City, W. had borrowed money from J. P. Morgan in the earlier 1920s to build a forty-acre tank farm of two hundred fifty thousand gallon tanks. He asked J. P. Morgan during the depression to accept interest only on the loan until the depression of 1929 was over; Morgan refused. Morgan had possession of an oil distributing company in Colorado. He combined the company in Colorado with E. W.'s company and called the new company by the name of the company in Colorado, Continental Oil Company. Then, he hired a man from Texas by the name of Don Moore (not his real name). Moore loaded E. W.'s "lieutenants" into a bus and drove them out into the desert. He had a desk in the back and called each back for an interview. If he did not like the answers he got, he stopped the bus and kicked that person off. It is a wonder one of them did not do Moore in.

Another story told Jay was that Moore was walking down through the refinery one day. He came across a man shoveling catalyst beads into a cracker. The cracker, jay was told, cracked heavier oils down into light oils such as gasoline. Moore asked the man what he was doing. The man said, "I ain't got time to talk to you now, ole Moore's coming." Moore said, "I am ole Moore, come go with me." He took the man to his office and promoted him. Another time Moore was walking through the refinery and saw a man sitting on a bucket. Moore kicked the bucket from under the man. That man jumped up and cold cocked Moore stretching him out on the ground. Moore jumped up and yelled to his lieutenants, "I want that man fired! I want him out of here!" His lieutenants said, "You can't fire that man." Moore said, "Why not?" The lieutenants said, "He works for the telephone company." Moore beat it back to his office and called the telephone company. He yelled at the phone company man in charge, "I want that man you sent to the refinery fired!" The telephone executive replied, "I'm not going to fire that man. He's the best worker I have." Moore died of cancer some time later, but left a legacy of weak and mean management according to folks Jay talked with.

A small refinery on the east side of the Continental refinery was eventually absorbed by Continental.

Many who Jay talked with about Marland thought it was an awful thing to happen to E. W. Marland who had worked so hard to develop his oil fields and refinery just to have it all taken away from him. There is a movie about the Marlands called The Ends of the Earth.

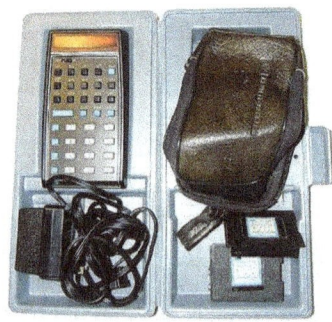

HP 35 Scientific Calculator

Jay's Oklahoma PE Stamp

The only significant industry in Ponca City is the Continental Oil Company. It has now merged with the Phillips Oil Company of Bartlesville, Oklahoma. It is called ConocoPhillips. While Jay was working at the oil company he studied for a professional engineer license examination. The first time he took the day-long test with a slide rule, he did not make it. He studied some more and bought a hand-held calculator, the HP 35 scientific calculator for four hundred dollars. It was one of the first on the market in 1972. It was very instrumental in Jay getting his Oklahoma license. His Oklahoma PE stamp is shown at right with the name modified.

Jay, now in charge of the engine test area after the young man from Pennsylvania resigned, was not as strict with the three technicians running the engine test on the dynamometers as he should have been. Other technicians told Jay they were sometimes forging data. Jay told his boss, who came to the lab with Jay at night to check the data; they found nothing unusual. The lab hired a young Arab to replace the man from Pennsylvania. He was said to be more "show than go."

The refinery workers went on strike and the salaried personnel were used to keep the refinery running. Jay worked on a tall condensing tower. He went to the top to loosen the goose-neck that handled the tower vapors. Then he crawled around on his belly scraping dried residue loose around bubble caps on the capture trays. The crude oil was heated in stainless steel pipes in a gas fired furnace and the vapors were fed into the condensing tower that condensed and separated the liquids into gasoline, fuel oil, etc. The different oils (gasoline components, kerosene, etc.), condensed on the trays and was captured and bled off. The remaining oil components flowed through under the bubble caps covering short stand-pipes used to separate the lighter oils from the heavier ones to the next tray. Each tray was the diameter of the tower and was two feet from the one above. Crawling around on the caps, held in place by sharp thin metal post with pins through the top, was pure torture. A huge vacuum cleaner on a truck had a hose that reached to the top of the high tower. Workers used it to remove the crud they chipped loose. When the hose stopped up, the hose was turned around. This was not an easy job.

Another job Jay did was using hones to clean the pipes approximately three inches in diameter in the catalyst crackers. The hones were air turbine driven. Each cracker had several pipes in them where the oils passed over the catalyst in the pipes. One day several guys were standing around the top of a cracker honing the tubes. The supervisor turned the air pressure too high and the hone Jay was using jumped off. The hose jerked out of Jay's hands and begin to whip around like a mad snake. The guys scattered like flies, but no one was hurt.

One night the pipe to the flare some distance away on a tower was to be closed off. The gas being flared was unwanted butane (highly flammable). Brass tools, used to prevent sparks, were used to separate the pipe at a pipe joint. To close the pipe a "blind", a round flat piece of steel, was inserted between the joint flanges. Butane was fogging down through the refinery area. Jay was nervous hoping that it did not catch fire before the blind stopped the flow. Fortunately, the blind was installed without a fire.

Jay was leery of the chemist he had been warned about, but decided to take two weeks of vacation in California in his sixth year at the oil company. He and Sandy, with her parents from Wichita, went to see Jay's sister in Baker's Field. From there they went to Santa Barbra to see Sandy's sister. They left the parents in Santa Barbra and went to Disneyland in Anaheim. The following day they tried to go to Universal Studios. The traffic was so bad they were frustrated trying to navigate it. After finding themselves off the freeways several times because they could not change lanes when they needed to, they went back to their motel in Anaheim. On TV was a program showing taxi drivers in New York City. They turned on their turn signals, counted to three and changed lanes. The next day Jay employed that technique; it worked.

Upon return to the oil company, Jay found that his job was assigned to the young Arab, who was not trained in supervision or rating engine tests. The old lab Superintendent retired about that time. His replacement was the PhD chemist with a big ego. The problem chemist lost no time getting close to this man. He spent a lot of time in his office giving his version of each member of the lab. His wife made the statement, "My husband is going to be promoted or we'll find out the reason why!" The trouble maker was promoted over others in the lab; he had only a bachelor's degree in chemistry. He was not qualified to be in charge of the other chemist and engineers in the lab, some were PhDs. It was not a happy place to be. The new superintendent was arrogant and did not like taking orders from marketing folks. Marketing ordered the materials they needed to be developed for their marketing outlets through the research and development lab. The superintendent told marketing to "go fly a kite" in so many words.

Jay was notified that he had three months to find another job. The lab personnel were turned upside down by the new superintendent. The PhD chemist Jay reported to was removed from his lead position and the trouble maker was made supervisor over the industrial lube formulation lab as well as the engine oils formulation lab. He was incompetent and the morale of the research lab was destroyed. The new lab superintendent thumbed his nose at the marketing department, the hand feeding the research lab. Marketing closed the lab shortly after Jay left and sent their formulation and testing to Southwest Research Lab in San Antonio.

Jay sent out more than two hundred and fifty resumes without a nibble over the three months he was given to find another job. In the meantime he helped the Arab learn the ropes and helped marketing where he could, especially with their computer programs.

A vendor that came to the lab regularly to sell specialty items such as hose fittings, restrictors, etc. had become acquainted with Jay. He offered to share the territory north of Tulsa with Jay. Jay took him up on his offer and became a tech rep for the products the vendor was selling. Jay went to the aircraft companies in Wichita offering the products.

Jay and Sandy's son was born during this time in Wichita. He was taken by caesarian and was "swimming" on his stomach when Jay first saw him through the window of the cleanup room. The nurse gave him a shot in one of his legs with a syringe that looked like it was as big as those for horses. His leg turned blue, and he yelled loudly. The doctor knew he would probably have to take the baby, named Josh, by caesarian, but decided to allow Sandy to go as far naturally as she could. Jay was there with Sandy in Labor.

He plotted the contractions and predicted the baby would be born at 11:50 a.m., but the progress stopped at 11:30 a.m. and the contractions became farther apart. The nurses, who were monitoring Sandy, came in soon after the contractions changed and took Sandy to the operating room. Jay was not allowed in the room where the operation was taking place.

Jay did not do too well at being a tech rep, but one week while in Wichita, Jay saw an advertisement in a Wichita paper for an engineer in a small company in a small town north of Wichita. He applied and was offered the job. He accepted and became the director of engineering.

Josh Birth Progress

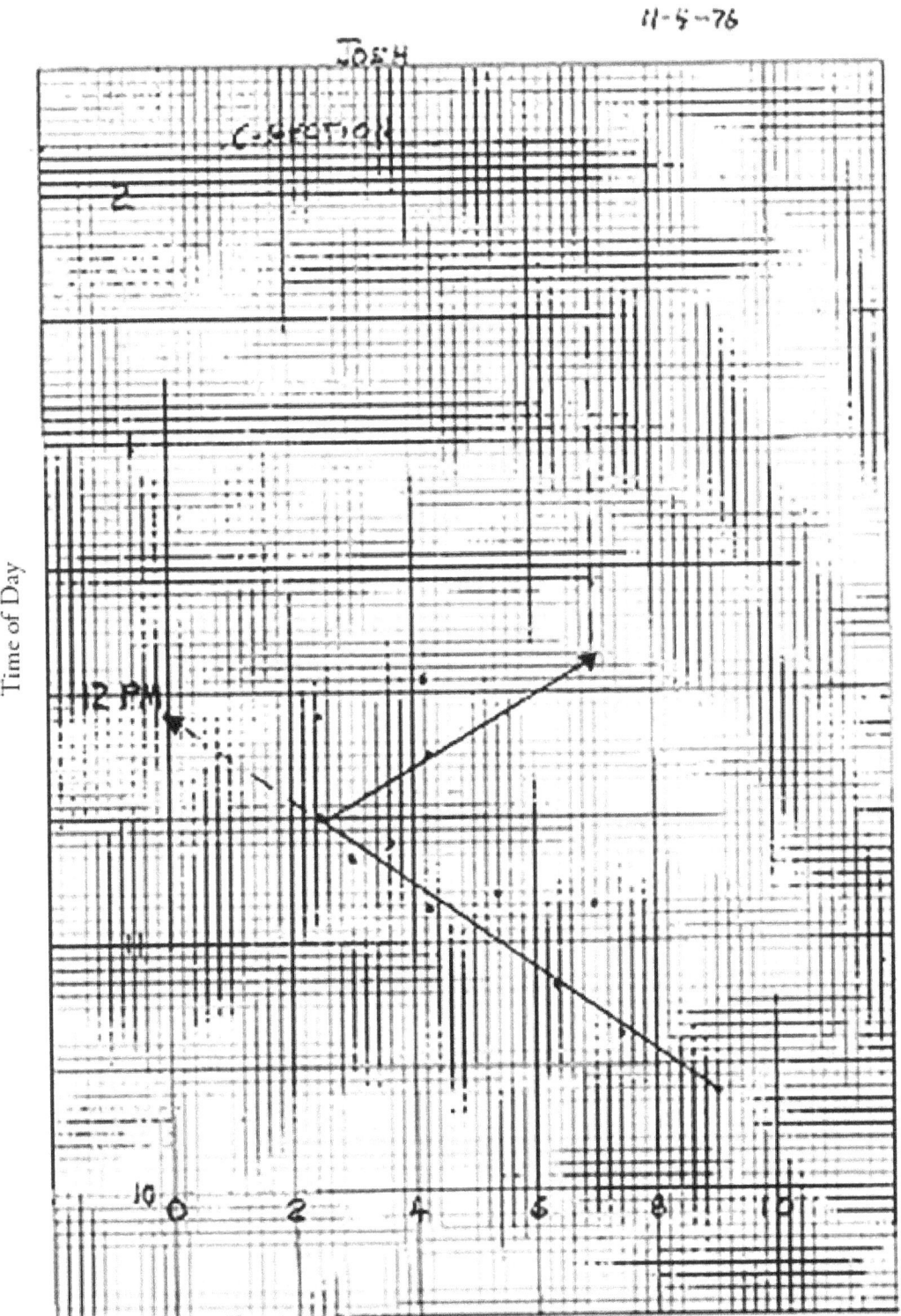

Time Between Contractions - minutes

Chapter 11

Director

Jay and Sandy moved to their new job and a new life. They found a nice house built of masonry blocks in a new housing development. It had a large lot and a large garage. It was built by the developer for himself. It had three bedrooms and a separate office with a safe in the floor.

The pay for the new job was less than Jay was getting at the oil company. However, it was a small company. Money was tight. The benefits were health care insurance and one week vacation each year. The three owners did not pay themselves any more than they paid Jay. The driving distance to work was approximately twelve miles. Jay was expected to be in his office on Saturdays and come in an hour early on Tuesdays. The work days were not limited to eight hours. These things did not bother Jay. He was raised on a farm where the days began at sun up and lasted sometimes into the night. Besides, Jay needed a job.

Being the director of engineering was a fun job. The small company was located on a deserted naval air base maybe forty miles north of Wichita. The town nearby,

Hutchinson, was a quiet little town. It had removed its parking meters in order to get customers to come down town to shop. The shopping centers were drawing their customers away. The hanger of the old airbase served to house the engineering, sales offices, owner's offices, etc. Manufacturing for school buses and wheel chair lifts were on the hangar floor. The earlier small school buses were built on vans. The tops were cut off and a raised top was added. The sides slanted in and were uncomfortable for the older children. The top was rounded and hung over the sides. Another building served as a facility for ambulance manufacturing.

When Jay came aboard, the company president asked engineering to come up with a design that gave straight sides. He wanted to use horse trailer bows down the sides and across the

The Bantam

top; the top was flat like horse trailers. Jay had his design engineers to buy a model of a van. If it was not yellow, paint it yellow and assemble straight sides on the model by cutting the chassis at the outermost line of the bowed sides. Then straight sides were built up from there. The model was built to scale and the plans were laid for the new, small school bus line. It was called the Bantam. The company president, who started the company, instructed Jay to go to Elkhart, Indiana to a horse trailer bows manufacturer and straighten out some problems with the bows that were giving the bus fabricators trouble. He did. Sometime after Jay left the company, the top was rounded because the flat roof was prone to leak. The president had marketed Wayne

President's Original Small School Bus Design

School Buses. He sold new buses to schools and old buses to Mexico. He was asked by his Wayne customers for smaller buses for rural areas. The larger bus companies were not interested in building them, so the president bought a van, put proper markings and lights on it, rigged a school bus handle on the door, put seats in it and sold it to a mid- Kansas school. Other schools were interested, and that is how the small school bus business got started.

The company built wheel chair lifts for buses and vans. The Veteran's Administration (VA) decided to write specifications for the lifts. They wanted to have the same safety factor for the lifts as was required in tall buildings, a safety factor of eight.

Jay went to Washington, D.C. to a hearing on the VA's proposal. He talked with the VA about the wheel chair lift specifications. Jay told the administration folks that a safety factor of eight was impractical.

The lift was designed to accommodate two two-hundred-pound persons, one in the wheelchair and an attendant. A safety factor of eight would mean that the lift would have to be designed and tested to

Wheel Chair Lift

St. Louis on Trip to D.C. With Sandy Looking Out the Front Door of the Ambulance

Sandy and Josh at the Washington Monument

withstand three thousand two hundred pounds load; that would be approaching the weight of the van. A safety factor of two would be more practical since the lift was seldom more than three and a half feet above the ground. The VA agreed.

The company's upper management told Jay to take an ambulance to D.C. and deliver it to a dealer there when he went to see the VA. The route included a detour to Elkhart, Indiana to explain the problems the school bus manufacturing folks were having with the horse trailer bows. The ends were not uniform with the rest of the bows. The bow manufacturer decided to change its press molds to hold the ends uniform. Sandy and six-month-old Josh went with Jay on the trip.

Jay and Sandy had a guaranteed room for late arrival the first night out on the trip with Holiday Inn. They arrived late, and Holiday Inn had given their room away. However, they set up the travelers in the bridal suite. The second night late arrival was guaranteed with Holiday Inn. They gave the room away and would not do anything to accommodate the couple. Jay was furious. He told the night staff that if he was billed for the room, he would press charges. They did not bill him for the lost room. The couple drove a few miles down the and would not do anything to accommodate the couple. Jay was furious. He told the night staff that if he was billed for the room, he would press charges. They did not bill him for the lost room. The couple drove a few miles down the road and stopped at a truck stop where they rented a nice room for less money. Of course, Jay's company was paying the bills.

In DC, the couple stayed in a nice motel in sight of the Pentagon. The next day, they drove the ambulance to New Jersey where Jay visited and toured an ambulance company that built box ambulances on truck frames. The president of the company Jay worked for wanted to see about the possibilities of buying the company to add a truck body ambulance to his line. From there the couple drove into New York City. They parked on the west side of the Empire State Building to check their map. The area looked like a ghetto. Someone came over and knocked on the window. He asked if they needed help. They, then drove around the building and entered the street leading back to the tunnel under the Hudson River to New Jersey. They were immediately caught in stalled traffic. It took a while to move toward the tunnel. Another ambulance was trapped in the traffic. It was sitting stationery with its lights and siren running full power. People came over to the ambulance Jay and Sandy were in. They looked in; Sandy and Josh looked at them. Finally the traffic cleared, and the couple was relieved to leave the area.

Six-Month Old Josh

After the meetings with the VA, Jay delivered the ambulance and rented a car. He loaded his family in it and drove to Richmond, VA. There they talked with Reynolds Aluminum about one forth inch armor plating. Jay's company was asked to consider building an armored vehicle on a van body. The trucks were too heavy and used too much fuel. Jay bought a four-by-eight-foot sheet for research purposes. While there the Reynolds contact took Jay and Sandy on a tour of the plant.

On the flight back from Richmond, six months old Josh was saying, "I" (meaning hi) while looking at the man across the aisle on the plane. The man asked, "Did you say hi?" Josh reached out his arms, and the man took him onto his lap. Josh was passed around the airplane; he liked every one at that stage of his life. Instead of going to the intended route to Chicago, the plane was routed to Atlanta because of storms in the way.

As a sidelight, one of the words Josh at six months was trying to say was a mystery to his parents. He said, "Bawter." Then one day when Josh was looking out the window at the water sprinkler watering the grass, Josh said, "Bawter." Mystery solved. Later, as Josh learned to talk, he said one syllable words such as crack for cracker, pape for paper, cook for cookie, etc.

After a long wait in Atlanta, the plane flew to Chicago. To catch a plane to Kansas City, the couple ran as fast as they could along the long corridors of O'Hara airport with Josh in a back pack on Jay's back. At KC, the couple was put up in a hotel for the night. Their luggage was who knows where. They were short on baby care things; however, it was a short night. They arrived after midnight and caught an early flight to Wichita. One of the engineers drove a company vehicle to the Wichita airport to pick up the weary family. They received their luggage three days later when they drove to Wichita to check on their luggage. The luggage folks said they did not know where the luggage was. Jay spotted it sitting in the unclaimed luggage area. It was a good thing he went to see the luggage folks in person.

A requirement of the ambulances was that they would start in very cold climate, like -10°F. Engineering rented a refrigerator trailer and put an ambulance in it. They put some dry ice in it to help the refrigeration system and let the ambulance cold soak. After the recommended time, the ambulance division manager donned breathing apparatus and started the ambulance easily.

Another requirement was that the ambulance would not overheat with a full load on a five- or six-mile run up hill with all electrical accessories engaged in cold weather. The electrical engineer contacted the Colorado DOT for permission to make a test run up from Vail to the Eisenhower Tunnel with one of the company's ambulances. The electrical engineer and Jay bought two fifty- five-gallon drums and put them in the ambulance.

Then they drove to Denver where they filled the drums with water and bought a set of chains in case the road had a chains only requirement. They drove the required distance up the required 7 percent grade hill from near Vail to the Eisenhower Tunnel. A camcorder monitored the gages and recorded the electrical engineer's comments along the way. The ambulance passed the test in flying colors. At the tunnel the ambulance was pulled over in a place where the snow had been shoved back, and the water in the drums was poured out such that it did not run out on the road. With the lights off, the siren silenced and the vehicle stopped to off load the water, the personnel at the tunnel came running to see if the ambulance had stalled with an emergency patient aboard. When they heard the explanation, they were dumbfounded. They had not been alerted about the test by the Colorado DOT. The drums were set out on the other side of the tunnel at a roadside park where there were other drums for trash collection. The ambulance was turned over to the manager of sales to deliver to a customer somewhere up north of Denver. The two engineers caught a plane and flew back home.

The wheelchair lifts were well designed by the company before Jay arrived. They did have a problem in that they had a tendency to bleed down while in the folded position; when they bled down they pushed the side doors of the vans open somewhat. The president stopped production and told engineering to fix the problem. Jay and the manufacturing manager went to Cessna, the hydraulic actuator manufacturer, to see if they knew why the hydraulic cylinders leaked down. Cessna said they knew exactly what the problem was. The original a very good young mechanical person to help. The electrical engineer had a good idea; he would put a limit switch on the lift that would run the lift back up when it bleed down a given amount. Jay asked the shop fellow to weld a rod to the cam operating the unfolding of the lift's platform. He asked that the rods be bent such that they hooked under the platform's folding support shaft when the platform was folded in its stored position. It worked. The two ideas were presented to the three owners of the company, the president, vice president and the purchasing manager. They chose the mechanical fix. The manufacturing person who worked with engineering, flame cut a cam with a hook on it and tried it on the lift. It worked. Another company was manufacturing the cams. Jay took a lift to their place of business and helped them to set up their pattern to cut the cams. Once the pattern was right, many were made. The customer service representative sent the cams to the distributers for replacement in the field. Later, the customer service rep suggested a block be welded on the cams to better lock the platform in place. That was incorporated.

Another problem the lift had was to chatter sometimes on the way down, especially on a hot day. Also, the lift would lock up and not open when it had been heat soaked on a very hot day. Jay was sent to Chicago to meet with a distributer to see for himself what was happening. Then Jay and a purchasing agent, a good friend, took a pump to the agent's house and studied it as well as the drawings. It became clear what was happening. The lift was outrunning the oil on the way down. The oil in the bottom part of the cylinder needed a restrictor to keep the lift going down at a slower and steady pace. The restrictor worked. It was installed such that the oil in the bottom of the cylinder would not lock the lift in the up position on a hot day as it expanded.

A school bus from Wayne arrived one day on the premises. The president called his management team together in the bus and examined it to see if there was anything that they were doing that would help his products. A panel along worked. It was installed such that the oil in the bottom of the cylinder would not lock the lift in the up position on a hot day as it expanded.

A school bus from Wayne arrived one day on the premises. The president called his management team together in the bus and examined it to see if there was anything that they were doing that would help his products. A panel along the side was opened, and Jay saw that the wires were numbered. Those of Jay's company were color coded. The electrical engineer had seen a numbering machine at Boeing's surplus store in Wichita earlier and suggested to Jay that the company should buy one. Jay spoke up and said that would help our work if we could get away from color coding and go to numbering. The vice president jumped all over Jay telling him that the company could not afford every idea that engineering came up with. The president spoke up and said to the vice president, "Damn it, Lee, you have enough color coded wire of different sizes to buy a bunch of wire numbering machines." After the meeting, the vice president told Jay to stay behind; he wanted to talk to him. Jay thought to himself, "I'm fired." When the others were gone the vice president told Jay, "How fast can you get that machine up here?" Jay lost no time having his electrical engineer get the machine. Now, only different sizes of white wire were kept in the electrical loft.

The company's president decided to build ambulances on vans to give paramedics a much bigger area to work in on critical patients. Most ambulances were hearses or made from same. Vans were not long enough to accommodate the gurneys and other equipment. Two feet were added to the rear of the vans by the ambulance department. There is a Truck Bodies Association for manufacturers of equipment on truck bodies. The association set up a trip for Jay to go to Chrysler's proving ground to see their new stretched van that would accommodate the ambulance manufacturing. They simply added two feet to the length of the standard van.

The electrical system was a big problem to the ambulance team. Sometimes drivers for sales companies had to wait for several days at the plant while shorts and open circuit problems could be resolved. Wires ran in all directions within the inner walls; they were constantly being pinched and drilled into. They were wired with color coded wires, but when the right color was not available, some other color wire of the same size was used making tracing wires extremely difficult. Also, the accessories for the ambulances, the sirens, lights, power outlets, etc. were run through power switches over the driver's head. They were big and awkward for the driver to locate while driving. Sometimes they fell down because the anchor points were not strong. The president wanted engineering to come up with something more user friendly. At first a pedestal between the driver and passenger was considered. Nobody liked that idea. Then, the electrical engineer came up with a brilliant idea. He would bundle all wires with pigtails for the accessories according to their location. The wires would be numbered by the numbering machine. The drawings would be changed to reflect numbering. The power to each accessory was to be handled by a relay in a box behind the driver's head. The relays were operated by miniature switches mounted on the dash in the driver's view at all times. The switches had tiny LED indicators to show green when on and red when off for each switch. The relays in the box behind the driver were all alike; if one failed on a run, a less needed one could be exchanged until the bad one could be replaced. On the electrical loft, the electrical engineer set up a test stand with simulated loads for the accessories; every wiring harness was to be proven before going to the ambulance. A pilot of this system was set up and demonstrated to the upper management. They liked it, and it was put into production. Electrical problems on the production line came to a screeching halt. Marketing showed an ambulance with the new electrical system at an ambulance show, and soon other manufacturers were using the design.

The president decided to buy a fire truck company. He wanted to build a plain Jane truck that small towns could afford. A company was for sale in Battle Creek, Michigan. The president sent Jay, the head of manufacturing and the head of the ambulance division to look at the drawings, parts equipment, etc. The president and the other two owners had been there already and the fire truck company owner asked $225,000 for the name, drawings and parts or equipment. Jay saw that the drawings were not up to snuff. The parts were obsolete for what the company needed. He felt the price was a bit much. When they got back, a meeting of the managers was held in the president's office. In the middle of the meeting, Jay was called out to meet with a Cessna person who had modified the lift electromechanical actuating system for the wheel chair lift somewhat. It met requirements. Jay returned to the meeting to find it had broken up. He told the president what he thought. The fire truck company owner had taken the three who went to evaluate the company out to dinner one night, and let it be known, perhaps not on purpose, that he needed money right away. Jay told the president that he felt that the fire truck company owner would take $190,000 if the president would offer more down-payment up front. The three owners went back to Michigan to deal with the fire truck owner. The president offered more money up front and held the total to $190,000. The fire truck company owner begged the president to give more, but the president held firm. As the president and the other two owners were sitting at the airport waiting for their plane the begging continued. The president went to the bathroom and the fire truck man followed. As they were holding themselves at the urinals, the fire truck owner gave in. They shook with their free hands.

The president decided to build a brush-fire fire truck on a pickup. He had the production department build it without asking engineering. It was a good idea that did not work. Water weighs over eight pounds per gallon. The two-hundred-gallon tank they used weighed more than sixteen hundred pounds. That, along with the pump, hose, and etc. overloaded the design of the brakes of the pickup. Engineering told the president of the problem. A short

Brush Fire Truck with Josh

time later, fire alongside of a nearby road was discovered. The ambulance supervisor and the director of engineering (Jay) responded with the original brush-fire truck.

They realized that engineering was correct. The truck was hardly controllable, especially around corners and when braking. A smaller version was constructed within the design limits.

The 1978 Federal Government released a set of safety requirements for school buses. Special seats spaced a prescribed distance apart were required, and the backs had to be padded as prescribed. They had to bend a set amount at the top when a given load was applied. Each seat had to be anchored per Federal regulations. The company president simply purchased his seats from the Wayne School Bus Company, whom he had worked with in the past before starting his own company.

President

In 1978, Federal school bus regulations that included roll- over protection were established. For small school buses, loading of the roof could be tested with a flat plate. The following photographs show the Bantam school bus under roll-over test. The first is of the company president addressing the engineering team, including its R&D department. The next photograph is of the president, Jay, technicians and an independent registered professional engineer. The test was completely successful.

Small school buses could be tested by simply loading the top with a load equal to the weight of the loaded bus and a margin-of-safety extra weight. The research department built a steel platform that covered the top of the bus. The four corners were supported by four-inch-by-four-inch square tubes with hydraulic cylinders inside of them. The company could not afford instrumentation to measure the load on Small school buses could be tested by simply loading the top with a load equal to the weight of the loaded bus and a margin-of-safety extra weight. The research department built a steel platform that covered the top of the bus. The four corners were supported by four-inch-by-four-inch square tubes with hydraulic cylinders inside of them. The company could not afford instrumentation to measure the load on the cylinders; therefore, a pressure gage was attached to the hydraulic lines to the cylinders. Camcorders (some borrowed and some rented) were stationed at each corner to record the pressure of the fluid in each cylinder. The load was calculated by the amount of pressure in each cylinder times its cross sectional area. The calculated loads were added together to find the total load. The system was calibrated by weighing each person invited to load the top plate and then placing them equal-distance apart on the plate. Enough people were placed on the plate to equal a calculated load to the top of the bus. The actual load was compared to the calculated load in the presence of a registered professional engineer (PE). The comparison was very good and was signed off by the PE. In the photograph at right, the person with his face showing at the right side of the photograph is the PE looking to his left with Jay in the middle looking to his right facing the PE. The president is at the far left of the picture looking to his right.

Bantam under Roll-over test

A bus was then tested with the plate applying the required load. The bus passed the test with "flying colors." All of the doors opened easily with the load applied. No windows were broken, though the top of the bus was distorted somewhat. All of the calibration and testing was recorded on VHS tape. The Tapes were spliced together by the electrical engineer, who had been a radio announcer, narrating. The president wanted the test shown the Department of Transportation (DOT) in Washington, DC. Jay and one of his engineering staff prepared a presentation for the U.S. DOT. They took the tape and a projector, along with their luggage, and flew to Dulles Airport in Washington.

The DOT brought several of their people to the meeting. Some "heavyweights" were in attendance. They were concerned about how much economic burden the new regulations placed on bus manufacturers. The tapes were shown and questions answered afterwards. One young DOT person asked about the "load cells." He was told that load cells (devices to measure the load on each mount of the load platform) were not available. The next best thing, measuring the pressure in the load-application hydraulic cylinders and calculating the loads from that was the method of determining the load on the bus top. He persisted until Jay and his engineer realized that he was questioning about the cylinders. They surmised that the young man was not familiar with load cells. The presentation went well.

On the flight from Dulles the two engineers were fed a large dinner. They changed planes in Atlanta and were fed a large dinner on the next flight. They ate their fill that evening.

The owner of the company bought some old cars at an auction in Kansas City. He wanted some of his salaried staff to go with him to KC and drive the cars back to the company site. Jay went, and on the way home they came upon an accident. A woman had driven onto the highway through a red light and a truck hit her station wagon car. It had knocked a young boy out the back window that was down, and the truck ran over him. He lay in a thin mass on the middle of the highway. Someone had covered him with their coat. The semitruck with a pup trailer lay in the ditch upside down with the driver trapped inside. A baby was being resuscitated beside the road by a paramedic. He died at the scene. Jay and a purchasing agent went to the passenger door of the car which was still upright. The mother of the lady driving the station wagon was severely wounded. She had glass in her eyes and her right arm was broken at the wrist and was at ninety degrees to her arm. Jay and the purchasing agent grabbed a bar from the ambulance (an ambulance made by the company the two worked for) and tried to pry the door open (it refused to open by the handle), but it would not give. After the prying they again tried the handle, and the door then opened. They helped the lady from the car and put her on a stretcher. More help arrived and took over. Some were trying to get the truck driver out, and others were helping the car driver, who was in shock. One of two pups in a cage wrist and was at ninety degrees to her arm. Jay and the purchasing agent grabbed a bar from the ambulance (an ambulance made by the company the two worked for) and tried to pry the door open (it refused to open by the handle), but it would not give. After the prying they again tried the handle, and the door then opened. They helped the lady from the car and put her on a stretcher. More help arrived and took over. Some were trying to get the truck driver out, and others were helping the car driver, who was in shock. One of two pups in a cage in the back of the car was yelping in extreme pain. His leg was caught in the wire cage and he was hanging upside down. The purchasing agent and Jay rescued the pup before going on with the different cars they were driving.

The president told engineering to fabricate a ten feet wide and thirty feet high frame made of I-beams with six inch webs and flanges. It was three-eighths inches thick. The sign was to have its legs ten feet in concrete and ten feet ground clearance. The day that the sign rigging was to be installed in the ground, a back hoe dug the holes for the legs. A crane was called from the local town. They brought a truck with a crane on it and with outriggers. The truck was parked alongside the road lengthwise to the sign. The outriggers could not hold the truck. Above the sign location was a highline with several thousand volts in the wires. The sign frame was heavy.

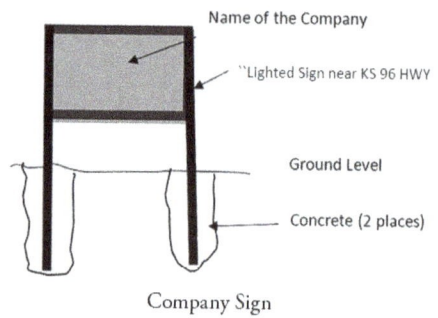

Name of the Company

"Lighted Sign near KS 96 HWY

Ground Level

Concrete (2 places)

Company Sign

The frame was hauled to the site on a trailer. The company owned a small crane.

Three concrete trucks were standing by. The crane on the truck, similar to the one in the photograph at right, was attached to the top of the sign frame. The small crane was attached to one of the legs to steady it.

The truck crane lifted the frame above the height of the highline. The holes for the sign were about ten feet closer to the highway than the highline. The truck with the crane tipped and the crane fell into the highline. Sparks flew. One of the legs of the frame was resting on the road's asphalt. The asphalt melted as the current poured into the ground. The truck driver took off running into the adjoining field when the truck began to tip. The driver on the small crane was in a precarious position. Jay, who was responsible for the overall situation was afraid the driver on the small crane would panic and step off the rubber tired crane. He ran to the small crane yelling for the driver

Truck with crane on it

to stay put. The driver climbed upon a tire and jumped as far as he could. He was safe. Jay sent word to the power company to turn off the power. Then the small crane pulled the truck away from the wires. The crane company sent out a much larger crane somewhat like the one in the photograph at the top of the next page. It handled the sign frame easily. It set the frame into the holes where heavy wire was set around each leg to reinforce the concrete. Then the concrete was poured. The power company sent a repair truck out to repair the damaged wire that had been in contact with the crane. A strand or two of power line cable had been severed. They spliced the damaged area.

The company president went on a trip the morning of the frame installation. He was well pleased that evening to find the job completed when he returned. It gave him confidence in his employees.

The sign itself was painted by professional sign painters on two-foot panels with the edges bent 90° for stiffening.

The panels were of twelve-gauge steel. When the frame was well set in the concrete, the panels were bolted to the frame. It turned out to be a very nice sign at the corner of the intersection of a state highway and the road leading to the company.

Large Crane Mounted on Truck

The back road to the manufacturing plant, the old abandoned Naval Aviation base, was treacherous. The village nearby was an Amish town. One late evening, a farmer was going home on his wagon with a hay rack on it when a vehicle running at high speed ran under the wagon and broke the back legs of the horses. Another time, a motorcycle rider was passing a car when he met a car going the opposite direction. The motor cycle rider went into the ditch on the a very nice sign at the corner of the intersection of a state highway and the road leading to the company.

The back road to the manufacturing plant, the old abandoned Naval Aviation base, was treacherous. The village nearby was an Amish town. One late evening, a farmer was going home on his wagon with a hay rack on it when a vehicle running at high speed ran under the wagon and broke the back legs of the horses. Another time, a motorcycle rider was passing a car when he met a car going the opposite direction. The motor cycle rider went into the ditch on the left hand side of the road, lost control, slid down a barbed wire fence, which acted like a saw on his neck.

Sandy's mother and father

Sandy's kin from Wichita came to see Jay and Sandy's family from time to time. It was a pleasure to have them. Jay had said that he did not feel it necessary to sacrifice to go see anyone who was not interested in coming to see him. That may have had some influence on visits. Regardless, the visits were appreciated and enjoyable.

The highlight while Jay was working at this company as director of engineering was a visit by Jay's three sisters from Joe's first family. Jay had three sisters from his immediate family, but none ever came to visit him. Needless to say, jay dearly loved the three who came to see him and Sandy.

Three Sweet Sisters

In the photograph at the right are of Jay's sisters from Joe's first Family. The picture was taken in 1977. From left to right are Olla, Lou and Vera. They were among the few of Jay's favorite people. They are of Jay's family who cared enough to come to see him. They are gone now and are missed. Jay thinks of them often. Sandy's parents are also gone.

There came a time when the personnel director thought the management team should go through a "take-em-apart-and-put-em-back-together-again" course. Jay had been through several of those already and did not want to go through another. It was a fad then for organizations to develop those things and sell them to companies. The electrical engineer, who had done so well, married the company's front office secretary and had taken a job at the nuclear weapons manufacturing plant in Kansas City. His job was field representative for the company. He had contacted Jay and said, "Boss, you should put in an application for a job here. The pay is good and they have excellent benefits." Jay was mulling it over in the back of his mind. The course was the straw that decided Jay to look into it. He sent in an application and received a letter back telling Jay that he did not qualify because only citizens of the United States could work there. Jay quickly corrected their mistake. He received an offer which was one and a half times the salary he was getting plus 33 percent of his salary in benefits. They gave him three weeks of vacation to start and

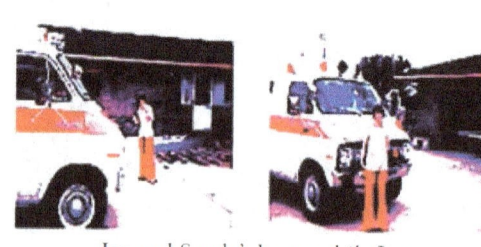

Jay and Sandy's home while Jay was Director of Engineering

another day of vacation each month up to five more days during the first year. Jay could not turn that down. He dearly loved his work at the place he was working in, but was not sure if the company would grow. It did. Looking back, Jay could possibly have become manager of one of the branch manufacturing companies such as one in Dallas or one in Florida.

The big job in moving to Kansas City was to sell the house that the couple had bought two years earlier. It was a nice house and Jay's family enjoyed it.Sandy stayed in the house until it sold. They were satisfied with the price and they rented a house in

Kansas City while trying to find a house to buy. Jay's philosophy was that engineers had to go where the work is. He looked forward to the new job.

Jay had bought a small Ford Courier to cut down on the cost of driving a big car to work. The truck was made by Mazda of Japan. Jay called it his "slant-eyed Ford truck." It was very light with thin medal construction. He undercoated it heavily at the bus plant. That was a mistake because the heavy undercoating dried and cracked leaving access for water and salt to attack the frame parts. It detached itself from the metal leaving a trap for the salt water to be held next to the metal.

1977 Ford Courier Pickup with Large Boat

Jay pulled his eighteen-foot boat with it; the boat looked bigger than the truck. Later, he bought a Suburban to pull the boat and other uses.

Suburban and Boat

Jay had stored his red 1966 Impala Chevrolet in the old Olympic-size swimming pool that the navy had for its cadets. The company owner had knocked out the wall at one end for vehicle entrance and had stored his large collection of old cars there. Jay had brought the Impala home when he left the company. The red car was bought new by Jay just west of Oklahoma City and was used primarily on trips. It was garaged always while another old car was used by Jay to get around locally.

1966 Chevrolet Impala

A short time after Jay left the company for the job in KC, the old, large wooden hanger burned down. It housed Engineering in the loft near the electrical wire-bundling department for buses and ambulances, the bus manufacturing line, the wheelchair lift manufacturing area as well as parts storage. The building was insured and the company recovered fairly quickly. Some of the files in engineering were salvaged with only scorched edges. Even though the file cabinets were not fire resistant, the packed files resisted burning. There was a pot that was heated most of the time keeping a plastic dip for manufacturing line, the wheelchair lift manufacturing area as well as parts storage. The building was insured and the company recovered fairly quickly. Some of the files in engineering were salvaged with only scorched edges. Even though the file cabinets were not

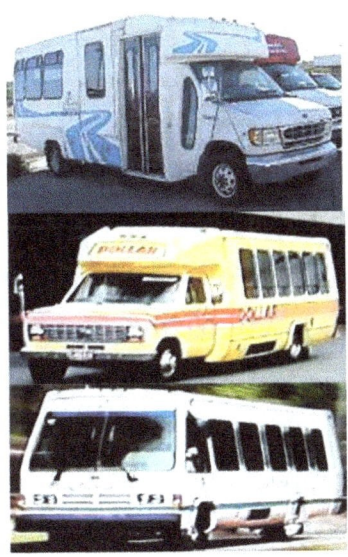

Commercial Buses

fire resistant, the packed files resisted burning. There was a pot that was heated most of the time keeping a plastic dip for handles for doors, etc., ready for use. It was thought it overheated when no one was around and burst into flames which set the hangar on fire.

It looked as if the company might not survive; however it did, and now has branches in Dallas and Florida. It has added a switch engine type of vehicle for railroad cars and a commercial bus line. The commercial buses are for shuttling people to and from parking lots at airports, etc.

When Jay was at the oil company he became a member of the Society of Automotive Engineers (SAE). The research lab personnel were all members; their membership was paid for by the oil company. They drove to Tulsa once a month for a regularly scheduled meeting. One year Jay was elected entertainment chairman. Now Jay was not a drinker, but he was in charge of the liquor for the meetings and kept it at his house between meetings. He knew nothing about mixing drinks and wound up mixing them too strong. The chairman of the chapter at that time became intoxicated and broke a glass with a spoon trying to call the meeting to order. Someone else took over the meeting. Jay was told later that the drunken chairman's boss was there and fired the guy for getting drunk.

Jay was still entertainment chairmen when he took the director of engineering job. He had one last meeting to cover to finish his tour. He and his him called the flight service station advising them that we were having some engine problems. They followed the I-35 highway and babied the engine, though it was running normal after the sputter. The smart thing would have been to turn back and set down for an engine check. They could see the glow of Wichita. They made it a point to pass by Wichita well west of the international airport. They arrived at their destination without further incident.

Looking back, Jay felt privileged to have worked as the director of engineer for the company. How many employees get to make trips with the President and CEO of a company? One time, Jay went with the CEO to the Wayne School Bus Company's plant to observe how the big buses are made. The CEO had sold Wayne buses before forming his own company. Another time Jay, the CEO and the director of sales went to a school bus convention in Dallas together. That was an interesting trip. Many times Jay wished he had stayed with that company.

The engineer that took Jay's place did well. He wound up being paid considerably more than Jay after a few short years as the company expanded rapidly. There was a time when the CEO's two sons came to work for the company. They got cross-wise with the stock exchange folks and slowed down progress, but they did recover from the problem.

The CEO had been a pastor of a large church in OKC. He and his wife had three children, two sons and a daughter. The CEO's wife ran off with a doctor in the church congregation, as the story goes. She was said to have been very attractive.

Jay wishes the best for that company, which has grown significantly.

Chapter 12

Nuclear Weapons

Nuclear Weapons Plant

The nuclear weapons plant was huge. It was eighty acres under one concrete roof. It was built in the 1940s for production of the Pratt-Whitney engines for the B-29 bombers. The roof was concrete to minimize bomb damage in case of an attack. Steel was in short supply at that time so the roof was of the gothic design (arched).

Eighty-five percent of each nuclear weapon was said to have been manufactured here. The plant closed when a new facility under construction became ready.

Jay arrived in February 1979 to begin his work as a nuclear scientist. He vowed this would be his last job because he wanted to give two-year-old Josh stability in his life. As a rule, engineers had to go where the work is. Jay had moved from five different cities before coming to Kansas City (KC). He wanted to settle down there.

The first thing to do was to find a house. Jay looked around the south part of KC and found only new houses made of "paper." The houses were made with pressed paper siding and slats covering the cracks. It was called bat and boards. Jay was used to masonry housing and would not accept the paper. He rented a house on Seventy-Sixth Street in Kansas City, Kansas. Seventy-Fifth Street was a busy street through the area. The house had a basement, three bedrooms and a fireplace in the living room. It had one single car garage; the red 1966 Chevy was stored in an old turkey barn in the northwest part of greater Kansas City; several old cars were stored there. The 1972 Tornado was parked in the garage. The Courier pickup was parked on the driveway. The house sat on a small lot. Most of the belongings were in boxes in the basement, which was full of bugs and spiders. Jay sprayed the basement but never got rid of the bugs.

When Jay started his work at the weapons facility, he was placed in what was known as the "red badge area." That was a holding area where new employees spent their days until the security people checked their backgrounds to be sure they were trustworthy. Some folks spent months there, others weeks. Employees must have a Q clearance to work inside the plant. There was one fellow of African descent that had gone to Africa on visits. He had been in the red badge area for nearly a year. Some started their clearances before they came to work and cleared in a short time. Jay had secret clearances with the aircraft companies he worked for. That may have helped.

The black dog, named Jig, was killed by a big dog in the last place where Jay and Sandy lived. The dogs were chasing a female in heat. Jig was getting old; a big dog crushed his voice box. The black cat, named George, moved with the family. He was harassed by another cat that claimed the territory on 76th street. One day George had his fill and worked the other cat over good. From then on there was peace in the cat kingdom. The cat ran some squirrels out of the backyard, also.

Meantime, Jay and Sandy looked for housing. Jay knew that it was desirable to live on the east side of the work place because it was difficult driving into the sun in the mornings, especially in the wintertime. They lived in the rental house in Kansas on the west side of the work place, which was in Missouri. Everywhere they looked east of the plant was too high, too ghetto, or were of paper construction. They found a new development in a suburb SE of the plant. It was fairly close and had back roads to the plant so that the crowded freeway would not have to be used to get to work. They bought a corner lot and had the builder build a house for them. They asked the developer/builder to leave a brick ledge on the foundation so that they could brick the house later. The house cost approximately seventy five thousand dollars.

Front and Interior of New House

Backyard Patio

The builder said, "I will brick the house for another three thousand dollars." The couple took him up on it. Also, the house was to have a walk-out basement. Jay had heard too many horror stories of basements flooding. The extra wide garage was under the house which was high on the West side. The garage, then, was part of the basement. The basement was large even at that. Any flooding could run out through the garage. The house had a hip roof; no gables. The builder built one more brick house in the development after that. He said he had a hard time selling it; people are like cows following each other around; they were brainwashed into believing paper siding was the better way to go. There were many law suits, it was said, over failure of the painted paper to endure.

Jay and Sandy's family watched as their house was being built. They were buying the house with a VA loan. Carter was president and inflation was rampant as high as 23 percent. The couple was able to lock in at 11.5 percent.

Ye Olde Cat house

They planned to refinance when and if the interest rates went down. Fortunately, rates did go down when Ronald Reagan became president. He "held the course," as he put it, and things did get better. With Reagan at the helm, the economy was straightened up and held for years after his presidency was over. Jay was well pleased with President Reagan.

The basement was finished by Jay and Josh with the fireplace of the same brick and design as the fireplace in the living room.

The cat house had a carpeted living area and a screened-in eating/protection area. One side of the roof lifted up for feeding and servicing.

The entrance door and center section door were each swinging doors for entrance and exit. It sat on a four-inch-by-four-inch post the same height as the back-rest on the deck benches. The cat loved it.

The new job presented new employees with different medical plans. One was an HMO that cost nothing to the employee. It had its own building and medical staff. The couple selected that one. Shortly thereafter , Sandy accidently kicked a bag of trash with a sharp can lid in it one morning. It cut her toe severely. Sandy called Jay at work; he came home and called the HMO with the urgent need for medical attention. He was told that they would have to wait until the HMO opened at noon. When Sandy was taken to the HMO at noon, a young doctor on the staff said that he could not sew up the wound because the couple had waited too long, and the wound had swollen. He bound the cut and sent Sandy and Jay on their way. At the HMO, there was no choice of doctors for the patients. Another time soon after the first incident, Sandy took Josh in for something. She checked in and waited for hours to be seen by a doctor. That did it. The couple changed to a better insurance the company offered. This insurance required the employee to pay part of the premium, but the patients could choose their doctors. It was a much better service.

The family spent the first year in KC, looking for a suitable house before having the new house built. Jay had been exposed to very loud machinery, along with lots of dirt, insects that tried to crawl into his ears, and, etc., when he lived on the farm. His hearing was impaired. Sandy was always saying, "Turn that TV down. The neighbors will complain." Jay told Sandy she had worn out his eardrums with her constant chatter. After Jay had been at Bendix for a year, his insurance would cover medical help for his hearing loss. A fellow engineer in materials testing had hearing problems and recommended an ear doctor that might help Jay. He went to the suggested ear doctor and took a hearing test on both ears. The doctor had said that if there was a lot of nerve damage he could not help. However, the test showed that there was a difference between the direct nerve response and response on the ear drum. First the sound technician placed ear muffs on Jay's ears and measured Jay's response to the different frequencies sent by the sound man on each ear drum. Then he put a sound device on the bone behind the ear to measure the direct nerve response. They were both plotted on a graph. Had the two lines for each ear been close or on top of each other, the problem would have been nerve damage.

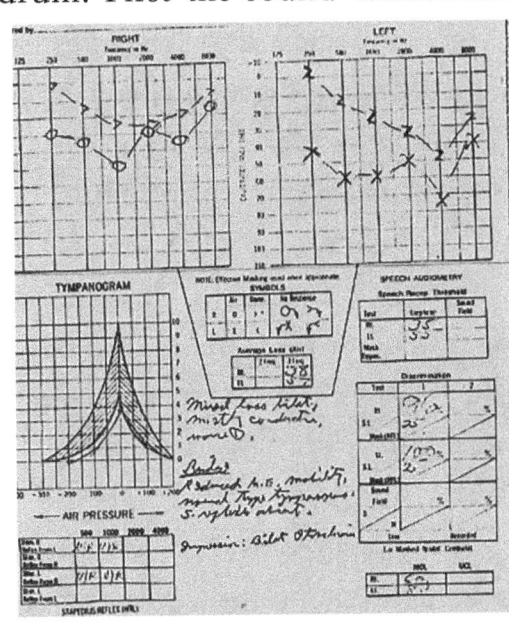

Jay's Hearing Test Results

The two graphs show there is hearing loss not due to nerve damage except at approximately two thousand Hertz (cycles per second). The area of the nerve damage was said to be in the range of women's voices; Jay thought that was OK. The right ear was selected for the first operation. To operate, the surgeon cut around the eardrum in the fleshy area and lay the ear drum back. Then he cut off the footplate of stapes (stirrup) attached to the inner ear. The footplate of stapes attachment on the inner ear had become incrusted with a stiff substance (plaque). After that he cut two strips of cartilage from the outer lobe at the ear canal entrance. The two were used for a seal on the inner ear. A stainless steel device that looks like a short nail with a bail on its head is used to replace the footplate of stapes and is inserted through the seal on the inner ear. The two strips of cartilage are sewed together around the pin and to the surface of the inner ear. It is all done through the ear canal with a microscope and precise instruments.

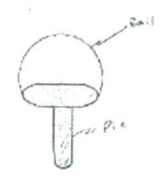

Sketch of Pin with Bail

The right ear operation was successful. Jay spent one night in the hospital and was allowed to go home. He should have spent some time in bed. He was told not to lift anything heavy. However, after a few days, he began to move around too much. He developed vertigo, vomiting and losing body fluids through the vomiting and diarrhea. His boss gave him a week off for sick leave. He tried to do some work he had been assigned; the process of studying and writing aggravated the vertigo. No water or food would stay down. The situation quickly caused dehydration. Jay could not stand. With help he was taken to the hospital emergency room in the hospital where he had the operation. The hospital was full, but Jay was stabilized and sent to the Jewish hospital in KC.

He recovered overnight on water applied IV and a shot to stop the vertigo. The doctor who performed the operation came by the next day and scolded Jay for being too strenuous in activity. He thought Jay had torn the stitches loose.

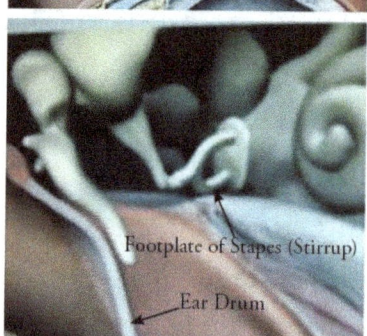

Footplate of Stapes (Stirrup)

Ear Drum

Cut-Away Drawings of Human Ear

Activity was not the problem as much as the studying was, and the stitches were fine. The ear healed quickly and was tested for correction. It had an over correction and was sensitive to loud sounds for a while. The other ear was operated on a year later and was successful, also. Even so, the hearing deteriorates after several years; a hearing aid helps after thirty years or so.

Jay is unique in that he was a bar tender working his way through college for a short time. He served as entertainment chairman for the Tulsa SAE chapter serving alcoholic beverages at monthly meetings though he did not drink (he did not like the taste of alcohol, or coffee either for that matter). And he served as church librarian though he did not like to read (he was burned out reading in college; he is a slow reader and reads only when he sees it necessary). He has controlled the sound systems in churches even though his hearing is not as good as it could be. Sandy, Jay's wife, has excellent hearing like a rabbit. If she claimed to hear a fly walking on the neighbor's roof, Jay might be inclined to believe it. Sometimes excellent hearing is a handicap; she is sometimes awaken at night by a passing car or noisy coyotes.

The first assignment for Jay at the Kansas City Plant (KCP) was in the materials testing area. His desk was located among the test machines. Jay developed a cough that was not serious, but it was irritating because he coughed when he tried to talk. As time went by, the cough improved somewhat when Jay moved from the test area into the upper office area. It remained a problem until one winter when Jay was running in cold weather. It became considerably worse along with wheezing. The doctor who diagnosed the problem called it asthma and treated it accordingly. Asthma medicines never worked very well, and treatment for asthma continued for the rest of the time Jay worked for the weapons plant. Many others at the KCP had pulmonary problems. One that Jay worked with is now on oxygen. There were more than eight hundred chemicals used there.

When Jay entered the work force in KC, there were two other new hire engineers working in the same test area. They were young and not long out of school. The three soon realized that the supervisor they were working for was doing things he should not have. The supervisor was using funds for a project to buy computer equipment instead of what it was authorized for among other things. The three knew they did not want to work in that department anymore. They met at one of the three's house and talked about what to do. All three had interviewed with another supervisor, Tim, at the time they hired in. The decision was to talk with him to see if he could use them. Jay cautioned the other two that management does not like to be told they have made a mistake; they hold grudges. They fear "whistle blowers." However, they agreed to go through with it. Management is the weak link in any organization, always.

After being contacted by the three, Tim told his superiors that there was a problem in its management over in the Test Lab. Upper management called in the three and quizzed them about the problem. The three wanted to be transferred to another department. Upper management asked if they would stay if the problem was fixed. Jay said he would prefer to work in another department. Another supervisor who had worked under the dishonest supervisor at one time confirmed what the three were saying was true. The supervisor in question was relieved of his command the same day and demoted to a working engineer. Some years later he got a patent and was promoted again to his original rank though not in materials testing.

One of the other two engineers, the one that was the valedictorian of his college classes, was looking into the Christian faith. He had been raised a Roman Catholic but was not satisfied with it. He was looking for a church that more closely held to his views of Bible teaching. He had investigated several Christian denominations and some cult type teachings. He revived the Christian spirit in Jay and directed him to books on religions such as one entitled The Kingdom of the Cults14. Jay knew that Christianity is not like other religions; it is a relationship with the Lord. Jay became active in a Baptist Church, sang in the choir, became the director of the Bus Ministry and became a deacon in the church. He studied the Christian faith in earnest. After becoming a deacon, he was elected to be the chairman of the twenty-three-member deacon body.

The church had a membership of approximately one thousand four hundred, though only approximately one-third ever showed up for services. The church had a family care ministry. Each deacon was assigned several families he was supposed to visit at the beginning of the year that they were assigned to him. He was to be available to help out in any matters that pertained to the Christian faith and be an extension of the Pastor. It did not work well; one big reason was that women usually came to church without their husbands and did not want strange men coming to their homes. They would have to explain to their husbands who were not too keen about what was happening. When a new pastor with a doctorate degree became the pastor, he did away with the family care ministry.

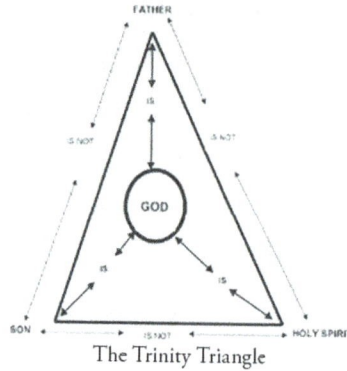

The Trinity Triangle

Jay never fully understood the trinity. See the diagram at right. Jay likened it to a company: one is CEO, one is supply manager and the other is the Operations manager with all equal owners.

Jay never fully understood the trinity. See the diagram at right. Jay likened it to a company: one is CEO, one is supply manager and the other is the Operations manager with all equal owners. That's an attempt to understand it but by no means comparing God to man.

Jay played in a gospel band, known as the Followers, which sometimes played an entire evening service at the church. They also played for other churches on both Sunday mornings and evenings. Jay normally played his eight-string Dobro.

Jay learned to play solo on the Dobro adding the background with the thumb pick and two finger picks keeping the rhythm as he went. It was pretty good and his style of presentation was copied by the church choir. The group enjoyed their music. The fellow on the banjo was one of the top banjo players in KC. He was also an ordained minister. His wife was a doctor. The group was named and lead by Molly, shown in the foreground in the photo to the left.

The Original Followers

The five member band promoted and ran an evening show at the Coleman Theater in NE Oklahoma in 1997.

They had three bands besides the Followers. One was a group from a nearby town headed up by a cousin of Jay. Another was a group that had a radio program in KC and was a member of the KC Blue Grass Club. The other, and feature band, was a semi-professional group called the Missourians that played the last of the three-hour program. All did well. Jay was the master of ceremonies and Mollie led the Followers' part. Proceeds

Followers at Coleman

went to the refurbishing of the theater. The black and white photograph at right was taken for the local paper to place in their paper, which they did, telling about the show to be performed in the Coleman Theater. Jay had made efforts earlier to get Roy Clark to come to the theater to do a program gratis to promote the restoration of the theater, but his manager wanted twenty-five thousand dollars. A few years later, Roy did perform there.

The Coleman Theatre

The theater was in the process of being renovated. When first built it was a very fancy and beautiful building that was financed and supported by a local wealthy man that had made his fortune from the nearby lead and zinc

Mr. Grayson, Manager.

mines in the first part of the 20th century. His name was George L. Coleman. Mr. Grayson was the manager of the theater during its refurbishing.

Chandelier

The Coleman Theater was as beautiful inside as it was outside. It had a chandelier in the center of the auditorium ceiling. A huge Wurlitzer organ used in the silent movie times was recovered and is now back on stage.

Ball Room

The theater has a large ball room on the second floor on the Main Street side. It is used for special occasions, including balls. Above is a photograph taken from the south end of the ball room. It is an impressive sight.

At the nuclear weapons facility a job for a process engineer was available in a department that rebuilt equipment for nuclear

Organ

weapons that had been tested. When cables, junction boxes that contained electronic safety devices for the weapons, etc., needed repair, an engineer was needed to look at the incoming inspection reports and write instructions for the repair. Jay was offered the job and accepted. The engineer doing the work was retiring at age fifty-three. He had eighty points (age plus years of service). He stayed long enough to train Jay somewhat.

Jay found himself taking work home to try to keep up. The supervisor of the department offered Jay one of his better technicians to help with the work. Jay was told that the technician wanted to be promoted to process engineer, but the company policy was that no more technicians without an engineering degree was told that the technician wanted to be promoted to process engineer, but the company policy was that no more technicians without an engineering degree would be promoted to process engineer. The tech did a great job. It gave Jay enough time to work with the computer department to develop a program to cover many of the routine repairs such as cable tears, etc. The program worked very well, and Jay was given a large digital alarm clock with the company logo on it.

Some of the special aspects of the job was reworking capacitors filled with oil, building dummy B-28 bombs of concrete for practice bombing, removing epoxy from cable connectors with many pins, etc. The connectors were out of production and used ones had to be salvaged.

For the dummy bombs, Jay had to buy a new concrete mixer along with materials. The technician who built the dummies before had left concrete in the mixer and ruined it. The B-52 carried four B-28s. Fighter bombers carried them, also. The concrete dummies had to be constructed of the right mixture of material to give the correct weight. They were cleaned and painted. They were about two feet in diameter. The B-28 bombs in the bomb bays of the B-52 were fired by a bank of capacitors. The capacitors were filled with oil with an air bubble in the metal containers. The air bubbles dissolved into the oil and caused the containers' sides to become concave.

B-28 Bomb

The cans had to be opened to relieve the bulged-in sides by a process not to cause fires or damage to the capacitors. Then a new air bubble was put into the containers and sealed. The capacitors were charged by batteries in the bombs. Jay was told that there was an incident where a B-52 had an accident on landing and either struck another B-52 or came close to it while the other B-52 was sitting on the ramp at the ready. The Nuclear Regulatory Agency, as the story install the batteries at a time when Russia could deliver nuclear weapons within thirty minutes. Later, the batteries were eliminated, and the weapons were connected to the aircraft bus to be charged in flight if need be.

The B-28RE bomb was a streamlined version of the B-28 for carrying exterior to the aircraft under the fusulage or wing. You can bet the enemy could not have enjoyed this weapon. The dummy concrete bombs were for training and accurcay determination.

To dissolve epoxy from the large connectors Jay used N2 pyrrolidone heated in a hood because the solvent was flammable. The out-of-production connectors were salvaged this way. When a new cable had to be made to replace one beyond repair, the salvaged connectors were used.

At one time some squibs, trigger devices for nuclear weapons about the size of pencils, were brought into the plant by mistake. Jay was told they were there for cable repairs. They had explosive material in them and were said to be radioactive. Neither explosives nor radioactive material were allowed in the plant. Jay did not know they were radioactive and examined the cables on the squibs.

Boating was a sport that the whole family liked. Jay bought an eighteen foot tri-hull boat with a 125 horsepower Chrysler outboard motor. The boat would cruise at around 35 miles/hour. They had lots of fun with it. One evening on Truman Lake the family stayed overnight on the boat with the enclosed top up. They pulled into a cove and tied up to a dead tree

Sandy, Josh and Boat

sticking out of the water. Early the next morning a boat approached them. Jay retrieved his lantern out of the tree and moved the boat away from the area. He just did not know if the on-coming boat was with a boat approached them. Jay retrieved his lantern out of the tree and moved the boat away from the area. He just did not know if the on-coming boat was with honest people. He did have a shotgun aboard. The boat was first pulled with a small pickup, the Courier. It grabbed lots of attention when the boat was pulled out of the water on steep ramps. It barely could handle the job. Later, a three-fourth-ton Suburban with a 454 CID engine was obtained.

When Josh was in grade school, he was asked to do a science project. He chose to determine the strength of several paper towels on the market. Using steel balls, each towel under test was stretched over a bowl held in place by a rubber band.

Josh placed one ball at a time on the towel until it gave away. He did it for each towel both wet and dry. He tested twelve different brands. The tests included strength and absorbency amount along with

Paper Towels

absorbency rate. The picture of the twelve brands of towels was blown up and glued to cardboard for display at the school. The Brawny and Bounty towels were considered the best from this test. They were also the most expensive.

Josh's was one of the better ones, though it did show adult help in a big way. The project was done as an engineer would do it. Josh did all of the work and was diligent in his effort. It took him a considerable amount of time, but he was proud of his accomplishment. It built self-confidence.

Absorbency Test

It was along about this time in Josh's life that he and Jay were on the roof calking a flashing between two sections of roof that were at approximately 30° angles to each other. Water ran down the larger section of roof, over the flashing and up under roofing past the flashing leaking onto the kitchen ceiling staining it. Afterwards, Jay was in the bathroom cleaning up. He was just out of the shower when young Josh came in and said, "I smell cock." Jay said, "What"? He was wondering who the kid had been talking with. Josh said, "Cock, cock like we put on the roof!" Jay corrected Josh saying, "It was calk."

Carla, Jay's daughter from the first marriage, called Jay for the first time since she was adopted at age six by Sadie and her new husband. Sadie worked in a hospital as a nurse's aide. She helped take care of a worker who had been injured on the job. He became her new husband. Carla's mother and grandmother had asked for the adoption when Carla was visiting with Jay and Sandy. Jay and Sandy hoped it had worked out alright for her.

Carla said that the situation was not good, and that she had moved out when her step father slapped her. She was eighteen then. Carla, at the age of twenty-five, had a three-year-old daughter. Her husband advised her against contacting Jay. The day Carla called, Jay and Sandy were surprised; they never expected to hear from her again. As mentioned before, her grandmother sent Jay a nasty, threatening letter along with a return of photos and a viewer Jay and Sandy had sent Carla.

After Carla called, she paid a visit to her dad and Sandy a short time later. She had just divorced her husband with her grandmother's help. She drove the three hundred miles distance with her daughter and a girlfriend. The girlfriend was a very sweet person. Jay and Sandy took them flying. The daughter sat on Josh's lap and became air sick.

They both were a mess. The girlfriend went to the hanger and brought back some paper towels to clean up the plane. Boating was also fun for the visitors.

Carla talked with her dad about coming to KC and finishing college there. They agreed that she could come there and stay while she finished her college. She was working at a school system where she lived. She quit her job and moved in with Jay and Sandy. She left her child with her folks in Tulsa. Jay rented a large covered trailer and moved her to KC. Sadie's mother and dad helped load the trailer, which seemed a bit strange to Jay. They seemed to hate Jay a lot. When the trailer was loaded, a guy that Carla worked with arrived. He and Carla went behind a large tree and appeared to be lovers. The three loading the trailer were bewildered. Jay knew he should unload everything and go home, but not smart at making good decisions, he went through with the plans. Sadie wanted to see Jay while he was there, so Carla took Jay to the hospital where Sadie came out to say hello from a short distance.

As usual, Jay's poor decision making did not work out. Carla went back home and a few days later she and the boyfriend came in a truck for her things.

Carla and her daughters and Jay's family have visited from time to time as they could. Carla brought her family to a family reunion near Columbus, Kansas, once. When Jay and Sandy pass through Tulsa, they visit.

Chapter 13

Product Engineer

The Original W82 Logo

Later Logo for W82

A product engineering job came open under Tim, the supervisor that the three contacted to get out of the materials test lab. He was a kindly man, a people person. Jay was glad to go to work for him. The product was a part for the nuclear warhead of the W82, a six- inch (155mm) diameter atomic artillery shell called an AFAP (Artillery Fired Atomic Projectile). The part cost thirty thousand dollars each to build; it was labor intensive and made of precious metals. The first logo (looking Down a NATO Gun Barrel) in the pictures shown here was for the six- inch W82 when the program started, but it was stopped after a couple of years. However, engineering continued for a couple of years after that until the program was restarted. Then, the logo was changed to the second logo in the second picture. There were several process engineers on Jay's team, one for each process in making the very precise part.

First, the material was purchased by a capable engineer on the team. The material was such that it could be formed in rough shape on a press. The part was heated on the press with an induction heater made of a copper pipe bent in the shape of the part to be formed. It had cooling water running through the pipe. It heated the part to be formed in a matter of seconds. Some problems arose, but capable process engineers solved them satisfactorily. The rough shapes were then machined to the shape needed to enclose a mandrel and be welded together for HIPping, a process described later.

A new building was constructed to house some of the processes and quality inspection. It cost somewhere in the neighborhood of $11 million.

One of the processes in the new building was HIPing (hot Isostatic pressing). There were two of the HIPpers in the new building.

The part was formed in two shapes. The two shapes were hermetically sealed by placing the two shapes over a mandrel and electronic-beam welding the two parts together in a vacuum forming a single part. Then the single part was placed into a HIPper chamber filled with an inert gas at a very high pressure and held there at a high temperature for several hours. The two parts had a flange on each side where the sealing weld was placed. The Flange was machined off leaving the part in its desired rough shape on the outside. During HIPing the two parts were fused together so well that it was difficult to see the seam area. The part was then polished by a special process and measured for size and finish using a depth measuring microscope and a Zeiss coordinate measuring machine.

Some of the parts had small marks on them after polishing. The cause was found and corrected.

When the first program began, Jay bought a $700,000 Zeiss coordinate measuring machine for the project and charged it to the project. The Precision Measurement Department "borrowed" the machine during the two years the program was down. They promised to give the W82 program priority when it restarted. Even though production was stopped, engineering continued while the program was down, as mentioned before. When the program was restarted, engineering asked for priority on the measuring machine, but Precision Measurement said it was too loaded with precision work and could not favor any specific project. Jay and his boss decided to purchase another unit, but put it in the program's manufacturing department. Precision Measurement personnel would operate it, but the program's parts would have 100 percent priority over any other parts.

Next, a hole was drilled through the part into the mandrel, and by a cyclic action of vacuum on the reservoir containing the part in a leaching fluid, the mandrel was dissolved. With the mandrel removed other equipment was attached to the part in a vacuum chamber. After final assembly, the parts were coated in electroless nickel to protect the surface. The nickel bath was started by a current and then the current was removed while the plating process continued. Sometimes the nickel coating came out mottled, and the part was scrapped. Jay looked into the hardness of both the nickel and the surface of the part and found that the nickel was not significantly harder than the bare surface of the part. He convinced the design agency at Livermore to eliminate the nickel plating process.

Now the part went to proof testing. The new building was designed to contain the part if it failed in proof testing.

Jay's job as the product engineer was to coordinate the processing efforts, budget the project funds, and see to it that all of the drawings were created, up to date and kept secure since they were highly classified. A liaison engineer from Lawrence Livermore National Laboratory (LLNL), Ben, came nearly every other week to see that the part was following the lab's design and to help solve any production problems or refer them to the PhD designers at the lab. He often brought another engineer, a brilliant lady engineer with a long pigtail, to help with the drawings. She was an older hippie-type. The Livermore design agency, one of three in the nuclear weapons complex and where the hydrogen bomb was designed under Dr. Teller, designed the weapon, and the production agency determined how to build it. That was a huge feat in itself. The other two design agencies were Los Alamos National Laboratory (LANL), where the first atomic bomb was designed, and Sandia National Laboratory (SNL) at Albuquerque.

The labs were nationalized when California governor Jerry Brown threatened to take over the Livermore Lab since it was operated by the University of California, Berkley.

Jay understood that Dr. Openhiemer, who led the team developing the atomic bomb, did not want to develop the atomic bomb further into the hydrogen bomb, it was said. He had been a card carrying communist, and that was probably used against him as he was stripped of his security clearance. Dr. Teller was set up on an old naval base at Livermore, California, to develop the hydrogen bomb.

The restart of the W82 in the mid-1980s found the design agency wanting to use a different material from the one that had been planned and setup for. The material they wanted to use was the same as that which had been used for the eight inch diameter W79 artillery fired atomic projectile (AFAP). It was decided that Jay should go to Livermore to convince the design agency that the Kansas City Plant (KCP) was set up to use the material that was originally planned and engineered for production with material on hand. To change would cost more and delay the project. The design agency agreed and the project moved ahead.

A young lady product engineer had under-budgeted her project, and Jay was asked if he could spare some funds from the W82 program. Jay had a modest reserve for unforeseen expenses. He told Program Management that they could use that. Jay's boss told Jay to budget to what he thought the project would cost and double it. That worked. Labor was only 50 percent efficient. Process engineers determined what they needed to set up a facility for their process, buy equipment and determine the manpower needed. That was incorporated into Jay's budget.

Jay and the design engineer became good friends. The Livermore engineer visited Jay at his home at times. He was a good entertainer telling stories into the night at times. He had a great sense of humor. He also had a half dozen or so old Chevrolet cars, most he restored himself. Jay had some old Chevys and was encouraged to join the club. One of Jay's cars, the 1966 red Impala, was pictured on the cover page of the old Chevrolet club's magazine, Vintage Chevrolet Club of America. The two enjoyed the old cars. Once when Jay was in Livermore, he visited the Livermore engineer's home. He drove the 1927 Chevy that the Livermore engineer had restored from a basket case. He had done an excellent job.

Another design engineer who sometimes worked with Ben became friends with Jay and family. He was from Japan and had a surname, Watanabe, that was common in Japan as Smith or Jones is in the United States. As Jay remembers, he told Jay that his family was a missionary family in the USA and had gone to Japan just before the war started. They were trapped when the war began. He said that he and his mother stood out in the yard and watched the aerial dog fights. Once they were strafed. They were demoralized, starved and just did not care about safety. He said that one day boys his age were called up to go to work in defense plants at Hiroshima. He had to go home to get his belongings and caught a train the next day. The train was stopped on the way, and the boys were told to walk home. They were told that an atomic bomb had destroyed Hiroshima (along with those who went the day before). After the war was over, he was seen in his starved condition (pot belly) and taken to a military base when it was learned he had a brother in the United States. He was sent to the United States before the time ran out for that. He received his college degree at Berkley.

The W82 part that was Jay's product responsibility had a large support group including process engineers, Program Management personnel who kept track of funds and progress, Quality Control engineers including the Precision Measurement folks, Non-destructive Testing engineering department and others. The LLNL engineer, Ben, is between the two ladies on the 1st row of the photograph at right.

W82 Team

Jay kept the drawings for the parts of the W82 he was responsible for in a safe near his desk. The process engineers used the drawings. Most were classified secret though a few were confidential. They were checked out for tracking purposes when needed. When auditors looked for the drawings engineers had, there was a big effort to find any missing prints. The investigation was kept open until they were found or accounted for.

One day Jay's boss's boss came down the hall and asked Jay what the part number of the part he was responsible for was. He had been told by a devious technician that Jay was not familiar with his part; he did not even know the part number. Jay told him the number and wondered why he had asked. The Manager made some remark and left. Jay stepped into the hall and saw the technician coming out of the manager's office with his tail between his legs. Jay had no more trouble out of him.

The manager of Program Management and one of his assistants scheduled a trip to Rocky Flats near Boulder to see a W-79 warhead being assembled with a part Jay was also product engineer on at the time along with the W82 part. They invited Jay along. The three watched the assembly of the KCP part along with the nuclear material and the high explosive around the nuclear material. Afterwards they toured the plant seeing the stored nuclear warheads, glove boxes used in the assembling, etc. They had protective clothing for their entire bodies. When they left, the protective clothing was left inside, and they were checked for radiation outside the door with a hand-held wand. The three were wanded several times, and after each time the wand operator went to the telephone and contacted someone. Finally they were released to return to KC. They thought they would glow all of the way back on the airplane. Jay feels that the exposure contributed to his prostate cancer that developed later. The genitals are highly sensitive to radiation. Jay caught the cancer early and the surgery was a complete success. Shortly after the trip the three made, the Rocky Flats facility was shut down (in late 1980s) due to radiation contamination. It was never reopened, and it took approximately ten years to clean up.

When Jay joined the nuclear weapons facility, it was run by Bendix for the Department of Energy (DOE). Bendix was a very well-run company attributed to CEO Blumenthal. However, Blumenthal was brought into Carter's administration leaving the reins of Bendix to Bill Agee. Bill met a woman by the name of Mary Cunningham, who was married to a black man. She was made his executive vice president. She divorced her husband and married Bill, who had divorced his wife to marry Mary. Together they tried to do a hostile takeover of the Martin Marietta Aircraft Company, but it backfired and Bendix became vulnerable to take over by Martin Marietta. Agee tried to persuade employees at Bendix to keep their Bendix shares. He wanted them to not sell their shares to Martin Marietta, who was vying now to take over Bendix. Agee asked the Allied company to take over Bendix. It did after Bill set himself up for a large "golden parachute." After a short time with Bill as an Allied employee, it is said that Bill was flushed out of Allied, and Mary went to work for the Seagram alcoholic beverage company. Later, Allied bought the Signal Company, and it became Allied Signal. Several years later Allied Signal bought the Honeywell Company and kept the name Honeywell. This was what was seen from Jay's vantage point.

Agee's efforts to save Bendix

At one time Jay was responsible for archiving the W76 earth penetrator nuclear weapon. Jay's boss told Jay that the penetrator was no longer needed. He said that the MX missile was so accurate that it could put one over the Moscow bunkers and blow off the ground cover. Another could be dropped in at practicallythesamelocationanddestroythebunkers.Drawings, correspondence, records, etc. were categorized and shipped to archives.

Jay was given the product responsibility for the W79, the eight-inch diameter AFAP. He had the responsibility of closing it out and disposing of extra material, archiving the paperwork, etc. A certain number of W79s were planned; their parts, similar to that of the W82, were built out. Approximately half of the W79 weapons were not yet built. That program was cut back and the remaining funds were used to fund the W82.

The W82 was to replace the W48, a six-inch AFAP that was deployed in Europe already. The W48 was said to be more dangerous to the users than the enemy. Too, it may be something that the enemy could detonate should they overrun an artillery post with the W48 present. The number of W82s to be built was the same as the number of W79s built. Though problems in forming, EB welding, polishing, HIPping, extracting the mandrel and final assembly were encountered, the team was blessed with good engineers from the supervisor through the final assembly. The parts were built out ahead of schedule.

The excess W79 parts were given to Jay to destroy their shapes and salvage the material which had some value. Jay contacted a scientific research supervisor at Livermore to see if he could use some of the parts for research. He took some of them at the salvage price. He told KCP Program Management to bill LLNL until the next physical year to charge for the parts. Livermore had a fit. The reason for the delay that Program

Management gave was that KCP had the same problem as Livermore, a surplus of funds in the current physical year. KCP was funding sidewalks and any other place where they could get rid of the funds on hand to avoid being docked the next physical year. Livermore never forgave KCP. Had Jay known that KCP had too much funding for the present physical year, he would have approached upper management to simply give the parts to Livermore for research.

Jay kept his membership in SAE (Society of Automotive Engineers). The Kansas City Plant (KCP) was getting low on work. Jay sometimes went to national SAE meetings. One was held in San Diego and Jay attended. He attended primarily to let

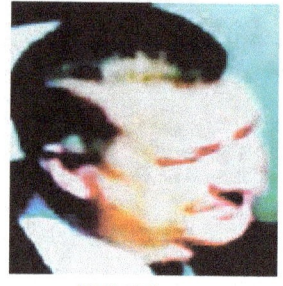

Kelly Johnson

other companies know that KCP was looking for work that their high skills and their high technological production equipment and facilities could handle.

One SAE presentation was by Kelly Johnson. After the meeting, Jay chatted with Kelly telling him that KCP was looking for work. He asked Kelly, jokingly, why his company, Lockheed, had not won the B2 contract. Kelly grinned sheepishly and visited with Jay for a few more minutes. As you know, or maybe not, Kelly was a capable engineer since his college days in Michigan15. He was instrumental in the design of the Lockheed Electra like the one Amelia Earhart flew when she was lost. Two of Kelly's greatest

Lockheed Electra

accomplishments were probably the U-2 and the SR71 Blackbird. The SR71 was our spy plane that the Russians could never come close to catching.

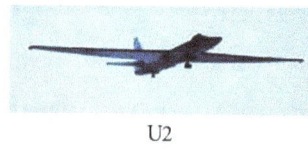

U2

This man, Clarence Leonard "Kelly" Johnson was a genius in the field of aviation. Only a few men accomplished his understanding of aircraft and flight. He will always be remembered as the man who moved flight into the future.

The guy was easy to talk with and was not aloof or arrogant. He seemed like an ordinary guy like people who are a pleasure to meet and visit with.

Sr71 Blackbird

The U-2, a spy plane worked well until the Russians came up with a missile that could reach the plane at its high altitude. It was replaced by the Blackbird and spy satellites which were being installed in space during the early 1960s.

Kelly contributed to the design of the following aircraft:

1. The Lightning P-38 fighter of WWII

P-38

2. The Constellation for Howard Hughes' TWA airline

Constellation

3. F-80 jet fighter

F-80

4. T-33 trainer

T-33

5. F-94 jet fighter

F-94

6. F-104 jet fighter

F-104

7. F-117 Nighthawk

F-117

8. C-130 turboprop cargo plane

C-130

Kelly ran Lockheed's Skunk Works with his famous fourteen rules of management. His motto was be quick, be quit and be on time. He received fifty- one honors and awards.

A lady engineer, actually a PhD chemist that was hired at the same time as Jay, had been promoted to supervisor. Jay understood that she had been promised promotion (affirmative action in action) when she hired in, along with others in her category, according to rumor. Jay did not doubt it; affirmative action was in full swing. Affirmative action was really reverse discrimination. One time when Jay sat in a manager's meeting for his boss, part of the agenda promised promotion (affirmative action in action) when she hired in, along with others in her category, according to rumor. Jay did not doubt it; affirmative action was in full swing. Affirmative action was really reverse discrimination. One time when Jay sat in a manager's meeting for his boss, part of the agenda was to ask for promotable people, "preferably women and blacks." White men were third choice or less. The chemist supervisor asked for Jay in her newly assigned electronics group, since the W82 was well under control. Jay's boss, Tim, was frustrated over the situation. He asked Jay what he thought; he did not appear to want to let him go. Jay said, "I will do anything you tell me." The boss reluctantly gave in to the chemist's demands.

The chemist was promoted to manager, one step above supervisor (senior staff engineer). A supervisor directly under her was for whom Jay was to work. He had an electrical group. Jay interviewed with him before starting to work in his group. Jay told him that he was not an electrical engineer, and that if he could he would have a hydraulic television. Electrical things seemed to be the cause of many problems in Jay's life. Electrical problems hide from you and will bite you if you are not careful. The supervisor nearly fell out of his chair. He then said, "If you know ohms law, you will do alright." Jay was assigned to work with another engineer on junction boxes and antennas for trailers that were designed to haul nuclear weapons. Nuclear weapons were hauled in trailer trucks at that time because The Nuclear Regulatory Commission had decided that it was too risky to the citizenry to haul them by air where nuclear material might be scattered over the countryside in case of a crash. Too, Rail was out; an idiot nuclear weapons protestor had sprawled himself in front of a train coming out of Rocky Flats where the weapons were assembled. He lost arms and legs because the engineer had strict instructions not to stop. It was decided that the railroad was too vulnerable.

Every morning Jay and the other engineer walked to the beverage machine. One morning the other engineer was limping. Jay asked him what he had done to his foot. The reply was that his legs were weak. Later that day, the other engineer was taken to his doctor by another friend in the same office area. The doctor put the friend in the hospital. X-rays showed a tumor on his spine. MRI showed that the tumor had wrapped around his spine; operating was out of the question. Radiation and chemotherapy reduced the tumor. Several years later, the engineer was going strong.

The junction boxes were not a big problem. Handling damage and repairs were the norm for problems with the units. The boxes had safety devices in them to keep the weapons from detonating accidently. There were approximately one half dozen safety devices to keep the weapons safe. They had to meet criteria such as the proper trajectory, proper acceleration, altitude, etc.

There was a problem with the trailer antennas. The original production was complete and, with new trailers coming on, more were needed. Sandia at Albuquerque was responsible for the trailer design, which had several safety features to safeguard against terrorists. Sandia sent Jay their drawings for the antennas, which had lightning arrestors built in. When the first units were built at KCP per the drawings, they would not work. Sandia gave Jay an earlier unit that did work. Jay had it x-rayed and discovered that capacitors in the unit were cascaded rather than in tandem as the drawings showed. Jay had one built like the old one and it worked fine. Jay then asked the Electronics Department to come up with one capacitor to replace the two for improvement of the unit. One was found, but it cost around six dollars compared to less than one dollar each for the original capacitors. The change was not incorporated.

By this time Jay had a serious pulmonary problem. Doctors had tried several different medicines without much effect. When Jay first came to work at KCP with his desk in the materials test area by the test machines, as mentioned earlier, he developed a cough that was not serious then, but it was a nuance because it interfered with his speech. Jay coughed when trying to talk. Jogging in cold weather had aggravated the problem. Since it was diagnosed as asthma and asthma medicines had little effect the pulmonary problem became serious. There were over eight hundred chemicals in the plant at one time or another Jay was told, and perhaps the worst was beryllium. Around the late 1980s or early 1990s, there was a large clean up around the plant with dirt removed and hauled to Alabama. Other employs were fighting pulmonary problems. Jay noticed that when he took certain medicines for other problems such as colds, the pulmonary problem diminished; a ray of hope.

A big layoff at the plant in the early 1990s took place. Most of the engineers with a C or less rating were laid off. Jay was then loaned to a new department that was charged with efficiency control of the plant. A young engineer was struggling to tabulate activities from several departments. He was behind, and the manual methods he was using were not conducive to keeping the reports current. Jay asked for and was granted permission to computerize the process. The engineer responsible was friendly and congenial. The computer department had lost people during the layoff and could not help with the programming for the automation Jay needed. Funds were made available to contract an outside source to do the work. The programmers were brought on site in an unclassified area, and worked directly with Jay. The problem was two-fold. A user-friendly program was needed to gather the data required from the departments. Someone in each department would load the department data on a floppy disc. The discs would be fed into another program that crunched the data and made a report. It worked well. The young engineer was promoted. Later, he became the president of the KCP facility after serving upper management positions and with management training. There was a pretty secretary in the group. The young engineer courted her. He and his current wife were in the process of divorce. He later married the pretty girl.

The PhD lady chemist had by now been placed in charge of a microcircuits department. She had an aggressive engineer in her group. He talked her out of keeping him in the job he was well trained at. The chemist supervisor drafted Jay into that group to replace the aggressive engineer that wanted to play at other things he had in mind. He had designed a carousel for processing hermans, which were flat pieces of ceramic used for plating gold microcircuits on. The carousel was to put the processing of the hermans in a close proximity arrangement for the new micro circuit facility that was being constructed. Jay and the other engineer went to Dayton, Ohio, to see the carousel in construction. Jay was not impressed with the design. He felt that the new microcircuit facility should have the latest in processing equipment. Since he was now responsible for the gold plating process, he budgeted over a million dollars to set up automated systems using robots. He put out request for a proposal (RFP) for each processing unit. That included coating the metalized hermans with photoresist (a light-sensitive semi-liquid material used on photographs), place the glass with the circuit pattern on it, properly expose the photo resist, move the hermans to the development tank of sodium hydroxide and dry the hermans after the photo resist on the circuit lines were removed.

The gold circuiting process was difficult, but the original engineer had walked away from it leaving Jay to learn it by himself. Jay asked the supervisor to keep the original engineer responsible for part of the process until Jay could come up to speed. The original engineer refused. The supervisor tried to trade the original engineer to another group, but no one wanted him; he was well known as a maverick. Jay had to learn the entire process from metalizing by sputtering through gold plating and verifying the proper line widths. He did that in a short while with the help of the technicians doing the work.

The instructions to the technicians, called travelers, were written on a traveler computer program. It needed help. After familiarizing himself with the traveler system, Jay tried to improve it. Some traveler folks viewed Jay as the expert with the system. People involved realized a new improved system was in order. It was being considered when Jay moved to another group.

The instructions to the technicians, called travelers, were written on a traveler computer program. It needed help. After familiarizing himself with the traveler system, Jay tried to improve it. Some traveler folks viewed Jay as the expert with the system. People involved realized a new improved system was in order. It was being considered when Jay moved to another group.

Now, ceramic is non-conductive. It cannot be gold plated bare. It has to be metalized. To do that the hermans were placed in a vacuum chamber and first sputtered with a conductive metal. Sputtering is done by placing a slug of metal in the vacuum chamber with the herman and vaporizing the slug with a laser. The vapor condenses on the hermans. Nobel metals were used to plate the hermans. One such as palladium likes ceramic and not gold while another such as titanium likes palladium and gold but not ceramic, or it is the other way around. Anyhow, the two metals were sputtered (plated) onto the hermans. Then the photoresist was applied. A positive glass pattern produced in the glass circuit pattern shop was used to define the gold circuits.

The technicians in the pattern shop were very good at their work. They worked with extra effort and produced excellent patterns. Jay put them in for a reward. Rewards were given to encourage extra effort and innovation. They both, a black fellow and a lady team member, were given the reward, a nice bonus.

The positive glass had the actual lines to be gold plated on it. With the positive glass pattern, positive photoresist, when developed by sodium hydroxide, would expose the bare sputtered-on-metal paths to be gold plated. Then, the hermans were clipped with alligator clips on each top corner. One was attached to a positive DC circuit post and the other to the negative. The hermans were then dipped into a large rectangular, clear-plastic tank (Plexiglas), and current was applied for a given amount of time. The tank contained gold cyanide, a clear liquid and poisonous. When the circuits were plated on the hermans, the developed photoresist is removed leaving the gold paths.

Next, a negative photoresist is applied to the hermans. When developed the negative photoresist, exposed to light with negative glass patterns, develop such that the gold is protected by the developed photoresist while the rest of the metal on the hermans is exposed for removal with strong metal dissolving chemicals.

The plated circuit widths were then measured with a measuring microscope which has two parallel lines that measure precisely the width of the gold circuit lines. It was acquired by Jay. The inspection department did not have as good equipment for measuring the lines and agreed to observe when production measured the lines on the precision scope. This is how they inspected and accepted the gold lines on the microcircuits.

For a new facility being built, Jay planned to do away with the Plexiglas gold cyanide tanks and replace them with a new design. The old tanks worked but the walls, cracks and crevices coated-out with gold during operation until they had to be disassembled and scraped clean. It took a long time to turn around the two tanks. Jay wanted to use two, smooth barrel-like tanks that were lined with liners similar to garbage bags and that could be turned around very quickly by simply removing the liners and replacing them with clean liners. The new system was to have a third tank that would be used to recover the gold from the used liners and the holders of the hermans which always became coated in the plating process. The holders with hermans were to be lowered into the tanks with movable arms through the top of the containers. Jay talked with Bell Labs about his gold plating system idea. The lab was interested and was looking into building a system for the nuclear weapons facility. Jay had budgeted several hundred thousand dollars for gold plating and related equipment as part of the more than one million dollars for the entire system upgrade for the new facility. About that time a different manager of the section that included the micro circuits group took over. He allowed the engineers to choose the areas of work that they preferred. Jay chose work that did not include gold plating tanks. That responsibility went to a PhD chemist from India. It was a better fit; however, she was not an engineer and chose to build two new plastic tanks like the ones there in the old department. What she did with the extra money budgeted to build a better system was not known to Jay.

One of the photoresist companies no longer produced a photoresist needed. Jay tried to develop the remaining photoresist to do what the unavailable photoresist did. An engineer at the Albuquerque design agency, Sandia National Laboratory, volunteered to help Jay. He had a lab and was familiar with photoresists. Jay spent a week in Albuquerque working with the Sandia engineer developing the resist application. They were successful. However, Jay moved to another department before the photoresist application was put into service. The physicist with an engineer title, who had originally worked the job Jay had, came back to the group as Jay was leaving and refused to use the new process; he developed one of his own later. Jay had put in a request for a patent for the new process. The original engineer demanded to see the details of the patent application before Jay left the group. The patent was not granted.

The company dabbled in new ideas for management. Jay was sent to a myriad of "take 'em apart and put them back together" courses, including diversity training to get folks to accept affirmative action, as well as other liberal ideas.

One good idea put into practice was "self-directed work teams" given to high performance engineering teams. Also, a program was in place to allow engineers to transfer from one group to another where there was an opening. One group, non-destructive testing, a self-directed work team, had advertised for a mechanical engineer but no one applied until the time ran out. Its manager was the supervisor that had come to the support of the three engineers when they wanted to transfer out of materials testing shortly after hiring in. Jay met him in member of the self-directed work team. Working in that group was a very enjoyable experience. It was somewhat like working for yourself.

Chapter 14

Nondestructive Testing

Self-Directed Work Team

The self-directed work team consisted of nine engineers and an administrative assistant. Each engineer was formally trained in each of the skills applied in non-destructive testing. Each had the overall responsibility for a specialty. The tests included X-Ray, magnetic particles, dye penetrants, ultrasonics, X-Ray CT, cobalt CT, real-time X-Ray and impact testing. For each technique of non- destructive testing, Jay had to go to school off-site. The training for dye penetrants testing was done in Houston. Jay and Ron attended together; they made the high grades with Ron at the top. He went to Houston again for magnetic particles testing, to Anaheim for radiation training for two weeks, and to Connecticut for ultrasonic testing training.

The team had administrative duties since they had no supervisor.

The team reported directly to a manager. The members of the team rotated duties at established time periods. The list of duties is described in the organizational chart on the next page with actual names blotted out. The self- directed team worked very well as long as it reported to a competent manager.

However, its manager was temporary sent out of state for a while and one of his lieutenants was assigned as his acting manager.

That did not work so well. A short time later, one of the manager's less competent lieutenants was assigned to be the team's manager. He did not fit as a manager of a self-directed work team. He promoted a young engineer from another group under his managerial department to be the team's supervisor. Jay, at that time had already begun the process of retiring. He had several weeks of vacation. When he went on vacation a young black lady (a 3-pointer as Tim said) in security took his badge away from him and he could not get back in the plant even though he was on vacation. Jay had enjoyed several years as a member of the self-directed work team though.

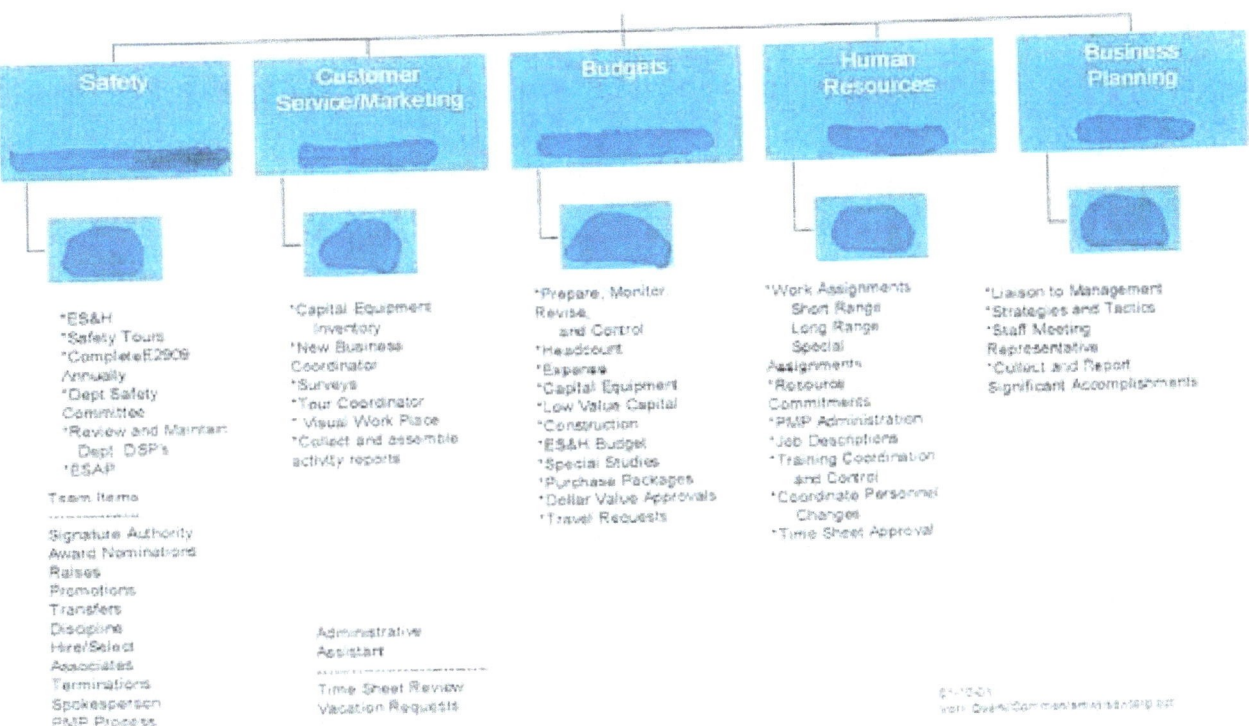

During the time Jay worked in non-destructive testing, Josh, his son, was attending college. He went one year to a local Junior college, but he did not show a whole lot of interest. He and a buddy took off after the first year of college for California. Sandy had traded him her small Dodge sports car for his 1966 Chevy Impala.

Dodge Sports Car

1966 Chevrolet Impala

When Josh turned sixteen, Sandy wanted Josh to be like his friends. She wanted him to drive to school as well as other places. When Josh was fifteen Jay and Sandy helped get a learner's permit. They let Josh drive on trips to begin with. Later they let him drive some around local places. He was a good driver and got his driver's license at sixteen. Jay wanted Josh to have a big car that he could work on. A 1966 Chevy belonged to an old lady in Fort Scott where Sandy's aunt lived. It had approximately forty-five thousand miles on it. Jay had it painted and brought up to date functional wise. Josh drove the car approximately thirty-five thousand miles in high school and junior college. He did not like the car; it was too old fashioned. He did have an accident in it.

Jay told him to stay out of the Kansas side of greater Kansas City; he did not and hit a small car. It did a lot of damage to the small car but not much to the 1966 Chevy. He hit the small car on New Year's Day. The lady driving the small car asked Josh not to call the police because she had too many tickets. Josh went along with it. When he went home he told his dad what happened. His dad told him to go to the police station and file a report. He went to the local police station and was told to go into Kansas where the accident happened to file a report there. Jay and Sandy went with him to the Kansas station. They found that the lady in the accident had filed a report accusing Josh of causing the accident. Josh and the lady had the same insurance company; it covered both cars to the owners' satisfaction.

Josh and a friend took the Dodge car that Sandy traded to Josh and went to Ocean Side, California. Josh saw himself as a surfer. He traded the Dodge for a new off-road vehicle. The boys could only find a fast food restaurant job each. It was not enough to keep the new vehicle. The dealer would not trade back, but did give Josh an old Electra that was worn out. While they were there, Jay was taking a two-week radiation course at Anaheim. Josh came up on a train on the weekend to visit. He did not tell his parents he was broke and had lost his car. Later, he called his mother and told her he was coming home and to keep his dad off him for losing his car. He went home with his tail between his legs.

Jay told Josh he would send him to college, but not locally. He had to go away from home to what is now Missouri State University. He first enrolled in computer science. Then he enrolled in accounting when he thought computer science was too hard. That did not work, and Josh's advisor set him up in business school. He flunked out. The school gave him another chance and hired a tutor to help him. The tutor was an attractive student the same age as josh. Her younger sister attached herself to Josh and later married him after he finished college. Josh graduated with a Bachelor of Science degree in Business administration. He obtained a job at Chrysler.

While Jay was in the non-destructive testing department he visited Los Alamos several times, Savannah River plant where special gases were manufactured, Rocky Flats where nuclear weapons were assembled, and Pantex where nuclear weapons were assembled, disassembled and stored. He had been to Laurence Livermore National Laboratories several times earlier. One place in the nuclear weapons complex he would have liked to visit was Y-12 (Oakridge plant in Tennessee) where many centrifuges separated the radioactive U-235 from the uranium ore called yellow cake. Jay understood that yellow cake was 99.3 percent U-238, which is not radio- active, is heavier than lead and is stronger than steel. It is used for bullets and armor plating. Since U-238 is heavier than U-235, the radioactive U-238 can be separated from the U-235 in a centrifuge. The heaver U-238 goes to the outside when spun in the centrifuge and is removed that way like separating milk from cream. It is separated one atom at a time. When the first bomb was dropped on Hiroshima, it was the U-235 bomb. Some U-235 was placed at one end of a large gun barrel. Some U-235 was fired down the barrel with a high explosive. It was not tested because there was not enough U- 235 for that. It was called the Little Boy, and it worked as intended.

The inert U-238 was called depleted uranium after the U-235 was removed. Two scientists at the University of California experimented with methods of irradiating the U-238. They found a way to do that. They called the radioactive U-238 plutonium. The scientists at Los Alamos were perplexed trying to get high explosives around the plutonium to implode uniformly. The firing squibs had to be placed in the optimum position, and the electric firing wires had to be precisely the same size, length and resistance. When the scientists arrived at the desired design they tested a unit at Alamogordo, New Mexico. It worked; the second nuclear bomb dropped on Japan was of this type. It was called Fat Man.

These two model units can be seen at the museums in Los Alamos and Albuquerque. They are open to the public.

On a trip to Los Alamos, Jay presented the status of the Federal Manufacturing and Technologies (FM&T) plant at Kansas City, known also as the Kansas City Plant (KCP), at one of the meetings on the status of the Nuclear Complex. As

Little Boy and Fat man

mentioned before, approximately 85 percent of nuclear weapons are manufactured at the KCP. No explosives or nuclear material were at the KCP except in instrumentation such as the cobalt computed tomography (CT) machine, which is something like the CAT scan machine in the medical field. At the time the KCP facility, covering approximately eighty acres under one concrete roof, was enhanced by three other buildings on the site, all with large floor spaces. A new facility has been built and the old one has been vacated of nuclear weapon production as mentioned before.

Jay was active in his church when Josh was still in grade school. Josh attended church with him regularly up into high school. Jay sang in the choir and was appointed the director of the bus ministry. The ministry had six large school- type buses and brought in several children each Sunday morning.

The new pastor that came to the church received his doctorate degree at a seminary in Canada. He was from KC before working on his doctor's degree.

In the small music band that Jay was a member of, Molly, the leader, and the banjo player, an ordained minister, were accomplished musicians. Jack is Molly's husband. The band sometimes practiced in Molly and Jack's basement, along with another band of the church, on Saturday nights. Jay and Jack both had Martin standard guitars. Mollie, Jack and Jay were members of the KC Area Bluegrass Club and played at their meeting place on Friday nights, sometimes on the program and other times sitting in with different groups in separate rooms of the building. Jay sometimes helped with the sound system. A friend of his was in charge of it controlling ten microphones for the weekly programs. Jay sometimes controlled the sound system at his church.

A coworker of Jay wanted Jay to take him and his girlfriend up for an airplane ride around Kansas City. The weather was not so too good, and Jay told his friend, "If the birds are walking, they would not go up either." When they reached the airport the weather was poor. As they walked around to the hanger doors there were several birds walking around close to the door. Jay asked the couple for a rain check. The coworker later got his pilot's license.

This same coworker, a young engineer, wanted Jay to fly him and two friends to Omaha. They wanted to go to the horse races. They flew to a nearby airport in Omaha after flying a long way around the KC International Airport, which is about fifty miles north of KC. When they arrived at the Omaha airport they could not raise the tower. They circled a bit and decided to land anyway. There was no problem with that; they called a taxi to take them to the track. Jay did not gamble. At the track, Jay remembered that he had forgotten to close his flight plan. He tried to call the flight service station in Omaha, but all outside communication was closed during the races. Fortunately for Jay, no one was looking for the plane since the flight plan had not been closed. When they arrived back at KC darkness had overtaken them. The airport they flew from had shut down the tower. While efforts were made to raise the tower, another pilot in the air said the tower was down for the night. Fortunately, the runway lights were left on.

There was an air show at Fort Scott where Sandy's aunt lived. Sandy and Jay, along with Josh, decided to fly down to the show and see Sandy's aunt. They were following the 71 highway in Missouri. US 69 highway was just a few miles west of 71 and parallel to it in Kansas. It ran through Fort Scott. Somehow the aviators switched over to 69 as a guide. When they saw the town coming up, they thought it was Nevada, Missouri, but it was really Ft. Scott. They turned right; Fort Scott is almost due west of Nevada on highway 54. After they had flown west awhile they realized something was wrong. They came across a town with a water tower. They dropped down to see the name on the tower and discovered it was Humboldt, Kansas. They backtracked following highway 54 to Fort Scott. When they arrived, the air show had already started. A bit anxious, they looked all around for show participants in the pattern. They saw none and came in hot to maintain full control. Being hot, they bounced back in the air two or three times. People were lining the runway both sides. They may have thought that was part of the show. They looked at the folks in the plane and the flyers looked back without showing embarrassment. The plane was taxied to parking, and Sandy called her aunt, a retired school teacher, to tell her they had arrived. At that time Omni was the best way to fly a course. However, Omni was limited to a short range at low altitude and would become erroneous at some distance from an Omni station. The stations were not close enough to be completely reliable at low altitude. When the three flew back to KC, the sky was overcast with broken clouds. They navigated with Omni, compass and highway 69, which ran close to the airport near Olathe, KS, where they flew from.

Sandy and Jay enjoyed their neighborhood. The neighborhood kids were around Josh's age and played around Sandy and Jay's house frequently. They liked to imitate Jay at times. The houses were new and the couples that moved in were young. Jay planted black walnut trees on their three acres plus the large corner lot they had. The trees grew rapidly and produced lots of walnuts. Along the east side of the three acres the walnut trees were planted ten feet inside the line and 10 feet apart. He planted walnuts to start the trees.

The government owned the nuclear weapons manufacturing plant. The Department of Energy controlled all nuclear energy including nuclear weapons.

Lawn Mowers

Ronald

Four Presidents that Jay Voted for

Winston Churchill

President George W. Bush and Vice-President Chaney

The photographs imbedded here are the items posted on Jay's office area walls. They were sent to Jay personally with his name on them for some reason unbeknown to Jay. It is a wonder that some liberal, or liberals, did not pitch a fuss over them. To see them, one had to enter Jay's office area. These were still posted when Jay retired. Folks in the nondestructive department gathered them up and gave them to Jay after he left. The nondestructive folks made a book with things that happened in it for Jay. Jay felt that it was a nice gesture and appreciated their efforts. Jay felt that overall the company, now Honeywell, was good to him, and he is continually grateful for the opportunity to have worked there.

Tank

A tank was on the screen of Jay's computer as a screen saver. Its caption said, "Kids can tear up a Sherman tank." Josh and his friends at that time were somewhat destructive. The picture of the tank was taken at Claremore, Oklahoma, at the Davis Gun Museum. It's out front of the museum along old US 66 highway.

Vera told Jay that she thought that someone from south central Missouri had come to the tristate area (Oklahoma, Kansas and Missouri) looking for Wiley, Jay's granddad. They said that Wiley was a bigamist, that he had not divorced his first wife.

THE TEN COMMANDMENTS

I

I am the Lord your God, you shall have no other gods before me

II

You shall not take the name of the Lord your God in vain

III

Remember to keep holy the Sabbath

IV

Honor your father and your mother

V

You shall not murder

VI

You shall not commit adultery

VII

You shall not steal

VIII

You shall not give false witness against your neighbor

IX

You shall not covet your neighbor's wife

X

You shall not covet your neighbor's goods

In the area in south central Missouri was a small town near the Arkansas border. Jay called a telephone operator in the town and was told the name and telephone number of an elderly lady said to be the matriarch of Wiley's former family there. Jay contacted the matriarch and found that Wiley's decedents of his first family were still living in that town. It seemed that most were of the line of Wiley's son from Wiley's first wife. Wiley's second family was invited to the town to a family reunion scheduled to take place soon. Lou, Vera, Jay, and Sandy did attend. They met their half cousins, decedents of Wiley's son and daughter of his first family. The contact was at the matriarch's home. Jay thought that one of the two ladies in the photograph, far right, is the matriarch. She was the last of her generation and was said to be the granddaughter of Wiley's son from his first wife; the son was named Wiley Jr.

Decedents of Wiley's First Family

Jay's Cousins from Wiley's First Family

Now, Wiley was the kingpin of Jay's family clan. As a recap, Wiley came back from the Civil war fighting for the North, found his family and farm not like he left them. His wife, two kids and farm were in the charge somehow of his neighbor, it seems. Wiley and his wife divorced, according to the wife of one of Wiley's descendants through Wiley Jr. The wife of the descendant kept the family history as well as she could; she said she found that there was a divorce and that Wiley had not simply abandoned his first family.

More of Jay's Cousins from Wiley's First Family

As a recap, Joe was the last of the second family of Wiley. He was born and raised in SE Kansas. There was a log cabin there, and it was said to be on Joe's home place. Joe's brother had established a farm in NE Oklahoma. Joe went to live with him when their dad died at the age of seventy-five; Joe was thirteen. When Joe was twenty-one he had his own farm in NE Oklahoma.

In 1959 the Tulsa world wrote an article on him shown on the previous page. Since the article was archived by The Tulsa World, and the reprint is hardly readable, the information is printed out for the readers here. The caption under the first photo says, "Milestone: Each new calf gets personal attention from Joe. He can recall the time when one calf was the difference between success and failure in his years farming."

The story written by Frances Baker on April 12, 1959 is as follows:

> Some of Oklahoma's pioneer farmers have let modern, fast-paced farming methods out-distance them, but not Joe, a tall, strong sixty- nine-year-old farmer of northeast Ottawa County, Okla. Though he has seen many changes in his half-century farming experience, "It's still the most rewarding life I know," is his comment.
>
> Joe has seen an average daily farm wage rise from fifty cents to ten dollars, the slow horse-drawn implements replaced by power driven ones and chores that required many hands now done with an all-in-one machine.
>
> With the years he has kept pace with the progress of the American farmer's research into ways to produce more and better products. Today, he commands the respect of youngsters of the Miami area who are starting out as farmers.

Joe was right in there when the Indian Territory was turned under the first plow and a new state was born. He is living proof that hard work never hurt anyone.

At thirteen, he did a man's work with a brother John not far from his home now. But progress was always of prime interest to him. Joe believes his success is the result of his willingness to discard obsolete varieties of seed, being constantly on the alert for more profitable hybrids as well as new methods of seedbed preparation and the use of fertilizers.

This spring his operations will include 1400 acres in cultivation with winter oats, the Arkwin variety that he says provides good pasturage after the crop is harvested, wheat and corn. Last year he produced one hundred thirty-six bushels of corn per acre.

His feedlot of eighty white face steers and two hundred head of stock cows thrive on his home-produced, home ground feed mixture ... the result of his experiments with different feeds to produce good marketable steers.

The mixture is ensilage, corn, oats and maize, with added soy bean meal. Summers he pastures four hundred acres of grazing land. This year he purchased two registered bulls from Ogeechee Farms at Fairland and some stock cows.

When we visited with Joe he was busy at the feed lot, hoisting the one hundred-pound bags of soybean meal around like a youngster. He believes the owner of a farm should be the top hand. "Things just runs smoother that way," he said. During planting he hires some help, but he is in the field every day.

Joe says he was raised on "hogs, cows, chickens and dogs," ... that much of the old time ways he carries on. This spring he has seven "bacon type" Yorkshire sows. He bought his Yorkshire start of swine in Illinois three years ago. And forty piglets are busy eating up some of his exceptional corn yield. He says the Yorkshire hog is the healthiest one he has ever raised.

The dogs? Three collies assist in the feed lot keeping the cattle away until the feeders are full.

Though personal tragedy of fire and death has hit him twice and "laid him low" as he put it, optimism is his way of life. He is the father of eight living children. The youngest son, Jay, twenty-three, is the only one of the children at home. He is a fourth year at Oklahoma University majoring in aeronautical engineering. Summers, Jay helps out on the farm.

The other children helped before they married, but the most impressive part of Joe's story is his steady battle to be a successful farmer from a small beginning.

"Nowadays young men think they have to have lots of equipment, a backlog of money and many acres of land but it takes something else to be a successful farmer," he says. "It takes the ability to see into the future and willingness to work with what you have toward bigger things. But, the most necessary thing is faith in the land and its people."

Joe is the energetic president of the Ottawa County Farm Bureau and a board member of the Cherokee Farm Loan Assn. of Vinita.

In co-operation with Ottawa county farm agent J. D. Blakemore, three years ago Joe began a seed wheat planting program aimed at producing certified seed wheat to sell. Last harvest his seed, grown, cleaned and tested by him and Blakemore, met top grade standards. His neighbors were glad to buy their seed from Joe. His pilot planting seed was obtained from Oklahoma State University Experiment Station.

Tine for rest for this busy farmer? Mr. and Mrs. Joe just take their vacations when they hop a plane to Oklahoma City, Omaha or St. Louis attending conventions of farm organizations. "My hens

buy the tickets," Faye remarked happily. Her fine flock of two hundred English White Leghorn laying hens are her pride.

This sturdy farmer says he doesn't plan to retire "just yet." "I came from a long-lived family and I've never been sick a day in my life," he says. One sister, eighty-two, still milks three cows and does all her own work. Another sister is eighty years young and brother, John, another active Ottawa county farmer, is eighty-five.

Joe, a good farmer of the horse and turning plow age and a better one in the age of mechanized agriculture, believes the next fifty years can be better than ever for men who team up with the earth to find their happiness and way of life.

His advice to youngsters who plan being farmers? "Don't be afraid of work and of making plans. Don't let little setbacks keep you from trying again.

MILESTONE—Each new calf gets personal attention from Joe ... He can recall the time one calf was the difference between success and failure in his years farming.

Half Century A Farmer And Still Going Strong

By Frances Baker

Some of Oklahoma's pioneer farmers have let modern, fast-paced farming methods outdistance them, but not Joe —, tall, strong 63-year-old farmer of northeast Ottawa county

Okla. Though he has seen many changes in his half-century farming experience, "It's still the most rewarding life I know," is his comment.

Joe has seen an average daily wage rise from to rush in $30, the slow horse-drawn implements replaced by power driven ones—there. Oil received many hands now done with so modest machine.

With the years he kept pace with the progress of the American farmer's research into ways to produce more and better products. Today he commands the respect of youngsters of the inland area, who are starting out as farmers.

Joe was right in there pitching when the Indian Terri-

tory was formed under the first plow and a new state was born. He is living proof that "hard work never hurt anyone."

At 13 he did a man's work with a brother John on a small farm not far from his home now. But progress was always of prime interest to him. Joe believes his success is the result of his willingness to discard obsolete varieties of seed, being constantly on the alert for more profitable hybrids as well as new methods of seedbed preparation and the use of fertilizer.

This spring his operations will include 1,000 acres in cultivation ... winter oats, the Arkwin variety that he says provides good pasturage after the crop is harvested, wheat and corn. Last year he produced the bushels of corn per acre.

His herds of 90 white face steers and 100 head of stock upon thrive on his home-produced, home grazed feed mixture ... the result of his experiments with molasses feeds to produce good marketable steers.

The mixture is ensilage, corn

cobs and grain, with added soy bean meal. Summers he pastures 400 acres of grazing land. This year he purchased 2 registered bulls from Openshaw Farms at Fairland and some stock cows.

When we visited with Joe he was busy at the feed lot, hoisting the 100-pound bags of soybean meal around like a rumatiza. He believes the owner of a farm should be the top hand. "Things just run smoother that way." he said. During planting and harvest he employs some help, but he is in the field every day.

Joe says he was raised on "hogs, cows, chickens and dogs." ... Gail think of the old-time ways he carried on. This spring he has 7 "brown type" Yorkshire sows. He bought his Yorkshire stock of swine at Illinois 3 years ago. And 35 shoats are busy eating up some of his exceptional corn yield. He says the Yorkshire hog is the healthiest one he has ever raised.

The dogs? Three collies assist at the feed lot, keeping the cattle away until the feeders are full.

Though personal tragedy of fire and death has hit him twice and "held him low," as he puts it, he fights in his way of life. He is the father of 4 grown children. The youngest son, Jay35, is the only one of the children at home. He is a 4th year at Oklahoma University majoring in accounting engineering. Summers, Joy helps out on the farm.

The other children before their dad before they married, but the most impressive part of Joe's story is his steady battle of a successful farmer from a small beginning.

"Nowadays young men think they have to have lots of equipment, a bankful of money and many acres of land but it takes something else to be a successful farmer," he says. "It takes the ability to see into the future and willingness to work what you have toward bigger things. But most necessary thing is faith in the land and its people."

Joe is the energetic president of the Ottawa County Farm

Continued on Page 26

PIN MONEY— Faye and her white leghorn layers.

FARMER

Continued from Page 12

Bureau and a board member of the Cherokee Farm Loan Assn. of Vinita.

In co-operation with Ottawa county farm agent J. D. Robertson, 3 years ago Joe began a pure-seed planting program aimed at producing certified seed wheat to sell. Last harvest his seed, grown, cleaned and tested by him and Oklahoma met top grade standards. His neighbors were glad to buy their seed from Beach. His pilot planting seed were obtained from Oklahoma State university Experiment Station.

Time for rest for this busy farmer? Mr. and Mrs. Joe had take their occasional when they buy a plane to Oklahoma City, Omaha or St. Louis attending conventions of farm organizations. "My hens buy the trips,"

Faye remarked happily. Her hen flock of 200 English white Leghorn layers, hers are her pride.

This sturdy farmer says he doesn't plan to retire "just yet." "I came from a long-lived family and I've never been sick a day in my life," he says. Our climate, he will make 3 cows and does all her own work. Another man is 60 years young and brother John, another active Ottawa county farmer is 85.

"Joe a real farmer of the horse and turning plow age and a better one in the age of mechanized agriculture, because the next 50 years can be better than the past 50 years who team up with the earth to find their happiness and way of life.

His advice to youngsters who plan being farmers? "Don't be afraid of work and of making plans. Don't let luck attacks keep you from trying again.

HOME GROWN—" Joe and some of his steers.

WHAT'S FOR LUNCH? Joe feeds some of his exceptional corn yield to his 60 Yorkshire, "Tempo-type" piglets. He says the Yorkshire hog is the healthiest he has.

GIVING DAD A HAND—Son Jay helping out on the combine last summer. Jay will never see the old time horse-drawn binder used, the method his father used to

This article was printed in the Tulsa World and archived on microfiche film. Photos are not well reproduced.

Caption under hog picture: What's for lunch? Joe feeds some of his exceptional corn yield to his forty Yorkshire, "bacon-type" piglets.

Caption under chickens: Pin Money. Fay and her white leghorn layers.

Caption under combine: Giving dad a hand. Son Jay helping out on the combine last summer. Jay will never see the old-time horse- drawn binder, the method his father used.

Joe lived to the age of eighty-four. The year was 1974. That is the extent of the family history of Wiley and his son Joe. Jay has a son, who is a confirmed bachelor at thirty-eight. J R had three sons, but two are dead without having fathered a family. The third has no family. Therefore, Jay's son, Josh, is the last male of Joe's line with Joe's surname.

Josh

Josh is in strong physical condition living at Ocean Side, California. He was surfing a lot until he was in an automobile accident where a truck rear-ended his Honda Accord. He had a neck operation that was successful, and he will be able to surf again in about a year. Jay would like for him to marry a good lady and have a family.

At the nuclear weapons facility, Jay went to Connecticut for a week's training in ultrasonics. He was then certified in that field at the Kansas City Plant. As mentioned before, each engineer had a field of specialty. Jay was responsible for the dye penetrants lab including certifying technicians and making sure that necessary

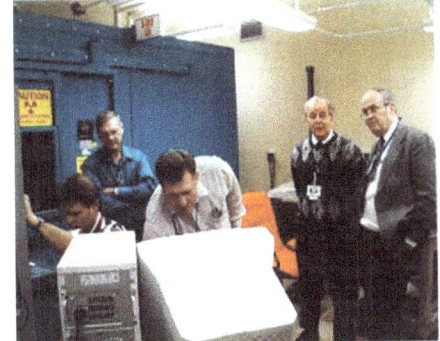

Real-Time X-Ray Machine

equipment and materials were available and functional. In addition, he was responsible for the real-time X-ray system. He budgeted and bought a large, modern display screen. The system was not performing as well as it should. Jay called in the maintenance department technicians to fix the electronics and any mechanical problems. The system had lead lined walls and a lead-filled glass observation window in the door.A camera was at one end and an x-ray generator was at the other. The object being examined was in between on a manipulation device to orient the object as desired. Jay worked with Los Alamos and Savannah River technical people to upgrade the system. They both had real-time x-ray machines.

The technical folks at Savannah River, where tritium was made and stored, helped Jay buy a much better camera than the one on the system at the time. The real-time X-ray system became better known around the plant and its use picked up considerably. Most electronic components, connectors, etc. were encased in epoxy. Real-time x-ray can very quickly examine the units for flaws without damaging the units. With this system there is no use of film or waiting for its development.

Jay helped some with ultrasonics, primarily verifying the integrity of stainless steel warhead storage container rims of various shapes designed to ensure positive sealing when welded to the mating covers. He spent some time at Pantex near Amarillo where warheads are assembled and disassembled. The W48 warheads on forty-mile range rockets were being returned from Europe at that time. They were stored in thick-walled stainless steel containers.

Jay also worked some with CTs (Computed Tomograpyhy like CAT scanner in the medical field). One used x-rays and the other used radioactive cobalt as sources. Both had a rotating platform between the source and detectors for the part being examined.

The platform rotated 360 degrees in increments of a few degrees for each exposure. Opposite of the x-ray source was a detector with a bank of sensors. After the turn table completes 360°, the computer crunches the data gathered from each exposure and forms a picture of what is in the object as if a slice was made with a cutting device at that level. Then the part is incremented in height and the process is repeated. The cobalt unit worked the same way in effect as the X-ray CT. The cobalt source gave off radiation that acted the same as X-rays. The part is exposed to the cobalt source by lifting off the lead container from over the cobalt pellet for a predetermined period of time at each increment of rotation. The detector array was considerably less than the one for the x-ray CT; the cobalt unit is less accurate.

Jay wrote travelers (sets of instructions for the technicians to follow when examining a part) for x-ray of various parts. One huge X-ray machine used R-12 refrigerant in its cooling system. Jay was the only one in the non-destructive department with a license to buy the material. Radical environmentalist painted the R-12 as a bad chemical destroying the ozone in the stratosphere; what a hoax. Dixie Rae Lee, the head of the Department of Energy (DOE), stated at the time that R-12 is four times heavier than air; there is no way it can get to the stratosphere. R-12 is harmless; its replacement, R-134A, is not as efficient as R-12 and requires workers who work with it to wear protective breathing apparatus. This was a bad joke on the using public. Also, there are no air conditioners at the North Pole where the hole in the ozone is. Jay bought R-12, still available at the time, with his license for the big X-ray machine.

In the X-ray department, X-rays were used to pass through the parts under inspection onto x-ray films. The films then were developed to display the images. Denser materials in the part allowed less x-rays to pass through than less dense materials. The images then are analyzed visually for defects in the parts. While working with the real-time x-ray machine and CTs Jay was shown some detector plates at Los Alamos. They were designed to replace the film and display the images on a computer screen. Jay looked into getting one for the non-destructive (ND) department. McDonald-Douglas in St. Louis had one and invited Jay and another KCP ND engineer to see it. The two engineers were impressed with the system. A set of specifications were written by Jay, and he requested funds for one. The funds were granted just before Jay retired. Another engineer in the ND department pursued the project after Jay's retirement.

The electronic plate is placed under the part instead of film. The plate is handled in darkness the same as film. After exposure the plate is taken to a computer designed for the purpose of getting an image from the plate. The image is displayed and stored on the computer. The plate is reset and used again. There is no industrial x-ray film produced in the United States. The three sources are AGFA (the largest) in Belgium, Kodak in Paris and Fuji in Japan. Ordering Film was a problem for Jay, who was in charge of stocking x-ray film for the ND department, because of its foreign locations. Often there were delays in delivery.

In March of 2001, Jay, who was already sixty-five years old, decided to retire. He had approximately ten weeks of vacation accumulated. Using up his vacation, he set his retirement date June 1. He planned to come in from time to time while on vacation to help transition those who took over his projects. However, the premium employee in Security, Tim's three pointer description (young, black and female) in affirmative action, took Jay's badge away from him. He was still an active employee and still on the payroll, but the lady in security insisted on removing Jay from access to the plant. Some folks thought Jay simply walked out without tying in to other coworkers on his projects, but that was not the case.

Jay used his vacation to fix up his house for sale.

He had recently finished the basement. A fireplace was built there. It was a mirror image of the one above in the family room. When the house was built, Jay had asked the builder to provide for a fireplace in the basement when the chimney was built. The deck just off the kitchen was large with seats all around the edges. Jay had fought the weather by trying to keep the cedar deck pretty yellow as it was originally. Several times he had sanded off the spar varnish and revarnished the wood that had been sanded to its original color. The varnish was only good for a couple of years at a time. While on

George on Deck

vacation, Jay painted the deck the same color as the trim on the house. The house had a roof with no gables by design (hip roof). The trim was at the doors, around the edges of the roof and around the windows.

The house was now twenty-two years old. It needed a few repairs. The driveway was cracked and settled. A new concrete slab was poured for the extra wide driveway. It improved the place a lot. Zoysia pads of green grass covering the bare places in the yard did wonders to the looks of the place.

Jay and Sandy went to the Kansas side of greater Kansas City and hired a real estate agency to sell their house. Jay told the agency he wanted tigers to sell his house and stated a reasonable price. He and Sandy had bought the brick house for approximately $76,000. He had a corner lot and added three acres behind that. He had finished the basement to living space leaving a work space on one side. Sadie and Jay decided to ask $146,000 for the house. They sold the house for approximately $140,000.

Chapter 15

Retirement

Jay had promised himself while living on the farm to retire in a warm climate. Sandy had two cousins living in Green Valley, Arizona. Early in 2001 Jay had a business trip to Los Alamos scheduled. Instead of flying to Albuquerque and renting a car to drive to Los Alamos through Santa Fe as usual when going there on business, Jay rented a car in Kansas City and drove to Los Alamos with Sandy. After business was completed the two drove to Green Valley to look it over and visit the cousins. The two were concerned that Green Valley was only thirty-five miles from the Mexican border. Bunches of Mexicans were in Kansas City crowding the stores there jabbering in their native tongues. Jay was not too eager to be close to the source of illegal immigrants flooding into the United States without being held accountable. Despite liberal views, wrong is not right!

Elaine, Josh, Sandy and Jay in KC

The house sold by November 2001, and they needed to plan for their next house. Jay and Josh laid out a series of flight maps of a route between Kansas City and Tucson. The route would begin at Lee's Summit and end at the Marana airport on the west side of Tucson. They would fly around the international airport and the large Air Force Davis-Monthan airbase which were close together. By passing between the large mountain ranges straddling Tucson on the north and south and flying south down the valley west of the Santa Rita Mountains they would avoid the congested air traffic. The maps covering the flight route were laid out on the floor and taped together. They would stop for fuel at Liberal, Kansas, and Magdalena, NM, enroute. Jay had checked out in a good four-place aircraft at Lee's Summit. It was reserved for the trip. However this was in November, 2001, shortly after the mohammedans, called muslims, attacked the United States by flying planes into the

World Trade center and the Pentagon. To encourage travelers to fly, airline tickets were very low in price. Jay, Sandy, Josh and Elaine, Josh's wife, all flew to Tucson for $118 each round trip. That was cheaper than renting a plane and flying to the Tucson area. It was much quicker, too. That is the way they went.

They spent three days looking for a home with a storage building that would store the pickup truck, three vintage cars and miscellaneous belongings. The realtor they were working with took them to a place where they could build a large storage building. The house had three bathrooms, one for each bedroom. It was on four acres. But it was more than Jay was willing to pay. He wanted to not go into debt for a house. However, Josh and Elaine said they planned to get jobs in the area and would live in the east room of the house. It was isolated from the other two bedrooms, which were on the west end.

The house has a two car garage and a carport under a deck for viewing the mountains and valley to the east. They agreed to help with the house payments. The owner of the house wanted $244,000. Sandy and Jay offered $220.000. The owner came down to $232,000 and the deal was set.

Green Valley Home

Back Side of Green Valley House

For the move, Jay and Josh rented two large trucks. They had around twenty-four feet long enclosed beds. Josh had never driven a large truck before. The trucks had automatic transmissions and diesel engines.

Outbuilding on 3 Acres in Grandview, MO

One was rated at approximately twenty-three thousand pounds max load and the other was around twenty-five thousand pounds. They were thought to hold all of the furniture and other things that had been accumulated over the many years that Jay and Sandy were married. It was amazing how much there was. Several boxes of files, etc., were stored in the attic. Some things, including the new Dodge pickup, were stored in a building Jay had built on the three acres attached to the house property.

The trucks each pulled a car. When the moving train started, the blue 1966 Chevrolet was to be driven by Josh's mother-in-law. The Honda Civic, belonging to Josh and Elaine, was to be pulled on the two-wheel dolly behind Josh's truck. Josh's father-in-law was to drive the new Dodge truck pulling a car hauler with the 1965 Chevrolet that had belonged to Sandy's parents. The in-laws stopped in Emporia, Kansas, to refuel.

Elaine, who was driving her late model Saturn, and Sandy, who was driving her new Honda Accord, stopped there for fuel, also. When the mother-in-law tried to restart the blue Chevy, the contacts on the starter would not release, and the starter continued to run after the car started. Her husband pulled the cable off the battery. Elaine tried to flag down Jay, who was in the lead, but he did not recognize her beside the

Loaded Trucks upon arrival in Green Valley

highway near the filling stations. When he realized Josh was not behind him in Emporia, he circled around in Emporia and came back to where he had seen Elaine. Josh was there. Jay analyzed the situation and decided not to try to find a replacement starter on that Sunday afternoon. The men pushed the Chevy off to one side at the service station and took the Honda Civic off the two-wheel dolly. They pushed the Chevy onto it. Jay knew that they could not pull the Chevy with its automatic transmission without dropping the drive shaft. He crawled under the car and removed the drive shaft connection at the differential. He tied the shaft to the frame with wire. The mother-in-law drove the Saturn and Elaine drove the Civic.

The two trucks drove together, and the others scattered except the two in-laws stayed together. The in-laws stopped in Oklahoma City and rented a motel room for the night.

The trucks stopped at a truck stop, refueled and weighed the trucks. They were over thirty thousand pounds each. That was several thousand pounds more that the max weight printed on the trucks. They thought sure they would be stopped at the highway scales. They might have to unload the trucks down to the max loads of each truck and leave the stuff. They debated about whether to drive on past the scales, but decided to take their medicine. They pulled onto the first scales they came to and were both waved on. What a relief! It was a good thing they drove onto the scales because there was a highway patrolman hiding behind an overpass support a quarter of a mile down the highway.

Because of the delay with the blue Chevy, the two trucks wound up at Oklahoma City after dark. As they crossed over from interstate 35 to interstate 40, the turn onto 40 was rather sharp and came up suddenly. Jay was traveling at a high rate of speed not expecting the quick turn. As he tried to negotiate the turn the truck, loaded somewhat top heavy, turned up on its wheels on the left side. Jay turned toward the left to keep from rolling over. Fortunately, there were no curbs on the side of the pavement. The truck came back down on all the wheels as the truck left the pavement and skidded in the gravel on the side of the pavement. Josh was behind some distance and saw the fiasco. He slowed for the curve. Dust was flying all over the place. There were cars in the area, but after Jay regained control, there were no cars in sight.

As the two trucks headed west out of Oklahoma City, the front end of the trucks bounced on the concrete highway as if they were going over a washboard road (resonance). The hoods shook loose and had to be refastened. It had to be a roughness frequency of the road surface that caused a resonance response by the trucks.

They arrived at Amarillo late at night at a motel that had been reserved for them. Sandy and Elaine were already there. After a short night of rest, they all headed west again. Josh was falling behind. Jay stopped at a small roadside park and waved Josh down. Josh said his truck was overheating. Jay told him to use full throttle as long as he was under the speed limit. That is what Jay was doing. Josh went out front and disappeared. Jay looked for him in Albuquerque but could not find him. He tried to call him on the aircraft portable radio that each had, but Josh did not answer. The next scheduled stop was Socorro, New Mexico. For Josh and Jay, they were to refuel just south of Albuquerque. When Jay pulled in, he tried to pull up to a pump, but some joker slipped in ahead of Jay as he was pulling up to the pump. Jay decided to try to make Socorro without waiting. As he pulled out, the trailer hung up on a wall at one side of the station. There was not enough room to maneuver. A professional truck driver came over and worked the trailer free. When Jay arrived at the motel in Socorro, the gang was there. They had a good meal together and headed toward their next stop in Tucson the next morning. Josh and Jay stayed together to Las Cruces where they refueled and ate. From there Josh went ahead. They refueled at a truck stop down the road. A couple came in to refuel there and asked Josh and Jay what gas mileage they were getting. They had a much smaller truck and were pulling a trailer with a car on it. Jay told them they were getting seven miles per gallon in both trucks with diesel engines. The couple said that they were only getting seven miles per gallon with their truck. Josh left in front from there, and Jay did not see him again until Tucson, where they all spent the night.

The Moving Train from KC

The Parade of Vehicles in Green Valley, AZ

They headed out the next morning for Green Valley. Sandy was leading the parade, but she missed the turn off to I-19. Elaine caught the mistake and got the group back on course.

All arrived at the real estate agent's office in the early morning. The agent took the group to their house.

The car dolly was designed for smaller cars, and it damaged the blue car. The vintage car insurance paid for the repairs on the car.

The location of the new home was approximately six miles southwest of downtown Green Valley. It is on the west side of the Santa Cruz valley and the view across the valley is fantastic. The picture on a post card and one shot from a camera at Jay and Sandy's house look a whole lot alike. The observatory seen on top of the large peak is as big as a house and the whole thing rotates. There are six or seven observatories there. The University of Arizona uses the observatories.

Jeep

Sandy and Jay had bought a four-wheel drive Jeep as a utility vehicle. They decided to drive up to the observatories one evening. That was a mistake! The road was open. It was paved at the beginning. There was a visitor's center there. As they drove up a ways the road became a dirt road, and there were no banisters along the drop-off side. The road narrowed to one lane.

A sign said ten miles to the top. A pickup with a camper was parked off to the side at a wide spot in the road. The further they went the more frightened Sandy became until she was past being scared. The sun had gone down and it was getting dark. After around eight miles up they found a spot wide enough to turn around. As they started down at fifteen miles per hour they looked back and saw two sets of head lights coming at a high rate of speed. The wide place where the pickup was parked was now vacant. The adventurers pulled into it and stopped. The two cars whizzed by leaving a cloud of dust. Jay and Sandy thought they may be found at the bottom of the mountain rolled up. They were told later that the speeders were University of Arizona students who worked at the observatories. Also, they were told that a girl with some friends had driven off the mountain road and were killed. Sometime later, Jay, Sandy and Josh, went to the visitor's center and rode the bus that took visitors on a tour of the observatories. They found that at the top there was a gate that was locked; Sandy and Jay could not have driven to the top anyway.

When Jay and Sandy were looking for a place that had a barn on it for storage of their three vintage cars and their new truck along with the things they had accumulated they found a place that was in a neighborhood that had restrictions, but they were unenforceable by the property owners' association. They decided to buy the house and build a barn. After much searching they decided on a steel barn forty feet by eighty feet by fourteen feet with clear span (no rafters). It was to have two ten feet wide doors, an entrance door, six skylights and roof metal capable of supporting masonry tiles. It was to be braced to accommodate concrete block walls (no movement in strong winds). The roof was to be insulated.

Site Preparation

Jay and Josh did the preparation of the floor and concrete supports for the main beams. A concrete contractor was hired to pour the concrete. The floor and footing were to be all poured at once, called monolith pour. ABC gravel was packed on the floor area before the pour.

Josh and Jay dug the trench too wide and the support column holes too big partly because of mis-location. The foundation trenches had two rebars running the length of them and spaced from the bottom of the trenches. The contractor showed Jay and Josh how to build the rebar cages for the support columns. They consisted of three square rings spaced evenly on vertical support rebars tied with wire ties fabricated for rebar.

The electrical wiring was run through the bottom of the concrete and up through it in an electrical conduit. A one fourth inch copper wire was attached to the rebar web work and taped to the outside of the conduit. It was called an Ufer named after George G. Uffer who thought the rebar would be a great source of grounding. Incidentally, when the electrical wiring was being installed in the building the primary ground came loose. The Ufer ground would not even run a drill adequately. The conduit was wrapped with foam where it came through the concrete. Jay wanted a bath room plumbed in one corner of the building, but the county would require another have another tank installed for that area because it just was not necessary for the small amount of use of the room. Plumbing was added later.

Before the concrete was poured, the floor area was surveyed by the contract workers (Mexicans). The forms Jay and Josh had installed were readjusted for better level accuracy. The Mexicans knew well what they were doing from lots of experience. They meticulously placed the bolts for the main support beams in the exact position where they were needed. There were six workers who were fast and accurate laying the concrete. A concrete pumper truck pumped the concrete into the forms. The workers drove stakes down in the middle of the floor to aid in keeping the floor level. The floor turned out to be level all over with

Foundation Trench

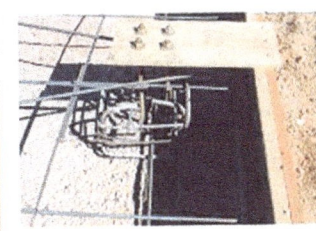

Steel Reinforcement for Concrete Support Column for Main Beams

Reinforcement Bars along Main Support Beam Column Re-Bar Cages

Ufer Ground Wire

Electrical Conduit into Building with Ufer Wire

high accuracy. The trucks with the concrete arrived around five AM and began pouring. It woke the next door neighbor, a bachelor, to the west. His house sat on four acres the same as Jay's. He did not let it bother him, though. The contractor counted on sixty-one cubic yards; it took ninety-eight. The problem was that the trenches and column support areas were too large. The cost of the floor concrete was twelve thousand dollars. The next day a fellow with a grooving machine cut grooves in the concrete to direct any

(A Detail Look at the Rebar) Layout

cracks. Unfortunately, the floor cracked all over it during the night. Jay and Josh filled the grooves with a round foam "rope" and epoxy made for that purpose.

Josh and Jay saw an advertisement of a fork lift for sale. It would lift seven thousand pounds thirty feet. It was in Phoenix. The two went there to see the unit. It was rough. The engine had a bad knock. The boys offered the owner, who was going out of business, two thousand two-hundred dollars delivered to the work site. The owner wanted more, but he took the offer. Jay ordered a replacement Continental engine from KC for seventeen hundred dollars. He and Josh put in the engine in the open on dirt. This was before any concrete was poured.

They bought an engine crane and put wheels with pneumatic tires on it. It worked well enough that the boys were able to get the job done; however, the tires were smashed nearly flat when holding the engine.

Fork Lift

The building that was bought had the calculations the county required done by the building company. The building was designed for ninety miles per hour wind. Jay did not have his professional engineer's license in Arizona yet and hired a registered engineer from Tucson. That was a mistake because the engineer told Jay and Josh they could not go higher than twelve feet with concrete block. He had charged $1200 and had his draftsman draw up the plans for the concrete floor. Jay fired him, but the county said the engineer was the engineer of record, and they would not take another engineer's changes. The neighborhood requirements were for masonry or stucco walls for buildings. After six weeks of delays, Jay decided to put on the corrugated steel siding that came with the building and stucco it. The

Building Framework Assembly

metal and stucco costs around twelve thousand dollars while the blocks would have cost approximately half that. Holes for the rebars for the block had been drilled in the concrete floors, and rebars cut to four feet lengths were bought. Jay was well aware that the world is full of crooks. Jay was fortunate to have found a professional engineer to finish out the building in spite of the county's objections.

The building parts were numbered and a set of instructions came with the kit. First the beams and legs of the main frames were loosely bolted together. Then the unit was lifted up at the middle with the fork lift and carefully set on the bolts at the support columns. There was no trouble matching the holes in the frames to the bolts in the concrete.

Jay and Josh built an eight feet by eight feet work stand of wood for the forklift. Later, they replaced the wood with steel. The wood just was not strong enough. Then the metal roof with insulation went on. The fiberglass insulation with a slick covering on one side went on and stretched on the perlins. The roofing was twenty-two-gauge painted corrugated steel. Before the roof could be

Josh and Jay Erecting Building

put on, the frame had to be squared. To do that, chain long enough to reach from corner to the corner diagonally across the building was purchased. A "come-along" was used to pull the corners with the longer distance between together so that both sets of corners had the same measurement between. The roofing cap at the apex of the roof has to mate with the corrugations of the roofing on both sides of the roof.

About this time Jay's pastor of the church he attended had been diagnosed with prostate cancer and was operated on. Jay decided that it had been a while since he had a PSA (prostate specific antigen) test. He asked his doctor to request the test. Jay's PSA test came back at 4.1. Anything over four is too high. The doctor asked for another PSA test. It came back at 4.6. The doctor sent Jay to an urologist specialist who sent Jay in for a biopsy. The biopsy was painless. There were nine samples taken through the rectum. Several were six on the gray scale, considered OK, but one was eight indicating cancer. The urologist asked Jay what he wanted to do. He said, "Do nothing and you have ten years to live." Use radiation pellets and you may live somewhat longer, but with treatment, cancer will always win. Only surgery can offer a complete cure." Jay chose surgery even though it meant the essential end of sex ability. At Jay and his wife's ages, that was not a problem. The surgery was completely successful. From then on, Jay's PSA test results were 0. The operation had opened his abdomen from the naval to the cancer area. Unfortunately, his pastor's surgery was not successful. His test every six months increased 0.2. His cancer location was not known.

Jay had a strong reaction to the pain medicine (oxycodone) and became dehydrated; he was taken to the local hospital emergency room.

He was barely conscious on the way to the hospital. When he was wheeled into the emergency room he passed out while Sandy was checking him in. The room was full of Mexicans, and Sandy was bracing for a long wait. When Jay became unconscious nurses came out and wheeled Jay in to an emergency room. Sandy accused Jay of faking to get ahead of the Mexicans waiting for free medical care, but it was not so. After a few minutes of water and saline IV Jay was revived. He stayed in the Hospital overnight. He took prednisone for pain killer until he was over the pain of the operation.

Working with x-ray was one of Jay's responsibilities in his job. He spent time as required in the x-ray test area where there were several X-ray machines for verifying the quality of nuclear weapon parts. He spent some time in the CT (computed tomography) lab that used an X-ray source. He was responsible for the real-time X-ray machine. He was found contaminated with radiation after touring the Rocky Flats nuclear weapons assembly facility before it was shut down because of radiation contamination. The department of health and human services decided that Jay's exposure to radiation during his employment at KCP was not a factor in Jay's prostate cancer though the groin area is more sensitive to radiation than other parts of the body.

Building Structure and Finished Inside

Finished Barn

Within three weeks after the operation, Jay was able to help Josh and a hired hand with the erection of the barn. The three had drilled holes along the edge of the floor for reinforcement bars to be used to support the concrete blocks planned for the walls of the building at considerable expense. Jay bought the rebars cut to four feet lengths, as stated earlier which were not cheap. When it was clear that the engineer of record would not cooperate, the three decided to put the metal siding on the building and then stucco it to satisfy the local home owner's association requirements for masonry. It costs approximately six thousand dollars for the metal siding and another six thousand for the stucco. As stated before, the masonry would have cost approximately half of that much. A neighbor said that her dad told her that the country's crooks came to Tucson in the old western days and they were all still there.

As mentioned before, when Jay hired into Bendix he developed a cough. Bendix operated the Kansas City Plant (KCP) building parts for nuclear weapons for Doe. Approximately 85 percent of each weapon was built there. Over eight hundred chemicals, including beryllium, was used in the KCP. At first the nuance cough primarily occurred when Jay talked. The only things that did help were antibiotics, for some reason, and steroids (prednisone). After Jay moved to Arizona he got prescriptions from his family doctor and bought prednisone from Mexico at a very reasonable cost. He took ten milligrams per day and had no symptoms of the cough. However, prednisone is a bad actor. It is habit forming, takes calcium from bones, causes high blood sugar, etc. It was an excellent pain killer; athletes liked it because they could exercise more without unbearable pain.

Jay did get hooked on it; he took it over a period of three years without coughing. He did have high blood sugar and had to treat himself as a type II diabetic.

Sandy developed a chronic cough about the same time Jay did. Her family doctor did a long series of tests of various substances checking for allergies. The tests were not completely successfully. She was reluctant to go to doctors after that and did not before arriving in Arizona. She then had the cough looked at there and was told that she had COPD (chronic obstructive pulmonary disease). She will not take medicines; she simply has a coughing spell from time to time just like Jay. She is on a health kick with organic foods. Jay thinks the organic thing is a hoax to sell produce at higher prices. Having been a farmer, he feels that sharing our food supply with bugs is unwarranted.

After coming to Arizona, Jay joined a local Baptist church. There he met a pillar of the church that played guitar and sang. The fellow is a high school teacher, the head of the math department. Not only did he and Jay play music together, but Jay substituted for him in his math classes in the local high school when he was away. Anyone with a college degree is allowed to substitute teach if they are of good character. Jay substituted in other parts of the school complex, but mostly he substituted for his friend. The friend asked for Jay when he was away. The friend was the top math teacher, and he had the cream of the crop students. It was a pleasure to cover his classes when he was gone.

The school that Jay substituted in was a campus type school system. Grades from the first through the twelfth were all on one campus away from town and enclosed with a fence. That is the ideal setup for graded school systems.

Later Jay was called by a local junior college to teach some math classes. Teaching in college is different considerably than teaching classes in high school. Students were adults and were expected to learn without as much teacher assistance.

Jay was given the leeway of establishing his grading plan called a syllabus. Jay knew from past experience that the best teachers were those that seemed the easiest. He told the classes that he did not give grades; the student gave himself the grade he wanted by getting as many points available as possible. He told them that he was there to help them to get as many points as they can by trying to make it as easy as he could to help them learn the course material. He decided to give the following percentages on performance for grading purposes:

1. Homework   20 percent
2. Participation   10 percent
3. Chapter tests   25 percent
4. Attendance   10 percent
5. Final test score   35 percent

He selected 35 percent for the final test scores because he intended to be lenient with the other scores, and the final test was not made by the instructor. The department head did that.

At the beginning of each class period the students initialed the attendance sheets as they entered the class. They picked up their homework that had been handed in earlier for credit. The classes asked for a copy of the lesson plan for each class period. Jay did that through the school copying service. Jay agreed because the students did not spend as much time writing and more of their time listening with the lesson plan before them. At the beginning of each class the students picked up the lesson plan along with their homework and their graded tests.

On chapter tests, Jay gave the students a review of similar problems that were to be on the tests. The students wanted ten problems on each test. If the students missed a problem, they were given the prerogative of reworking the problem correctly for 25 percent credit. If a student missed more than four out of the ten problems on a test, Jay gave that student five similar problems to each of those they missed beyond four to solve correctly (from the text book with answers in the back of the book) for full credit. That way there was no excuse for any student to get less than a C (70 percent) on a chapter test. Emphasis was placed on learning the course work as well as encouraging the student to succeed. Students who missed a test were allowed to make up the test without question.

Homework was due the following class period. However, Jay did not hold the students strictly to that. They were required to have all homework in by the end of the semester. It was for their benefit. Jay did not assign a huge amount of homework. He assigned enough to cover the principles presented in a class period. He assigned those with answers in the back of the book. When he checked homework, he only looked to see that the problems were worked and then posted the assignment as worked.

Jay grilled the students on the most important mathematical principals of the course. He reviewed often. Also, the students were required to keep a journal, which they did not do well. Jay told them what to put in it. At the end of the semester, Jay gave each student a copy of the one Jay completed for their reference in future math courses.

Jay made good use of the smart board in each class room. It was a white board about the size of a standard classroom chalk board, operated by a computer and activated with special color pens about the size of white board pens. Work on the smart board could be saved and printed. It was a boon to teaching.

The table on the next page shows the scores of eight chapter tests given to one of Jay's classes. The students were allowed to discard two of their lowest scores. The table on the second following page shows the two lowest scores for each student removed as indicated by the blank cells.

The tables are of one unique class and actual scores are shown; only the names were changed. The five scoring attributes (attendance, class participation, homework, chapter tests and the final test) are all based on one hundred points of which the percentages for grades are derived. For example, only eight homework assignments were given. Each homework assignment was worth one point before evaluation if completed (actually, it was worth two and a half points toward the final grade). To reach one hundred points for the eight, the actual homework points gained were multiplied by 12½ (12½ x 8=100). Then 20 percent of the number of assignments turned in (the homework is only worth 20 percent of the final grade) multiplied by twelve and a half determines the points gained by students toward their final grade. Therefore a maximum of 20 points toward the grade is possible for homework assignments. As mentioned before, home work was for the students' benefit; answers were available in the back of the book. Students had until the end of the semester to get all of their homework in; however, it was not a good idea to get behind.

The tables were set up by Excel spread sheet. Excel was programmed to calculate the results.

CHAPTER TESTS AVERAGES

MATH CRN C108
INSTRUCTOR JAY
12/7/2006

NAME	TEST 1	TEST 2	TEST 3	TEST 4	TEST 5	TEST 6	TEST 7	TEST 8	TEST AVG
	60	73	60	70	70	90	50	100	72
Katy	85	93	73	70	78	70	100	100	84
Nello	80	70	70	85	90	60	90	90	80
Rose	78	78		90	100	90	50		61
Mary	100	100	100	100	100	80	100	100	88
Lou	90	80	70	80	60	60	80	100	80
Alma	80	80	70	100	70	78	93	100	84
MarDe	80	50		73	80	70	93	100	72
Malinda	100	80	78	85	100	80	70	90	85
Maxine	100	50	60		100	100	100	100	80
Brenda	78	100	70	85	90	90		100	77
Olivia	70	80							19
Romona									0
Sandy	93	80		73	100		70	100	65
Sarah	90		80	60	100			100	54
Carol	80	70	73	60	73	30	60	100	68
Darala									

Original Chapter Test Results

CHAPTER TESTS AVERAGES

MATH CRN C108
INSTRUCTOR: JAY
12/7/2006

TESTS

NAME	TEST 1	TEST 2	TEST 3	TEST 4	TEST 5	TEST 6	TEST 7	TEST 8	TEST AVG (BEST 6)
Katy	60	73		70	73	90		100	77
Nellie	85	93	73		78		100	100	88
Rose	80	70		85	93		90	90	85
Mary	78	78		90	100	90	60		81
Lou		100	100	100	100		100	100	100
Alma	90	80		80		80	80	100	85
Marce	60	80		100		78	93	100	89
Malinda	80	80		73	80		93	100	84
Maxine	100	80		85	100	85		90	90
Brenda	100	80			100	100	100	100	97
Olivia	78	100		85	93	93		100	92
Ramona	93	80		73	100		70	100	86
Sandy	90		60	60	100			100	72
Sarah	80	70	73		73		60	100	76
Carol	90		60	60	100			100	54
Daria	60	70	73		73		60	100	76

Two Worst Results Removed

CHAPTER TESTS AVERAGES

MATH CRN C108
INSTRUCTOR: JAY
12/7/2006

TESTS

NAME	TEST 1	TEST 2	TEST 3	TEST 4	TEST 5	TEST 6	TEST 7	TEST 8	TEST AVG (BEST 6)
Katy	60	73		70	73	90		100	77
Nellie	85	93	73		78		100	100	88
Rose	80	70		85	93		90	90	85
Mary	78	78		90	100	90	60		81
Lou		100	100	100	100			100	100
Alma	90	80		80		80	80	100	85
Marce	60	80		100		78	93	100	89
Malinda	80	80		73	80		93	100	84
Maxine	100	80		85	100	85		90	90
Brenda	100	80			100	100	100	100	97
Olivia	78	100		85	93	93		100	92
Ramona	93	80		73	100		70	100	86
Sandy	90		60	60	100			100	72
Sarah	80	70	73		73		60	100	76
Carol	90		60	60	100			100	54
Daria	60	70	73		73		60	100	76

Two Worst Results Removed

Column Headings:

HW – Homework

H SCR–Homework Score (HW x 12 ½ x 0.2) note: 0.2=20 percent

PARTN - Participation (Based on attitude and Behavior)

C SCR – Chapter Test Scores (Average of six tests)

FNL SCR – Final Value of Chapter Test Scores (C SCR x 0.25)

ATTN – Attendance (Classes attended)

ATTN SCR – Attendance Score (each absence costs 1 percent, or -1 point, off the total number of points that determines the grade for the course) Up to a maximum of 10 points can be subtracted since attendance is only worth ten points, or 10 percent, of the final grade.

FT SCR – Final Test Score

W T SCR – Weighted Test Score, (35 percent of FT SCR, the final test score is worth 35 percent of the grade)

T SCR – Total points for the grade

When tests were given, Jay never pressed the students for time. However students seldom spent more than thirty minutes on each test, including the final. Jay made the chapter tests from a disk of test problems given to him at the beginning of the semester. All had answers to them for the teachers. The head of the math department made two finals to choose from by the instructors. They, too, had answers to make it easier for the instructors to check the students' test results. The teacher's book had all of the answers to all of the problems as well as how to work each problem. This took a lot of work off the instructors, but the instructors had to understand the math before trying to teach it.

Jay's students did well in each class. No one failed, and most took advantage of the student-oriented method of teaching. Several students asked Jay if he was going to teach the next higher class. The top class was made up of all women. They made a good effort to learn and made the best grades.

During the latter part of the fall semester of 2006, Jay developed a discomfort in his hips and knee joints. He just could not get comfortable enough at night to sleep. He went to his family doctor who sent Jay to a specialist. A cat scan and X-ray film revealed an irritated area between the fourth and fifth vertebrae in his back. An operation was performed on Valentine's Day in 2007.

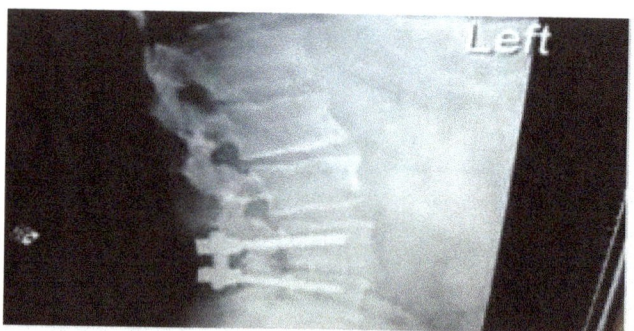

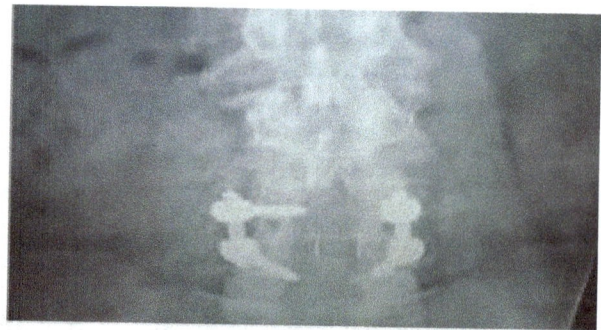

Side View of Back Pinned   Back View of Braces Installed

A block was attached to each of the fourth and fifth vertebrae, and a pin was inserted into each block to stabilize the two vertebrae with respect to each other.

There is a small wire cage placed between the vertebrae at the front to keep the gap from closing there. The cage fills with a stable substance over time. The operation was a complete success. It, in itself, gives no problems. Jay can lift as much as he is able, which is not much as he gets older. He feels good and has no trouble with his back at night.

At the time of the operation, prednisone pain killer was injected into the area of the surgery. It lasted for three days. Jay went home after a couple of days. He was given hydrocodone pain killer which made him extremely sick. He became dehydrated to the point he had to be taken to a hospital emergency room. He was given a shot of cortisone and perked up right away. He stayed in the Hospital over several days while the doctors tried to evaluate his problem. They thought that the gall bladder may be part of the problem. It was not. Jay had become hooked on prednisone. He took prednisone for pain killer until he was over the pain of the operation. Then he spent a year and a half getting off the steroid, prednisone. Prednisone is a good pain killer but a bad actor since it softens the bones, drives up the blood sugar, increases the appetite, etc.

If anyone were to ask Jay for his advice beginning a career he would tell them to try to pick a field that they really like, check it out and stick with it. Do not be moving around. Folks who stay put in a good job fare much better than someone who moves around a lot. Jay picked Aero/Space engineering, which had an inherent requirement of changing jobs a lot. Since several aircraft companies bid on a contract for a new aircraft, and all were required to have an engineering staff capable of developing the new aircraft, each hired a staff of engineers. The bidders who did not win were left with an engineering staff without work. Also, the new aircraft was put into production within a year or two. Then the engineering staff was reduced. Those companies who did not get the contract had to immediately reduce their engineering staff. Not a good situation. That may have changed somewhat by dividing up work on new aircraft among the aircraft companies. Also, several aircraft companies have merged.

Prepare yourself well with education, etc., and you will be in a position to be where you want to be. Do not sell your soul for position, rank, money or any other prizes of this world. Do the best job you can at whatever you do. No matter what you do, remember that everyone has a boss. When you are working directly for a boss, keep in mind that you are answerable to him first, and you are only there to help him get his job done. The key to success in this world and the next is to do the right thing. But most of all focus on this: the only successful people in this life and the next are those who accept Christ as their Savior and Lord and serve Him. Do not waste your time consorting with the enemy, the friends of the evil one (1 Psalm and 1 Corinthians 15:33); they will corrupt your thinking and lead you astray! When you marry, marry within your faith; you will be much happier and effective if you have an agreeable mate. Accumulating physical wealth makes living easier in this life, but it does not go with you when you leave; lay your wealth up for the next life. That is the mark of success.

FINIS

Acknowledgments

1. 1936 International Truck By permission of Henry Suderman, Hank's Truck Pictures Photograph

2. Permission granted to use photograph of Bonnie and Clyde showing Bonnie holding a gun on Clyde while removing his revolver by the FBI, Kristin K. Vidovich@ ic.fbi.gov

3. Information from Tulsa Tribune, April 7, 1934

4. Pacific Reporter 2nd series, page 1062, OK Methvin vs State

5. Drought's Footprint by the New York Times, PARs/NYT, Http:www.nytreps.com/,212 221 9595 x-201

6. Permission to use photograph of laundry machine by Karen Baney, www. karenbaney.com, Karen@karenbaney.com

7. Permission to use picture of Coleman Iron by Antiquesareus, Oxford Mills, Ontario, Canada

8. Permission to use photograph of antique Singer sewing machine by Pamela Kellogg, pkellogg@mc.net, Kitty and Me Designs

9. Old US 66, Wikipedia

10. Allis Chalmers combine and hay rake, picture help, Harber Village, Grove Oklahoma

11. Talent, Julie Granone's Gelding, Julia@healthyfeetandlegs.com

12. Jack's brown mule, Jack Childs, permission to use in this book granted

13. DC Case tractor photograph on disk by Sarah Stevens, Marana, AZ

14. Ray's horse drawn mower, Ray Bell, permission granted

15. Kelly Johnson, genius aircraft designer, Wikipedia

About the Author

I, the author of the true Hard Way Jay book, am an engineer who witnessed the information presented herein. Efforts were made to include humorous incidents and inform younger folks of bygone tools, equipment and culture for their edification. The book is planned to be informative to all readers about the experiences of an American citizen of the midwest who succeeded the hard way and the rewards of hard work. In addition, technical information was presented in such a way that all readers could understand it. A little bit for everyone was my goal as the author of this book.